MONMOUTH

THROUGH TIME

Keith E. Morgan

AMBERLEY

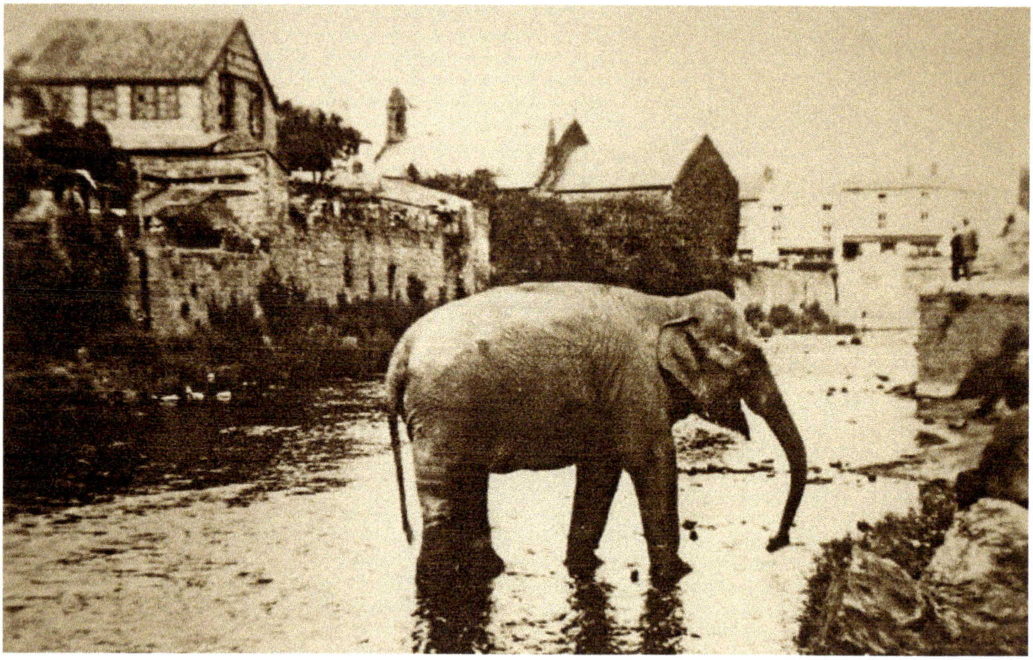

Time to cool off! According to a report in the *Monmouthshire Beacon* of 9 May 1930, just as the circus was leaving town after the Mop Fair, this elephant decided that he wanted to stay and escaped from his handlers to have a dip in the River Monnow.

This book is dedicated in memory of Malvina, 'My Special Angell'.

First published 2016

Amberley Publishing
The Hill, Stroud, Gloucestershire, GL5 4EP
www.amberley-books.com

ISBN 978 1 4456 5676 2 (print)
ISBN 978 1 4456 5677 9 (ebook)

British Library Cataloguing in Publication Data.
A catalogue record for this book is available from the British Library.

Origination by Amberley Publishing.
Printed in Great Britain.

Introduction

Monmouth (Welsh: *Trefynwy*), meaning 'town on the Monnow', is a traditional county market town in Monmouthshire, Wales, and is located on the confluence of the River Monnow (Welsh: *Afon Mynwy*) and River Wye (Welsh: *Afon Gwy*). According to the work carried out by the Monmouth Archaeological Society over the last few years on 'The Lost Lake', Monmouth's history stretches back some 8,000 years to when the post-glacial lake was overlooked by a Stone Age hunter-gatherers' camp. There were subsequent settlements here covering the period from the Bronze Age to the Iron Age. Finds include a 5,000-year-old building set on stilts in the lake as well as a unique prehistoric boatbuilding industry with the latest discovery being that of a possible prehistoric boat.

Following the Roman invasion and occupation of Wales, a small Roman auxiliary fort called 'Blestium' was built here, but it had to wait until the Normans arrived in 1067 for Monmouth to become established as a town. The Roman fort has been the subject of archaeological research and digs throughout the town and local area since 1986, but there are, unfortunately, no physical remains to see above ground level. The castle, originally of the motte-and-bailey type, overlooks the confluence of the rivers Wye and Monnow in a strategically important border area; it was originally built by the Normans as part of a system of fortifications to establish their dominance of the Welsh Marches, and as a base for extending their control into Wales itself. The Monmouth town walls and gates were built between 1297 and the early part of the following century. There were four external gates, Wye Bridge Gate, East (Dixton) Gate, Monk's Gate and Monnow Bridge Gatehouse. Only the latter survives intact, albeit in a substantially modified form to that of the original structure. The Monnow Bridge Gatehouse is the most renowned and visible portion of the town walls and defences and is now the only surviving medieval fortified bridge in Britain with a stone gatehouse, which is positioned on the bridge itself.

Monmouth was the birthplace of Henry V in 1387, hero of the Battle of Agincourt; a legacy that has been reflected in the name given to the town square. In 1536, Monmouth became the county town of Monmouthshire and, three years later, troops were mustered here, becoming the foundation of the Monmouth Militia, making the regiment one of the oldest in the country. Monmouth is also the ancestral home of Charles Stewart Rolls, the well-known motoring and aviation pioneer. There are statues to both Henry V and Charles Rolls outside the Shire Hall.

Monmouth, once a thriving port, became a market town and a tourist centre at the heart of the Wye Valley. Today, it acts as a shopping and service centre and focus for educational and cultural activities, including the well-known river-rowing sports. I trust that the reader will enjoy this illustrated history book, the contents of which cover a period of 8,000 years to the present day.

Keith E. Morgan

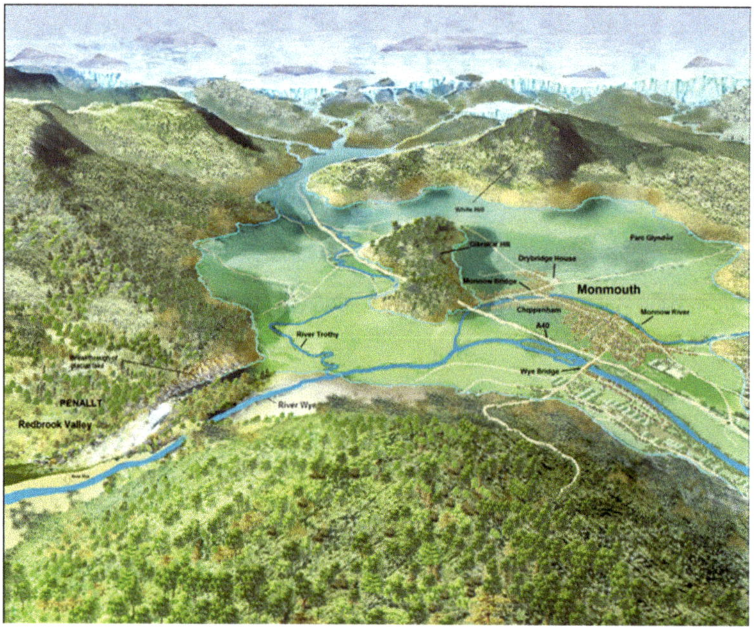

The Lost Lake

> It is almost impossible to imagine, but where we go shopping now in Monmouth was once deep under water, until little more than 2,000 years ago. Ice Age debris dammed the lower Wye gorge and the whole of the Monmouth basin was submerged under the biggest lake in South Wales.
>
> Stephen Clarke, chairman, Monmouth Archaeological Society
> Preface to *The Lost Lake,* revised edition, May 2016.

The top illustration is a reconstruction of the Monmouth Pleistocene Lake by Peter Bere, environmental lecturer and technical illustrator, Monmouth Archaeological Society, while the lower photograph shows archaeologists hard at work on the bed of the lake, which is covered by alluvial deposits left by the ancient River Monnow.

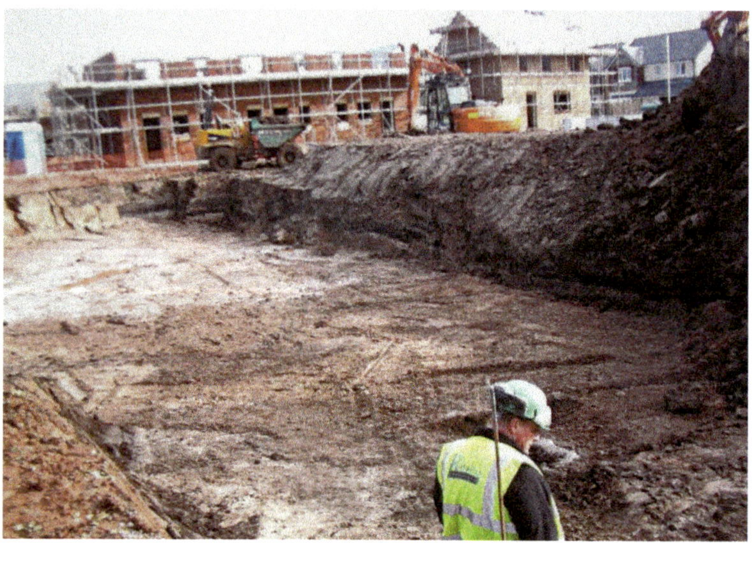

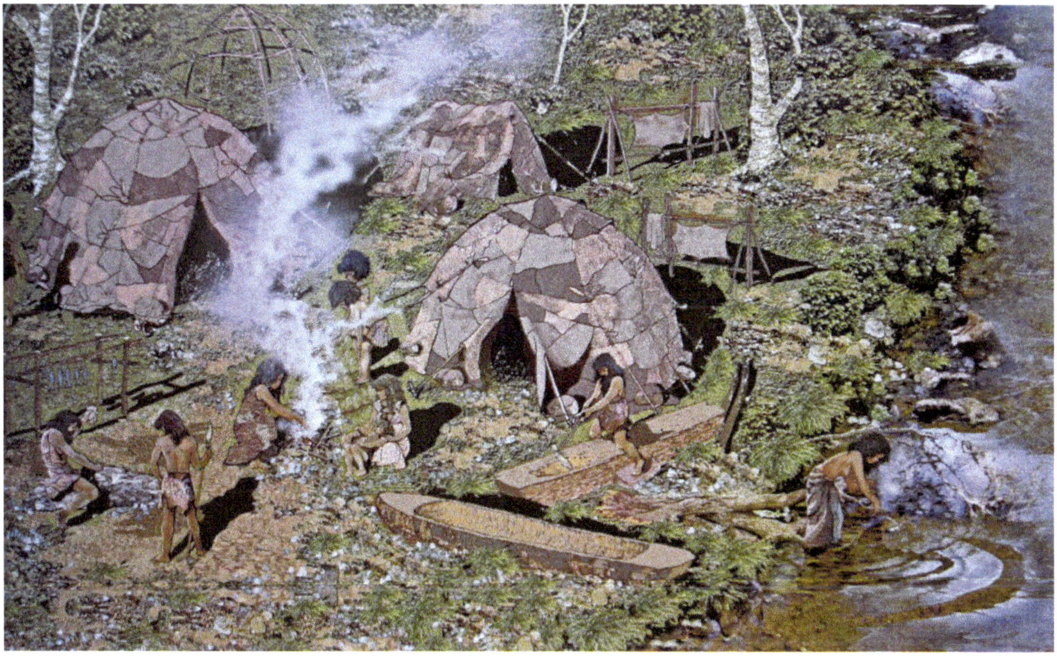

The Lost Lake and Ancient Prehistoric Boatyard

In the top image, Peter Bere has brought back to life in his fine illustrated reconstruction what a Stone Age camp beside the lake would have looked like some 8,000 years ago. The lower photograph shows the three parallel 'channels' from what is assumed to be an ancient prehistoric boatyard that was discovered during their first exposure. The photograph looks north-west at the Charles Church Wales Parc Glyndŵr site of the archaeological dig. It is thought that the three 30-metre-long parallel 'channels', cut into the clay at right angles to the edge of the lake, were created for assembling and launching a twin-hulled outrigger vessel after the component parts had been formed.

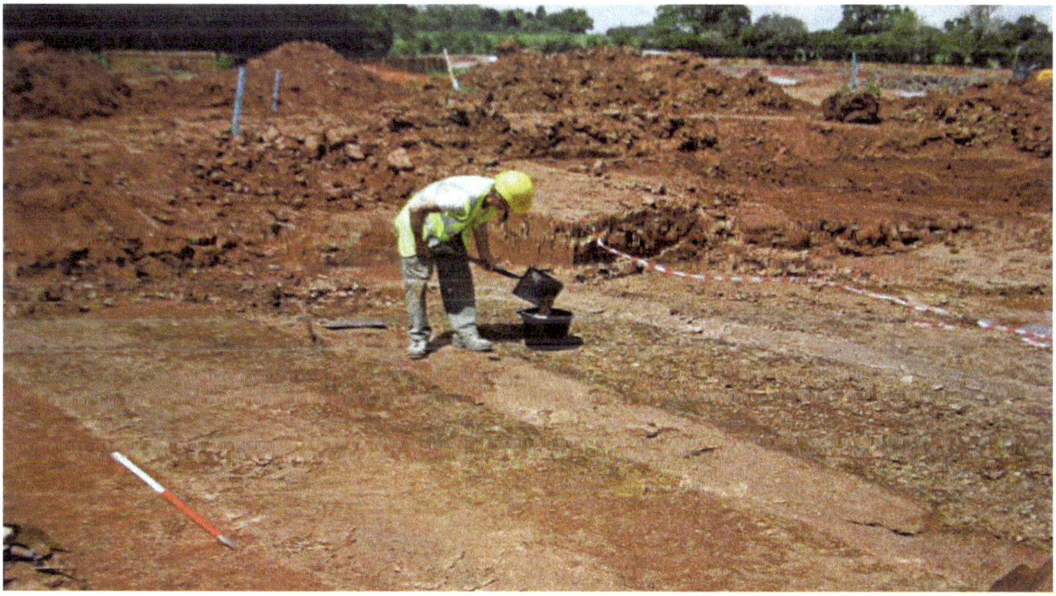

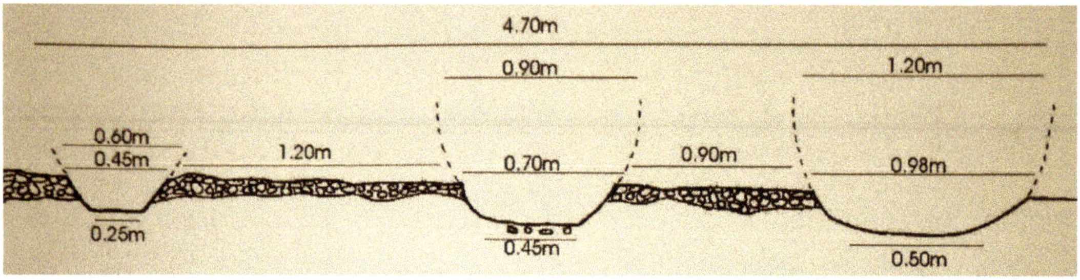

Ancient Prehistoric Boatyard

The drawing and photograph on this page show the cross section and plan view of the three 30-metre parallel channels thought to be the moulds for building a twin-hulled outrigger as illustrated on the following page. By comparison, the Eight Sweep Boats (eight rowers with cox) used by the Monmouth Rowing Club and the Monmouth Schools are on average only 19.9 metres long! Would the present Monnow or Wye rivers be able to accommodate the Bronze Age vessel today?

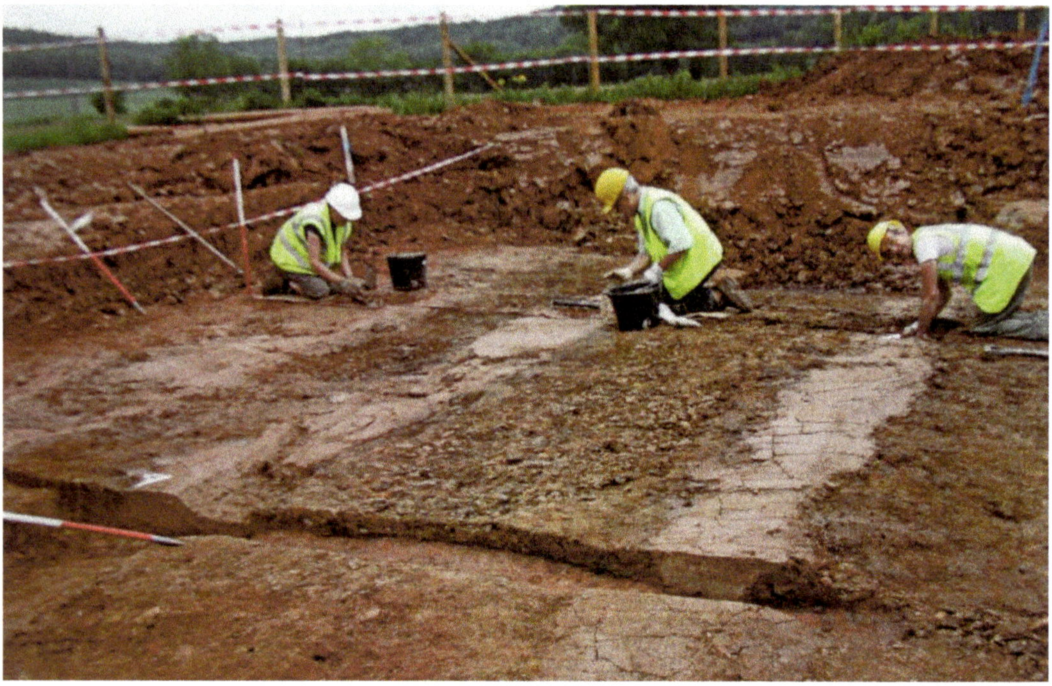

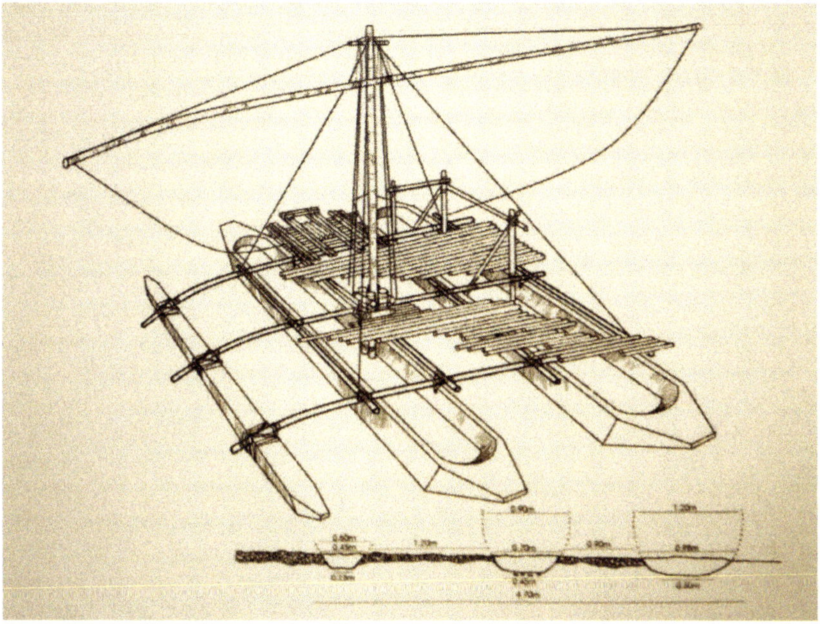

Ancient Prehistoric Boatyard and Twin-Hulled Outrigger Vessel

Peter Bere's clear drawing illustrates what the twin-hulled outrigger vessel must have looked like when it had been completed and launched, ready for sailing in the Bronze Age. Research by the Monmouth Archaeological Society has discovered that similar double-canoe vessels with outriggers were still in use in nineteenth-century Fiji. The lower photograph, with the three parallel channels outlined in white, serves to illustrate the possible construction of the Parc Glyndŵr twin-hulled outrigger vessel. Now we know why Monmouth, although it is 18 miles from the Severn Estuary, has such a strong shipping and rowing heritage. The medieval town's seal is of a ship, a reflection on times past when seagoing vessels could reach the harbours at the Wye Bridge.

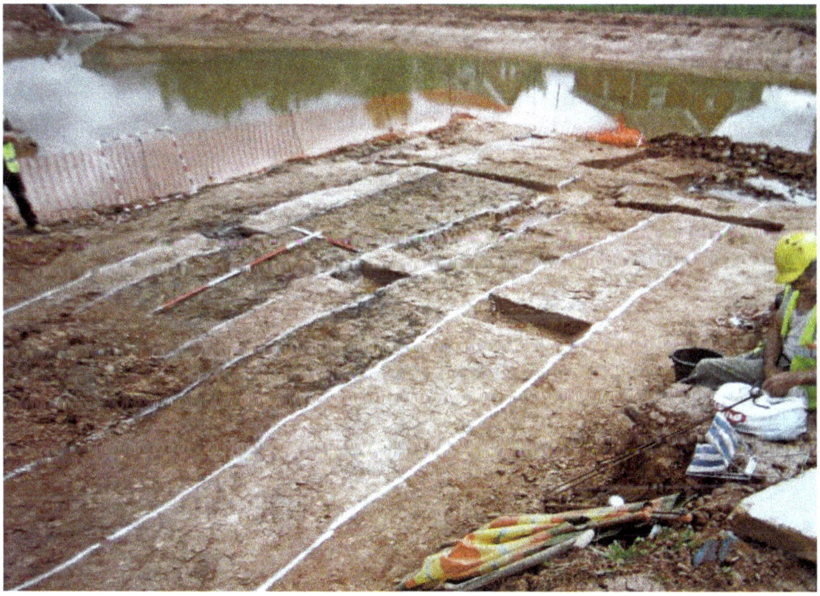

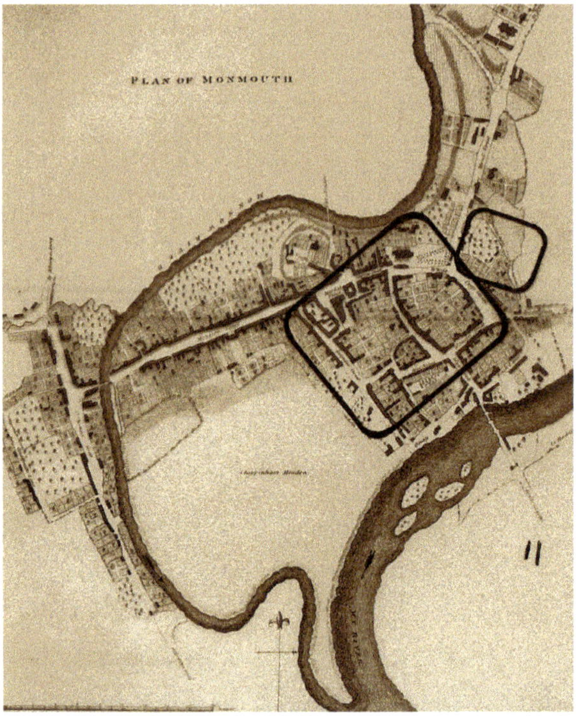

Roman Monmouth

The probable site of Monmouth's pre-Flavian vexillation-sized Roman fort, as suggested by George Boon of the National Museum of Wales, has been superimposed on William Coxe's 1801 map of Monmouth in the top illustration. The fort would have housed around 2000 soldiers. Based on discoveries made near the East/Dixton Gate, the possible layout of a smaller, but later date fortlet is also shown on the map. The fort was established at the very outset of the Roman advance into Wales, around AD 55. If this date is correct, it makes Monmouth the site of the first Roman fort in Wales. A blue plaque commemorating the fort is mounted on the wall of No. 20 Monnow Street, an eighteenth-century Georgian town house and now Lloyds Bank.

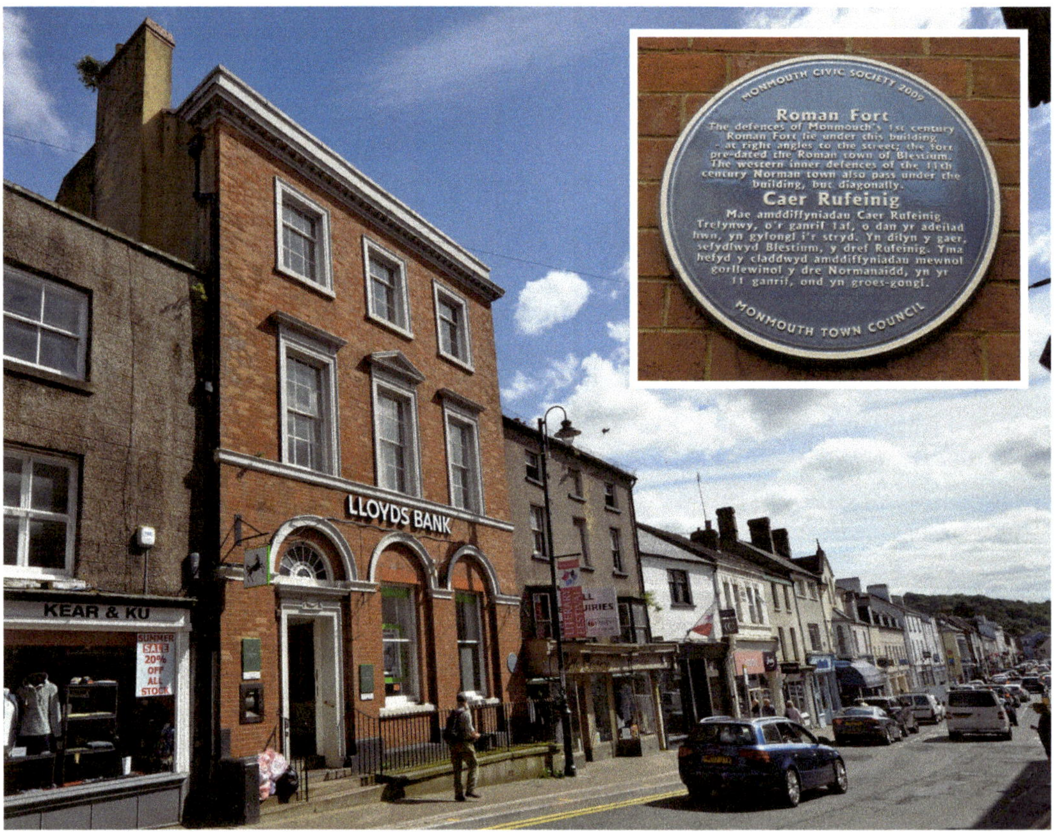

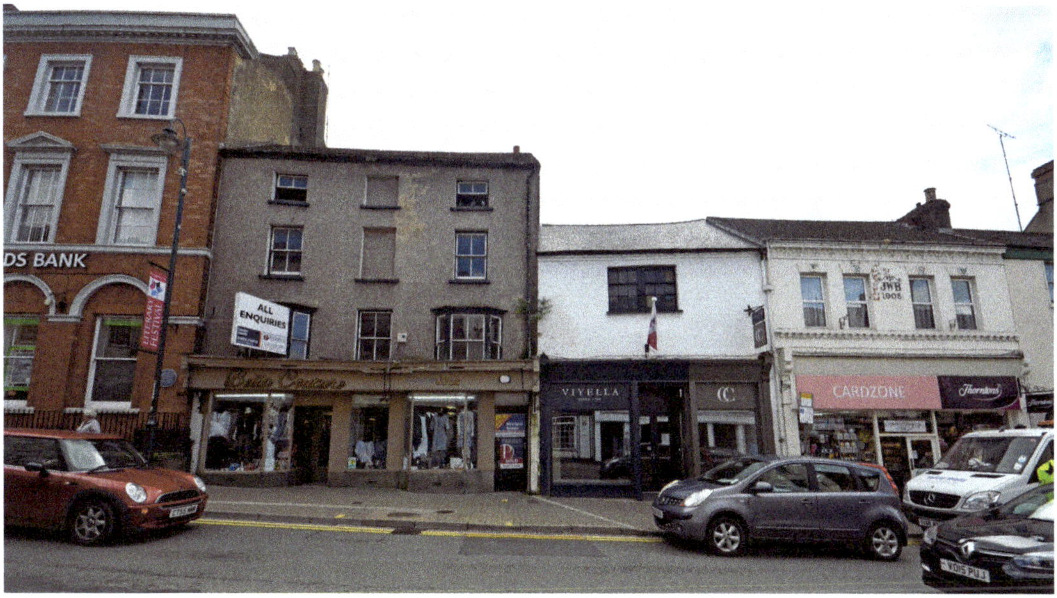

Roman Monmouth

The fort at Monmouth was a focal point on the route between the fortresses at Usk and Gloucester and important for the invasion of Wales by the Roman imperial governor of Britain, Ostorius Scapula, in AD 48. The Monmouth Archaeological Society ran the largest long-standing urban amateur archaeological excavation in Britain, at Nos 22–24 Monnow Street, Monmouth, from 1990 to 2000. Nos 22–24 is the white and grey building with one window on the first floor, as shown in the top photograph, while the bottom image shows Stephen Clarke, chairman of the Monmouth Archaeological Society, giving a conducted tour of the dig to members of the visiting Kenfig Society on 18 July 1992.

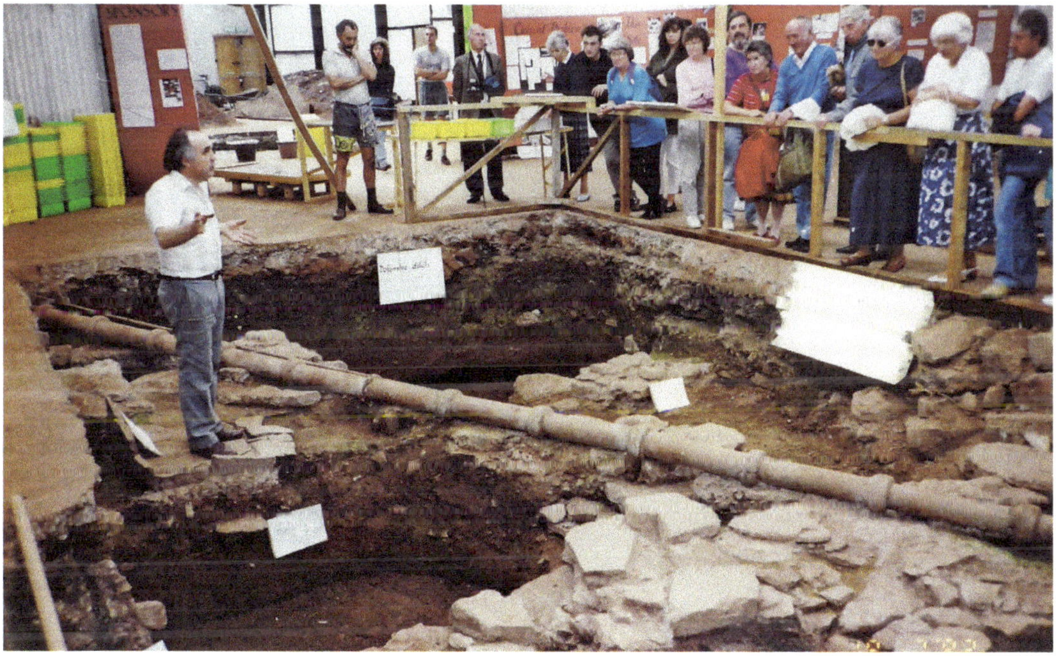

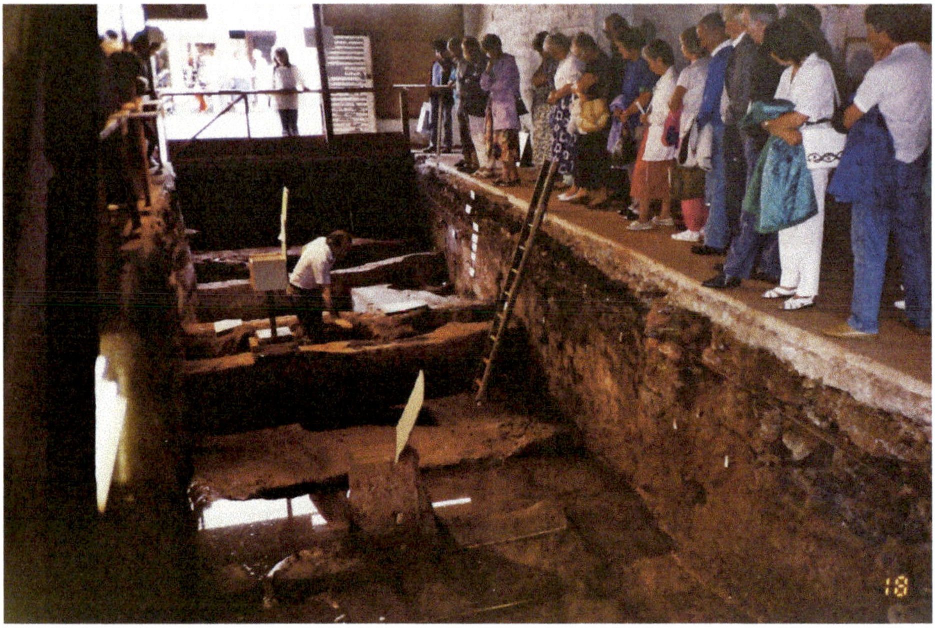

Roman Monmouth

Two more photographs taken of the dig at Nos 22–24 during the visit of the Kenfig Society in 1992. The dig opened onto the street and passers-by were encouraged to pop in and see how the work was proceeding. The Monmouth Archaeological Society was awarded the Pitt Rivers Award in 1988, as well as the Silver Trowel Award for the greatest initiative in archaeology. As a result of his contribution to archaeology, Stephen Clarke was awarded the MBE in the 1997 New Year's Honours List. Other than the blue plaque, there are no visible remains of the time the Romans spent in Monmouth.

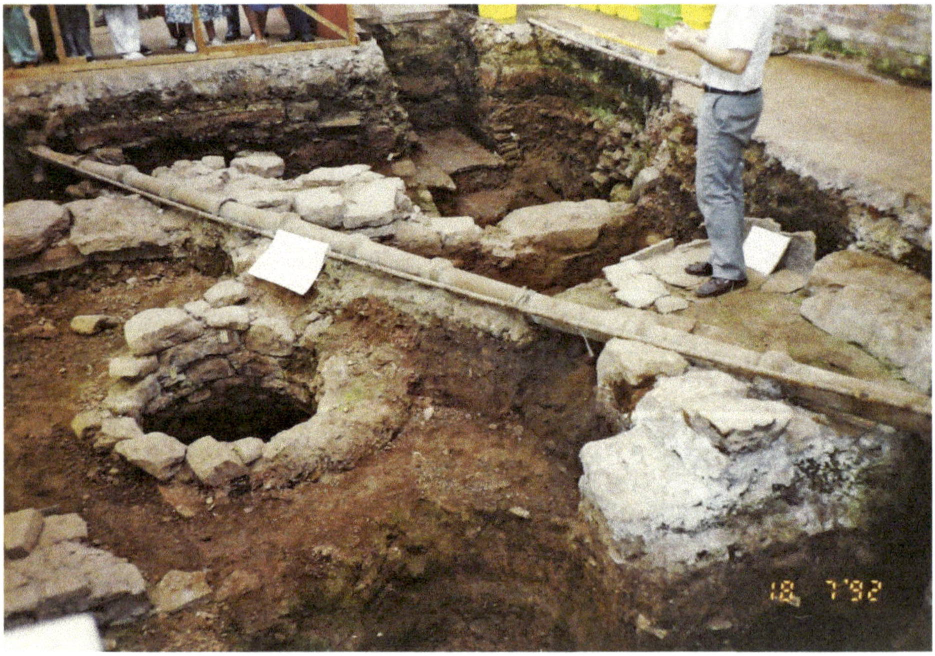

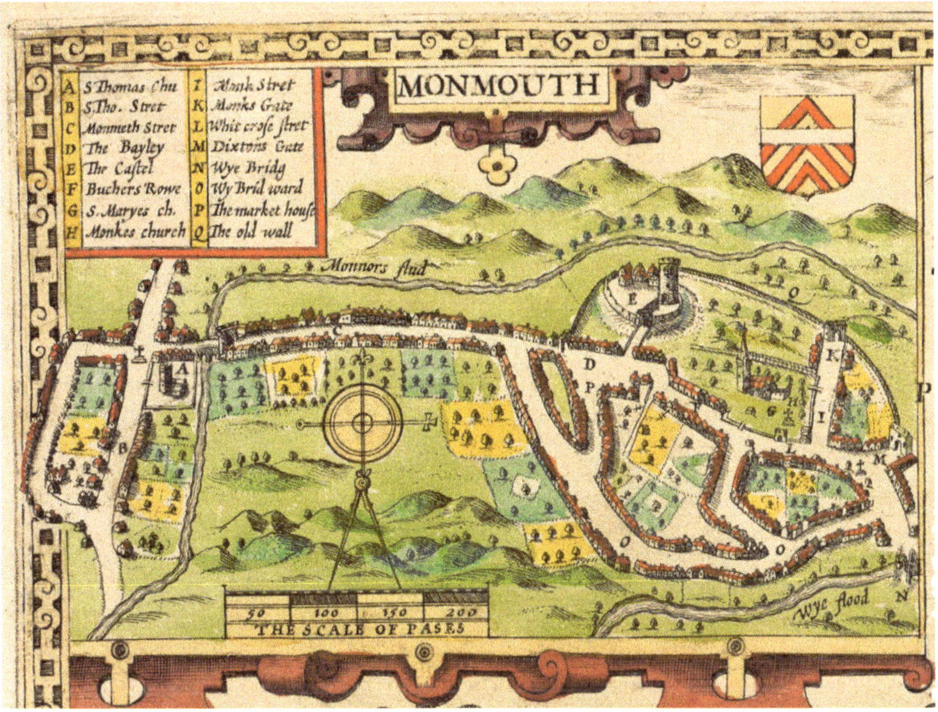

Monmouth Castle

Monmouth Castle, originally of a classic motte-and-bailey design, overlooks the confluence of the rivers Wye and Monnow in a strategically important border area. It was originally built by William Fitz Osbern in 1067 as part of a system of fortifications to establish Norman dominance of the Welsh Marches and as a base for extending their control into Wales itself. John Speed's Map of 1610 shows the castle and its strategic position in relation to the rest of Monmouth.

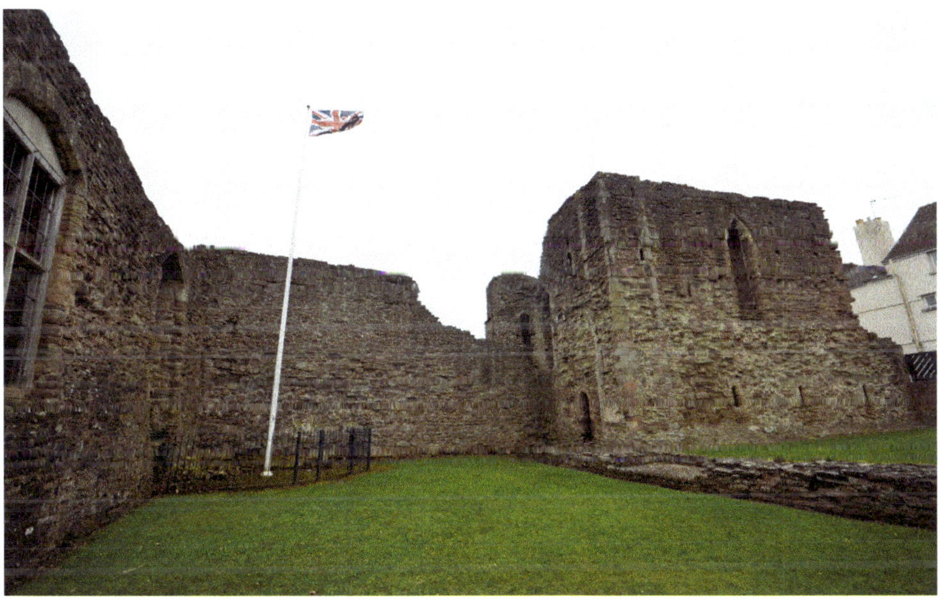

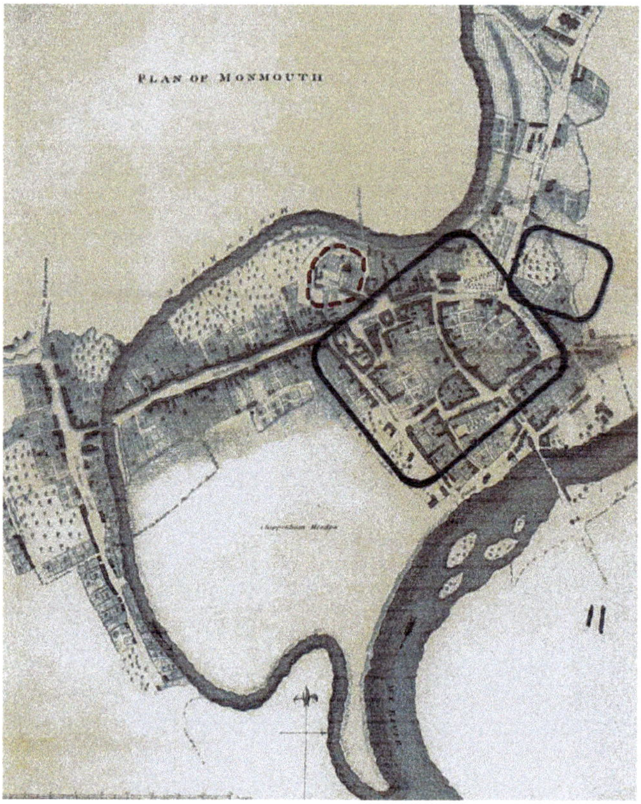

Monmouth Castle

In the twelfth century, the Breton lords founded the stone castle, which was completed by 1150, but sadly only fragments of the curtain wall and ditch, the Great Tower and the thirteenth-century Great Hall remain. The top map of 1801 shows the site of the Norman castle, outlined in red in relation to the Roman forts. Even though they arrived centuries after the Romans, the Normans recognised the military significance of the site and built their castle in virtually the same location. However, the Roman fort must have had its buildings made of timber rather than stone as there appears to be only one example (as shown in the inset photograph), of where the Normans have used quarried red tiles from the possible Roman remains.

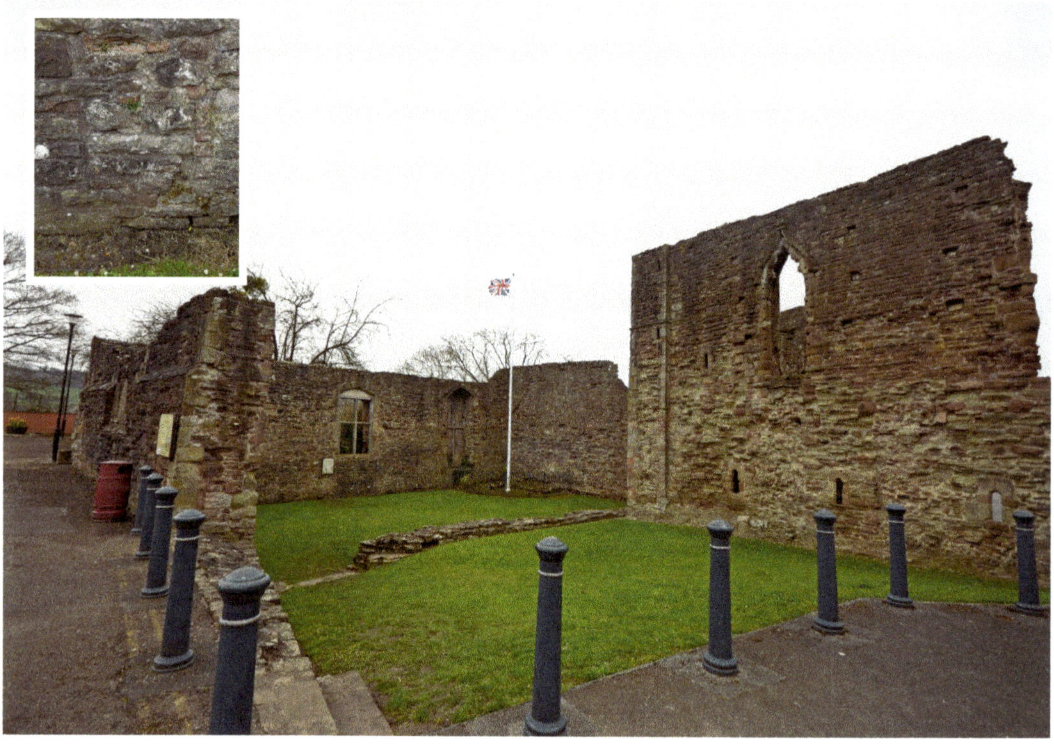

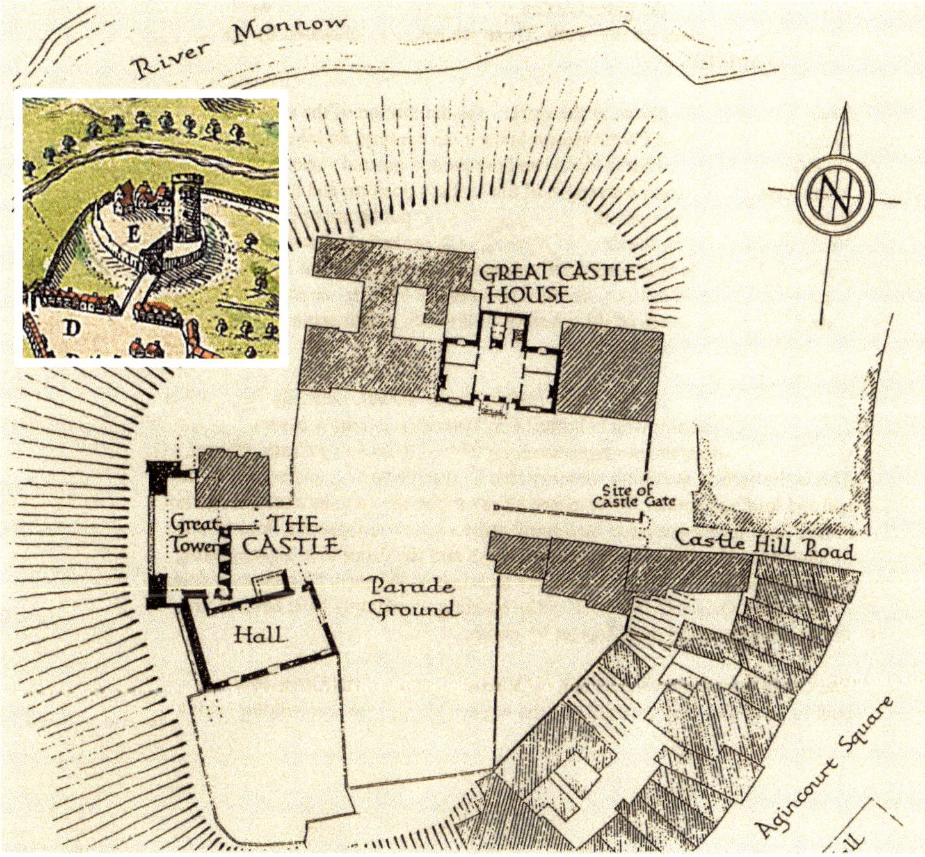

Monmouth Castle

The Great Round Tower of 1230, as shown in the insert blow-up of Speed's 1610 map, was demolished during the Civil War when Monmouth was taken by the Parliamentarians. The 3rd Marquess of Worcester built the Great Castle House in its place in 1673.

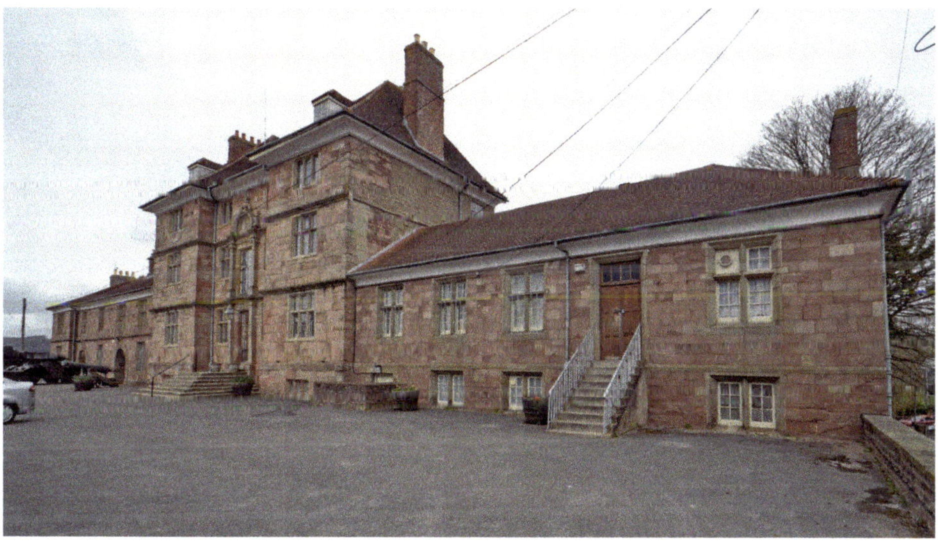

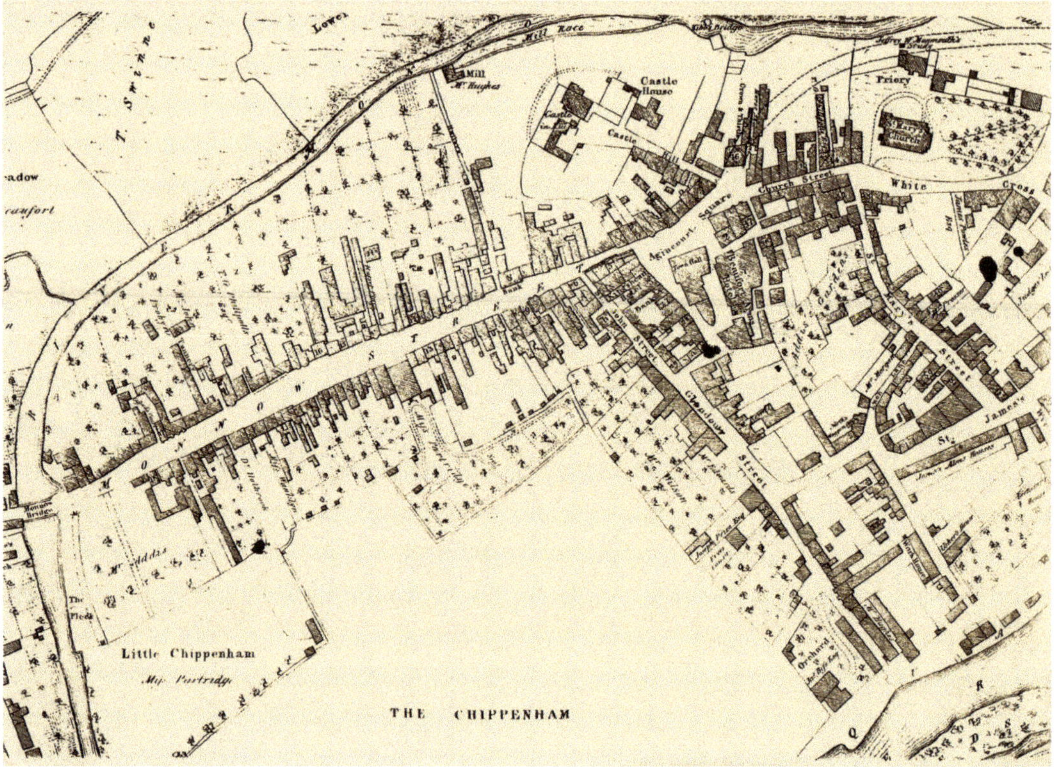

Monmouth Castle

The top Ordnance Survey map of 1834 shows the location of the castle in relation to the growing size of the town of Monmouth. The photograph is of the south-facing walls of the castle overlooking the Remembrance Garden.

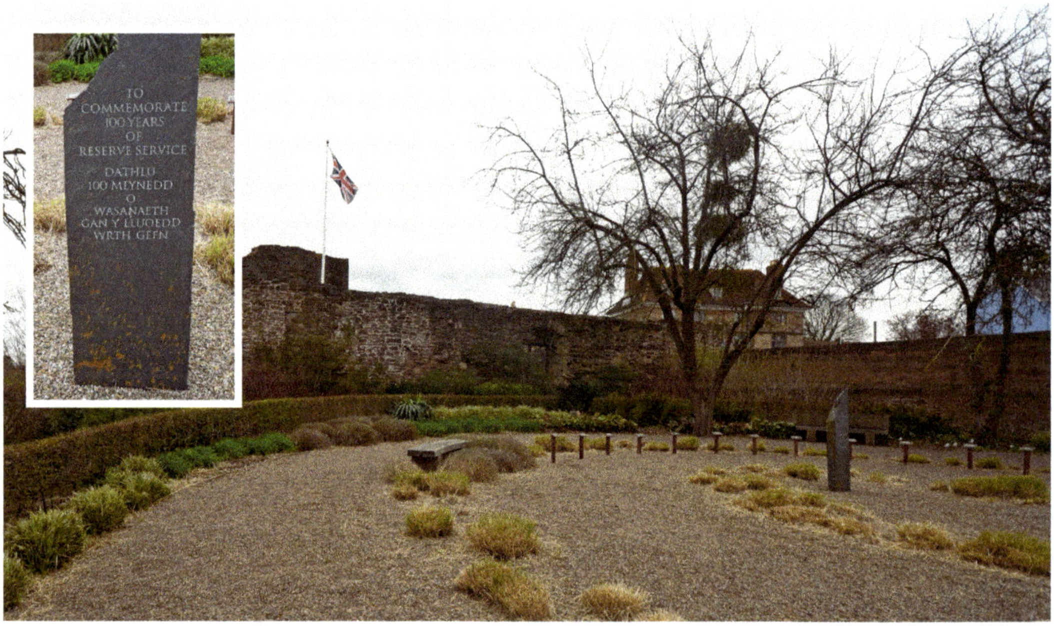

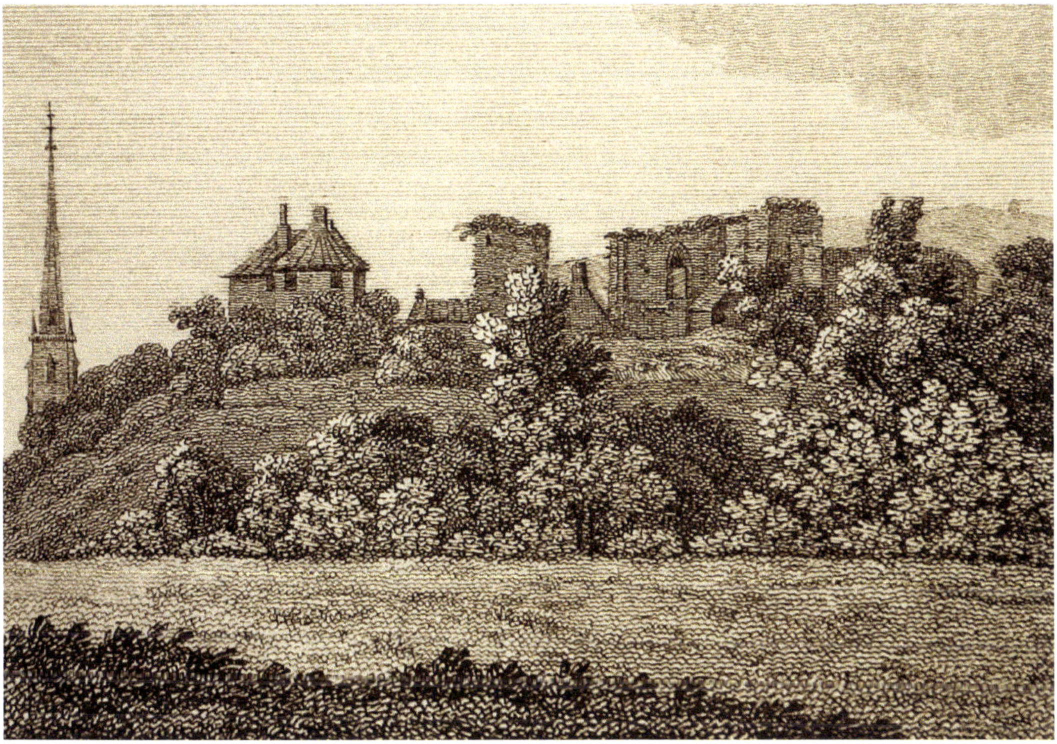

Monmouth Castle
The castle as viewed from Vauxhall Field in William Coxe's print of 1801 and today.

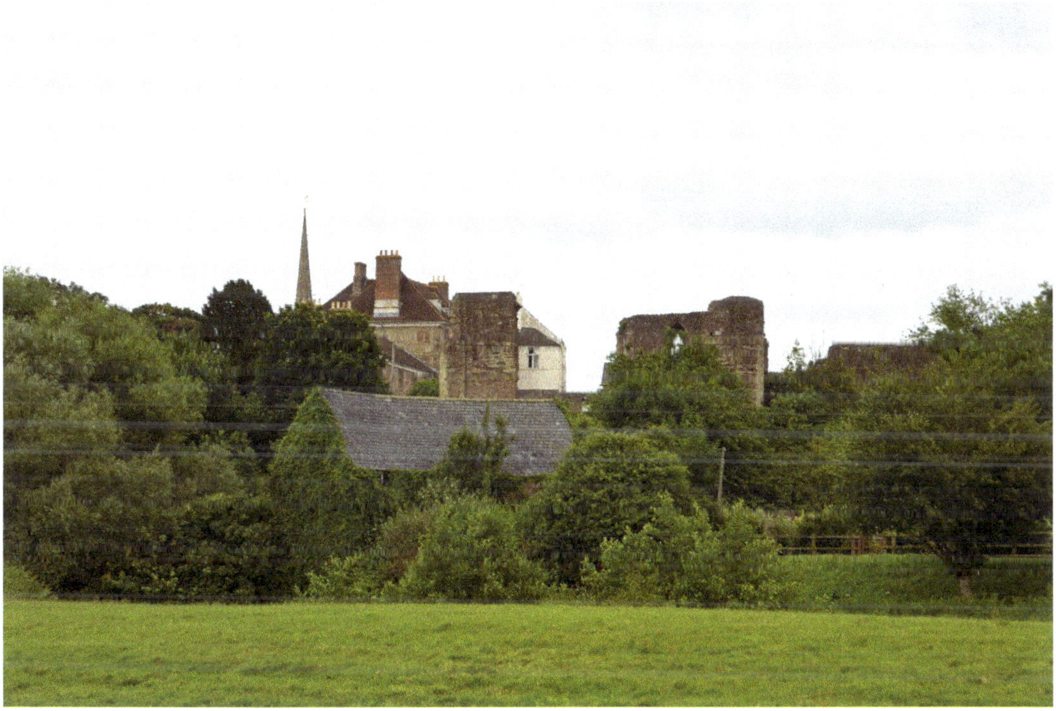

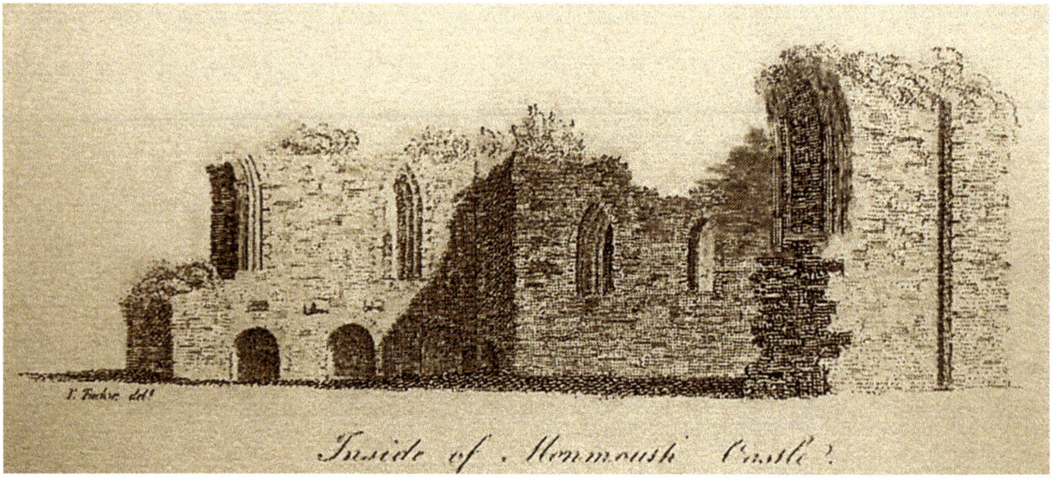

Monmouth Castle

Another view of Monmouth Castle sketched by William Coxe in 1801, together with a postcard photograph taken in the 1920s showing the same scene.

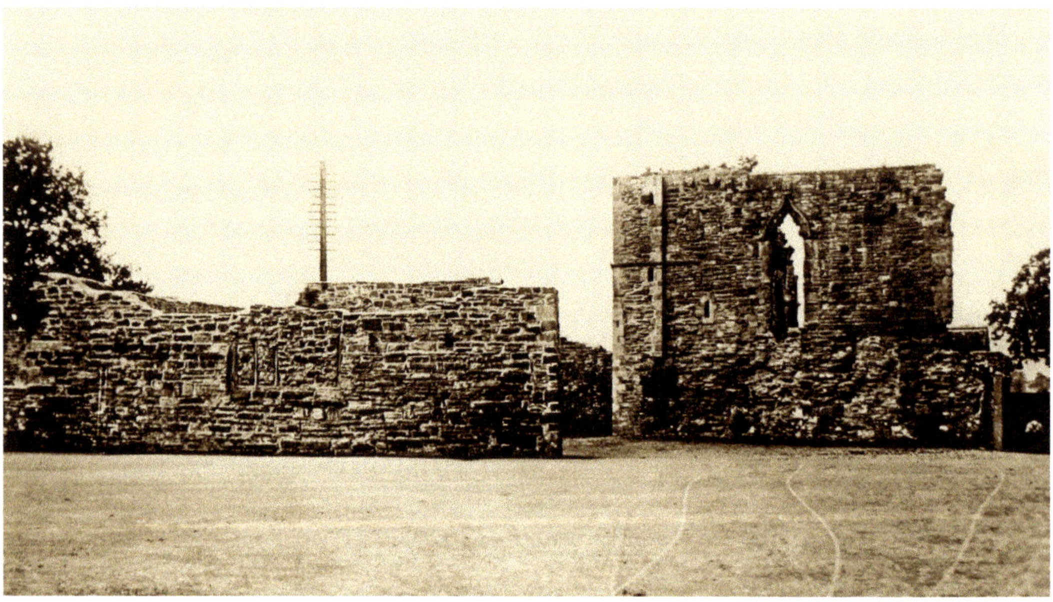

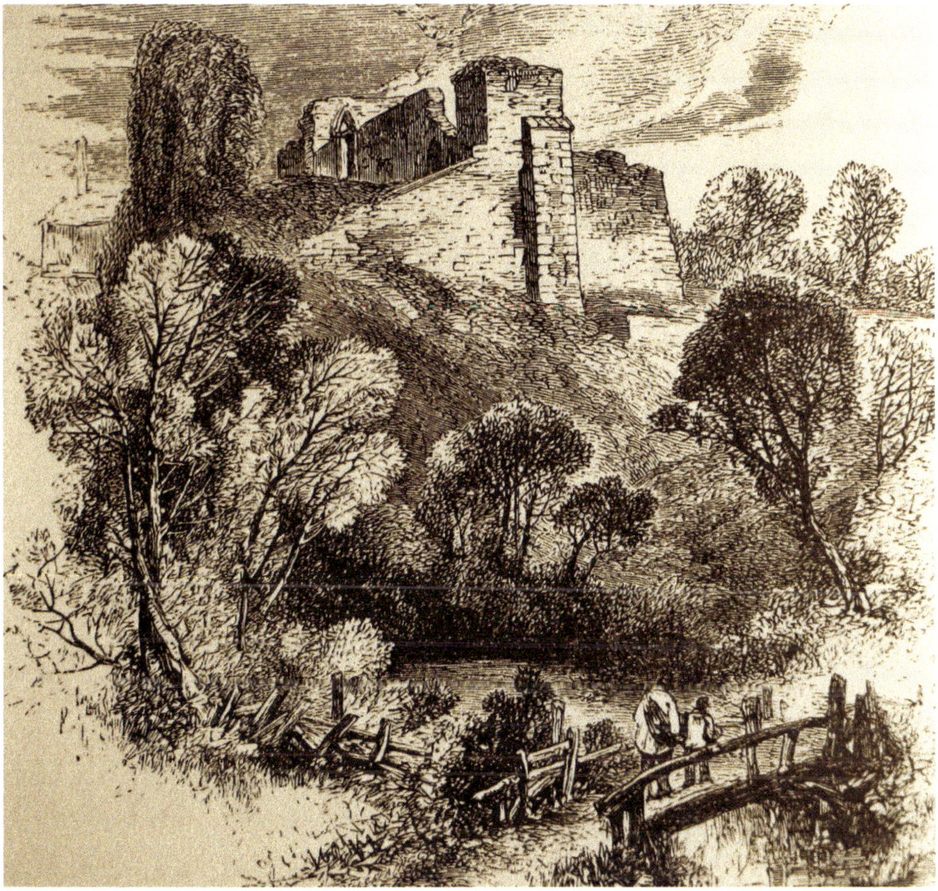

Monmouth Castle

The top engraving of 1861 has been taken from the *Book of the Wye* and shows Monmouth Castle as viewed from the River Monnow. An attempt has been made in the lower modern photograph to replicate the same scene, but not without difficulty due to modern buildings and tree growth over the intervening years.

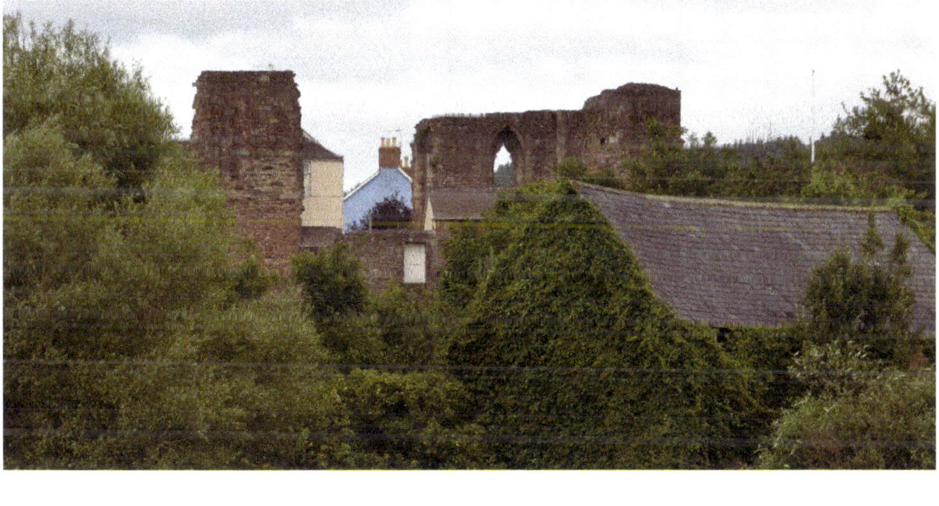

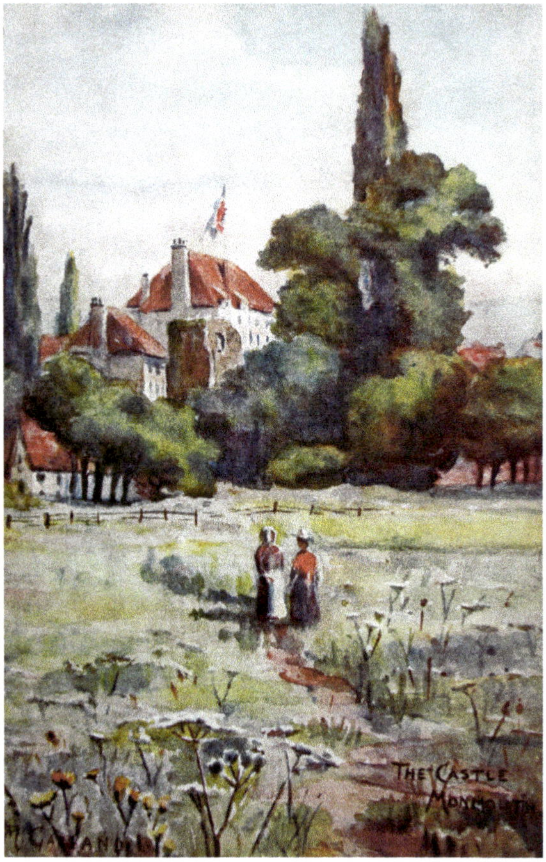

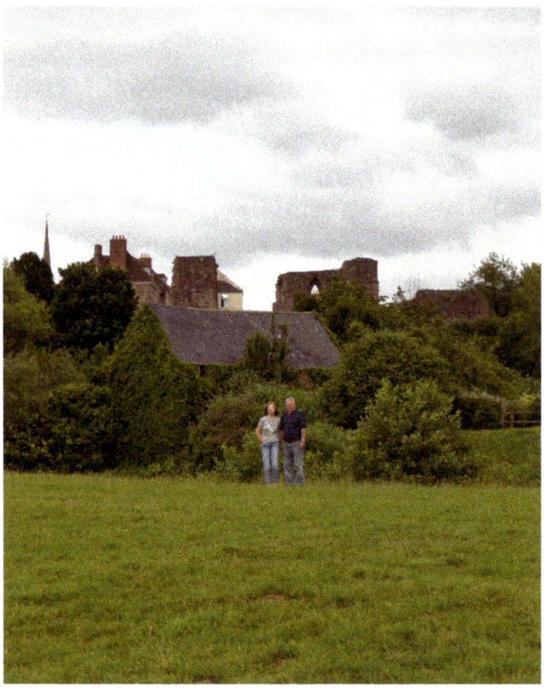

Monmouth Castle

The top colour postcard is of a charming 1900s' painting in the style of Monet showing Monmouth Castle overlooking the River Monnow. The author has tried to replicate the scene in the lower photograph, even enlisting the aid of Chris and Mike Smith, two locals born in Monmouth, as suitable subjects. Again, building development and tree growth together obscure the view of the castle.

Monmouth Castle and Henry V

In the fourteenth century, John of Gaunt transformed the upper storey of the Great Tower and in 1387 it was the birthplace of his grandson, Henry V, who became the hero of Agincourt. The battle, which took place on 25 October 1415, is one of the best-known events in British history, the story of Henry V's forces defeating a much larger French army having been immortalised in tales, poetry and plays, especially those by William Shakespeare. There is a stained-glass window in St Mary's Priory Church depicting Henry V, as well as a statue to the famous king in a niche on the front of the Shire Hall in Agincourt Square.

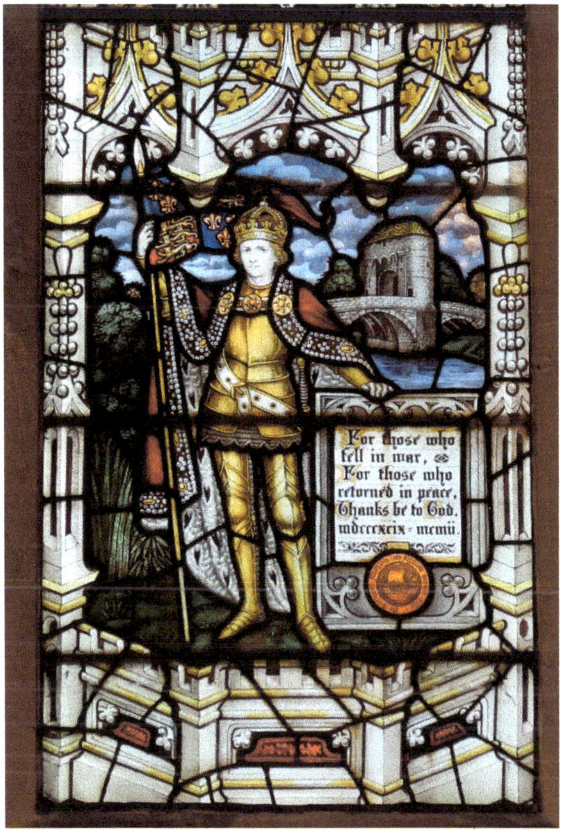

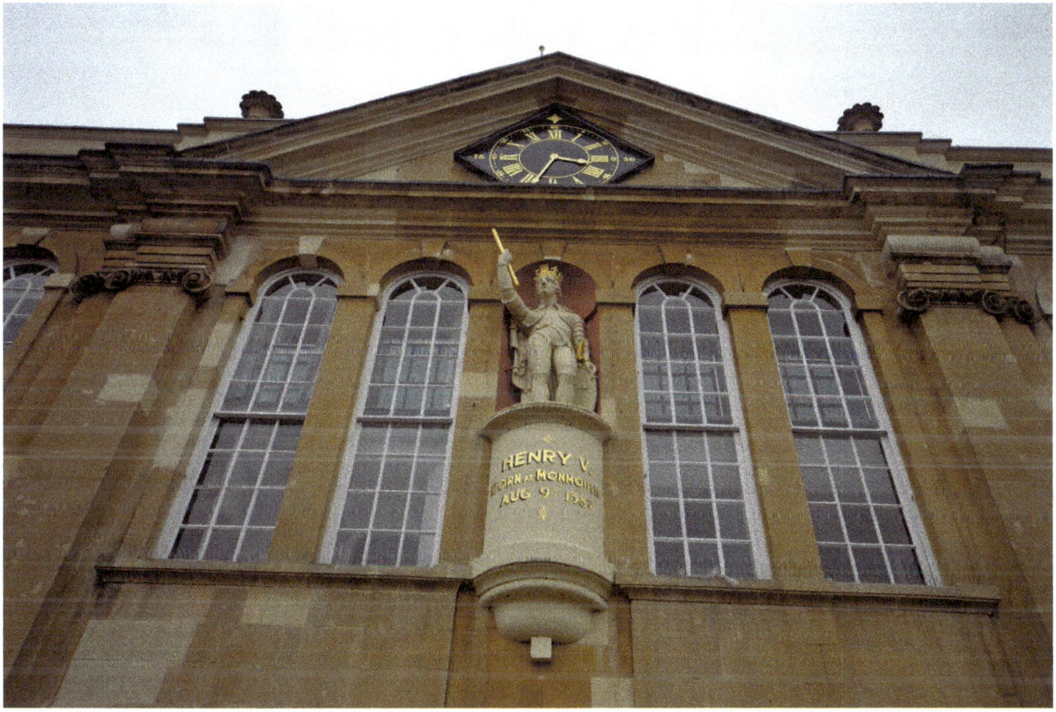

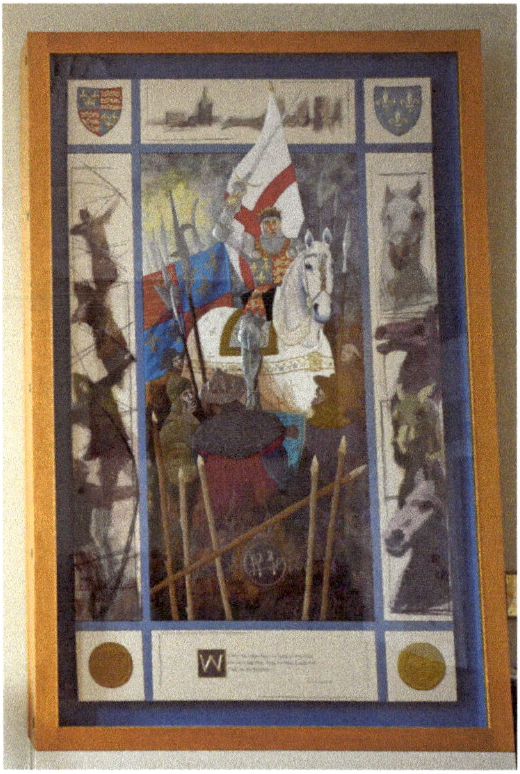

Henry V and the Battle of Agincourt

Mounted in the Shire Hall is a beautiful tapestry wall-hanging depicting Henry V on horseback addressing his troops before the Battle of Agincourt on 25 October 1415. This was designed by local artist Richard Wills and presented in 2015 by the Monmouth Broderers as a gift to celebrate the 600th anniversary of the famous battle. Henry V's army of around 8,000 was outnumbered by five to one, yet 500 Welsh longbowmen cut down the heavily armoured French knights and won the day, marking a major turning point in the Hundred Years War. The bottom picture shows Graham Anderson of Porthcawl, a modern-day Welsh longbowman, demonstrating the skill and strength required to pull a 3-metre (6 foot) longbow and shoot an arrow.

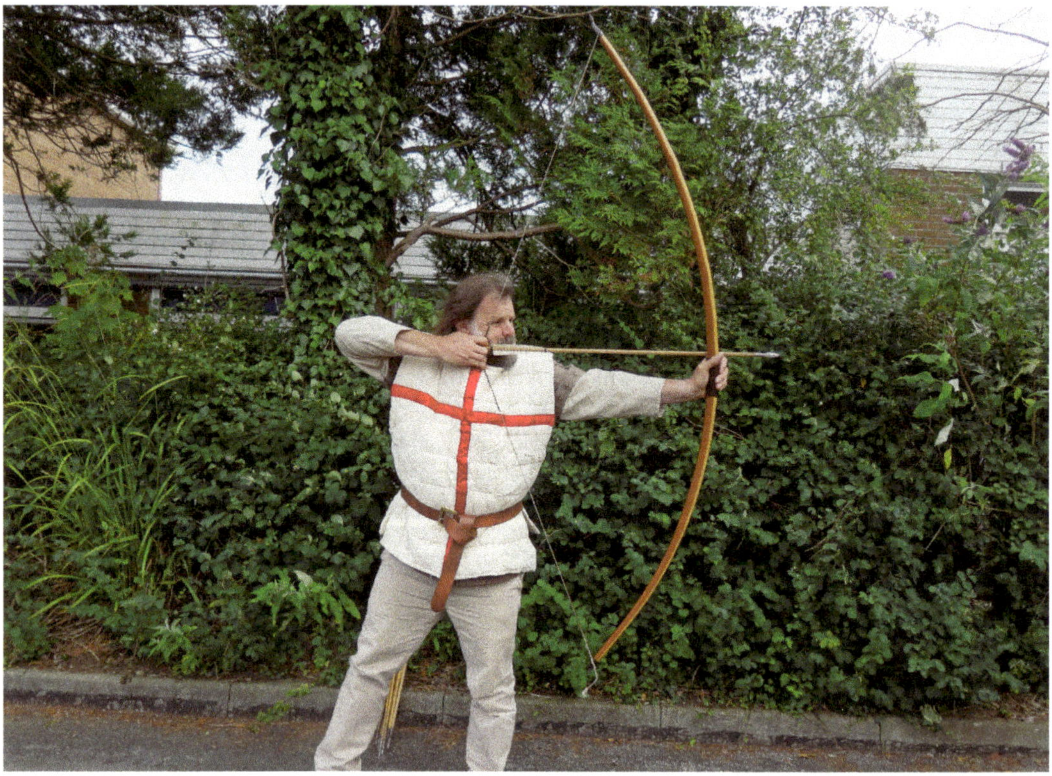

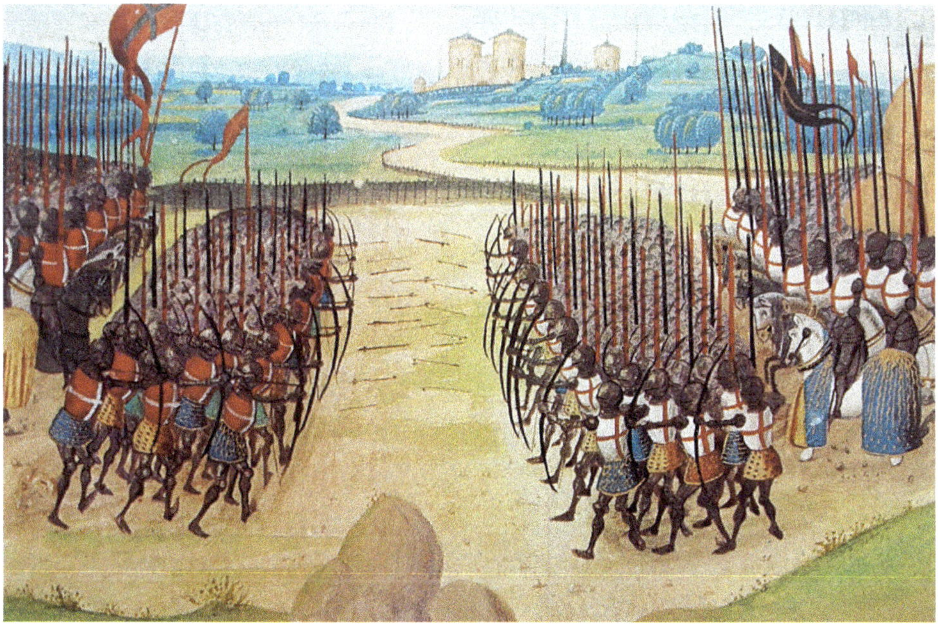

Henry V and the Battle of Agincourt

The top illustration, entitled 'The Battle of Azincourt', is from a fifteenth-century miniature by artist Enguerrand de Monstrelet and depicts the French (on the left) and English bowmen letting fly at each other at the commencement of the battle. To celebrate the 600th anniversary of Agincourt in 2015, many re-enactments took place in the county, as shown in the lower photograph. The Battle of Agincourt is the centre piece of the play *Henry V* by William Shakespeare and many famous quotations from the play have remained throughout history and are still in use today.

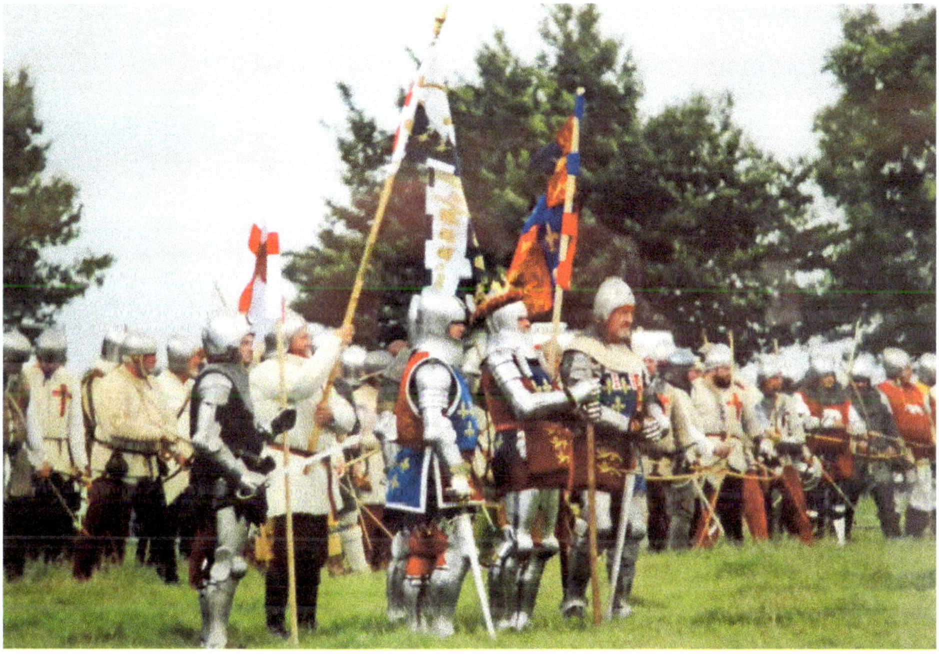

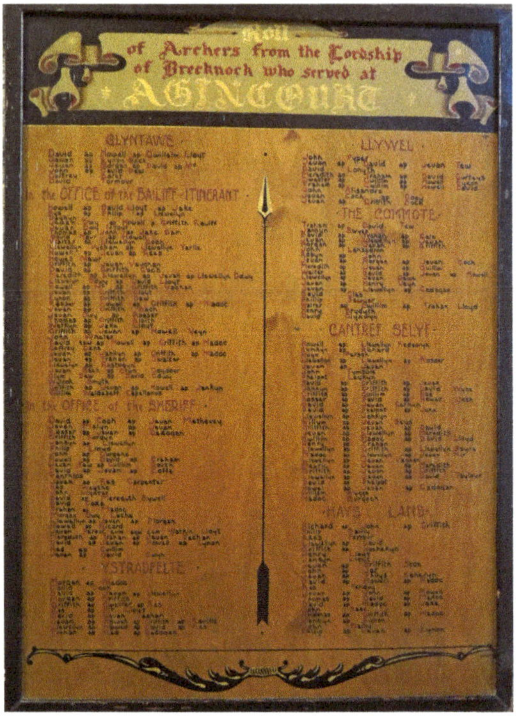

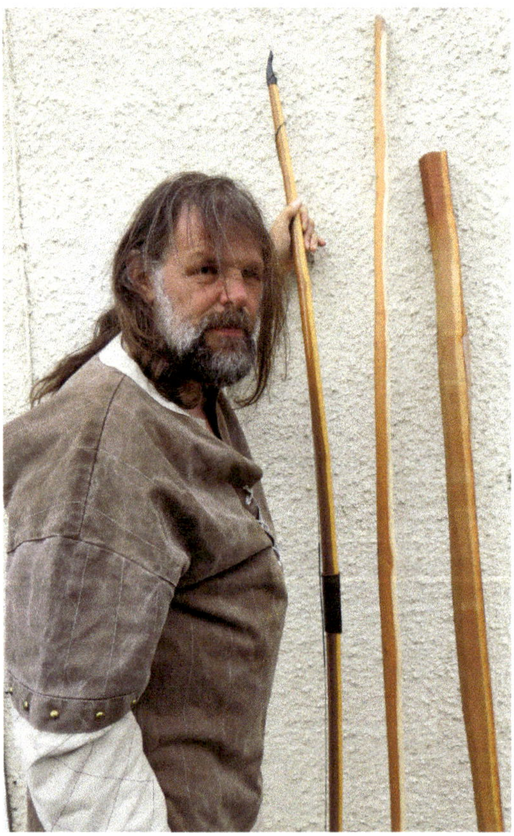

Henry V and the Battle of Agincourt

Shakespeare went to town in his play *Henry V* and gave us quotations such as:

'Once more into the breach, dear friends, once more; or close the gap with our English dead!'

'The game's afoot; follow your spirit; and upon this charge, cry – God for Harry! England and Saint George!'

'We few, we happy few, we band of brothers; ... that fought with us upon Saint Crispin's day.'

Some 500 Welsh archers and twenty-three men-at-arms, led by Watkin Lloyd of Tir Marchog near Trecastle, took part in the battle and it has even been said that 'Welsh archers were the reason Henry V, Harry of Monmouth, won the Battle of Agincourt'. The top photograph is of the plaque in Brecon Cathedral that records the Roll of Archers from the lordship of Brecknock who served at Agincourt.

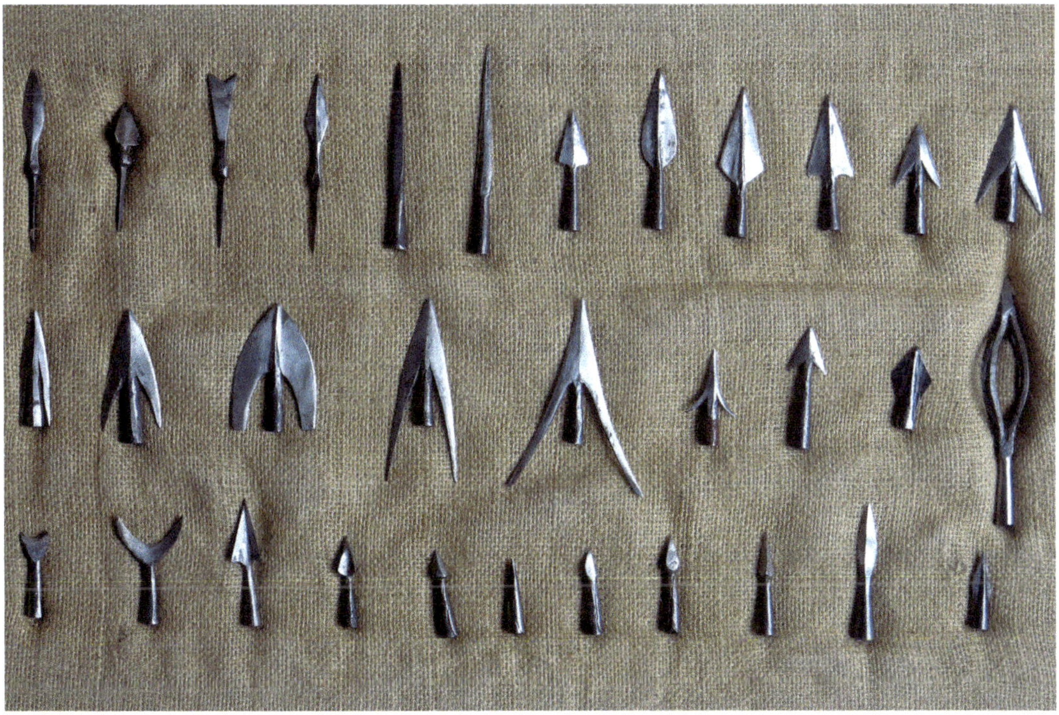

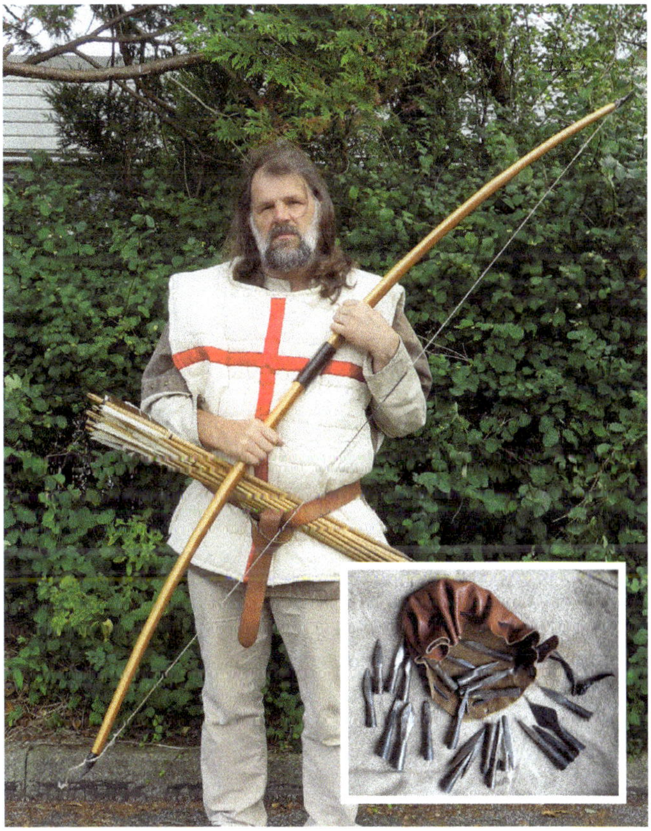

Battle of Agincourt and Longbowmen

The Welsh and English longbowmen at the Battle of Agincourt would have been equipped with an array of weaponry, as depicted in the photographs on this and the previous page. Graham Anderson is a modern-day longbowman who makes his own 3-metre (6 foot) longbows out of seasoned yew and his arrow shafts out of ash. He takes part as an extra in many films and documentaries made in Wales at the Pencoed Film Studios near Bridgend. Not just a picture-postcard longbowman, Graham participates in competitions and can bend a bow with a 13-kilogram pull on the bowstring before releasing an arrow that flies 201 metres before falling back to earth.

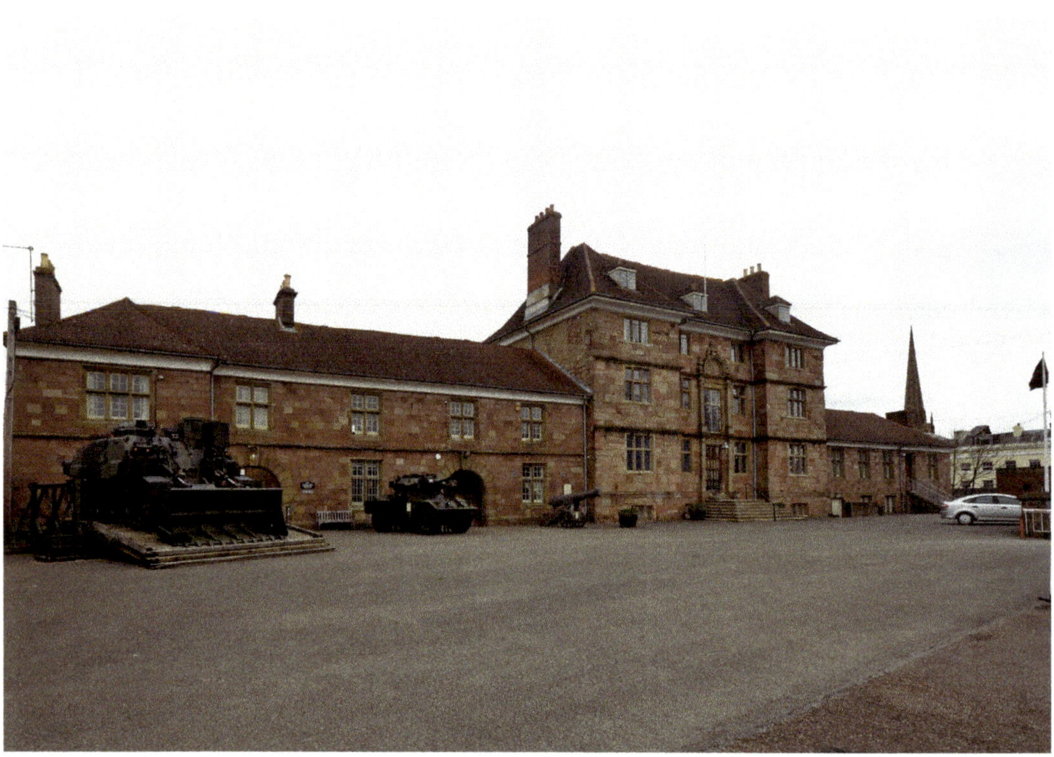

Great Castle House and the Royal Monmouthshire Royal Engineers (Militia)

Monmouth's regiment is one of the oldest in the country, its roots going back to the 1530s when Henry VIII split from Rome, divorced his wife and dissolved the monasteries. In order to control and tax Wales, Henry VIII passed an Act of Union (1536–43) and created the new county of Monmouthshire. During the same period, troops were first mustered in Monmouth in 1439. Originally know as a Posse Comitatus (the power of the county), the troops eventually evolved into militia regiments. Today the regiment is called the Royal Monmouthshire Royal Engineers and its headquarters are in Great Castle House.

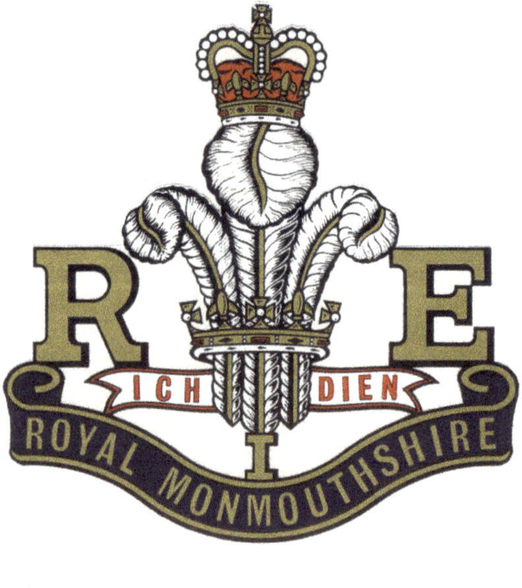

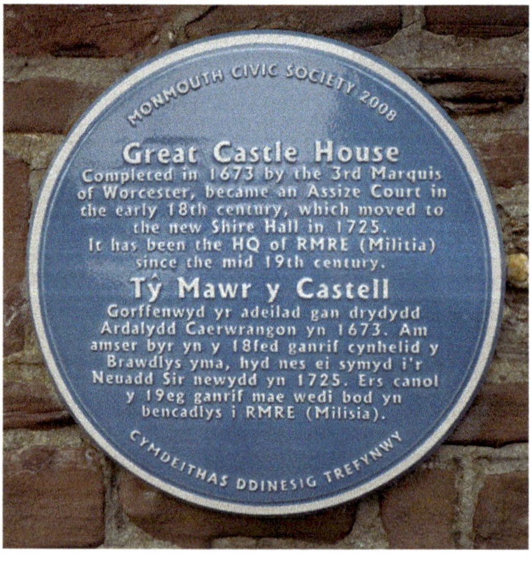

The Royal Monmouthshire Royal Engineers (Militia)

The Crimean War took place from 1853 to 1856, but the militia was not allowed to serve overseas and the regiment was embodied and posted to Pembroke Dock. However, many men joined other regiments to get to the action. One of these men who made his own way to the Crimea was Colonel Vaughan, an energetic officer who served with the regiment for forty years. He was so stirred by the squalor and chaos he found there that he wrote an influential booklet urging reforms within the army. The lower photograph is of a Russian Fortress Gun that was given to Monmouth after the Crimean War in gratitude for the service of its men. The gun fired a ball of 32 pounds over 2,500 yards at an elevation of 8 degrees using a powder charge of 10 pounds.

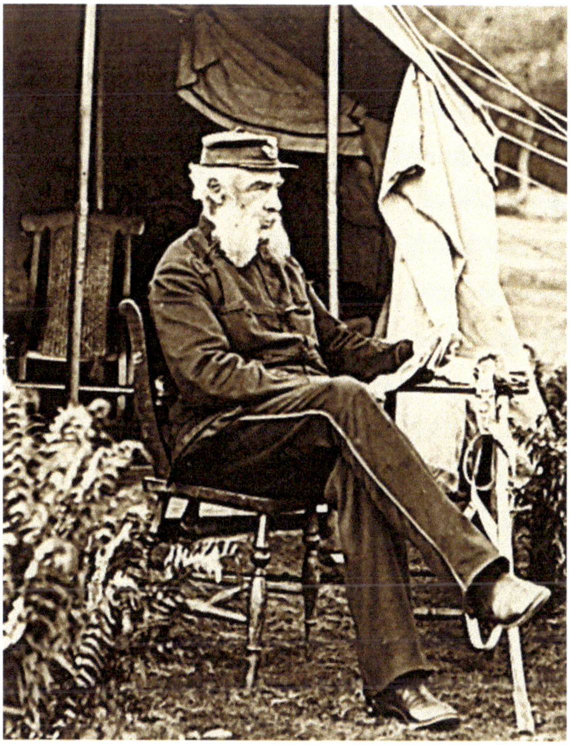

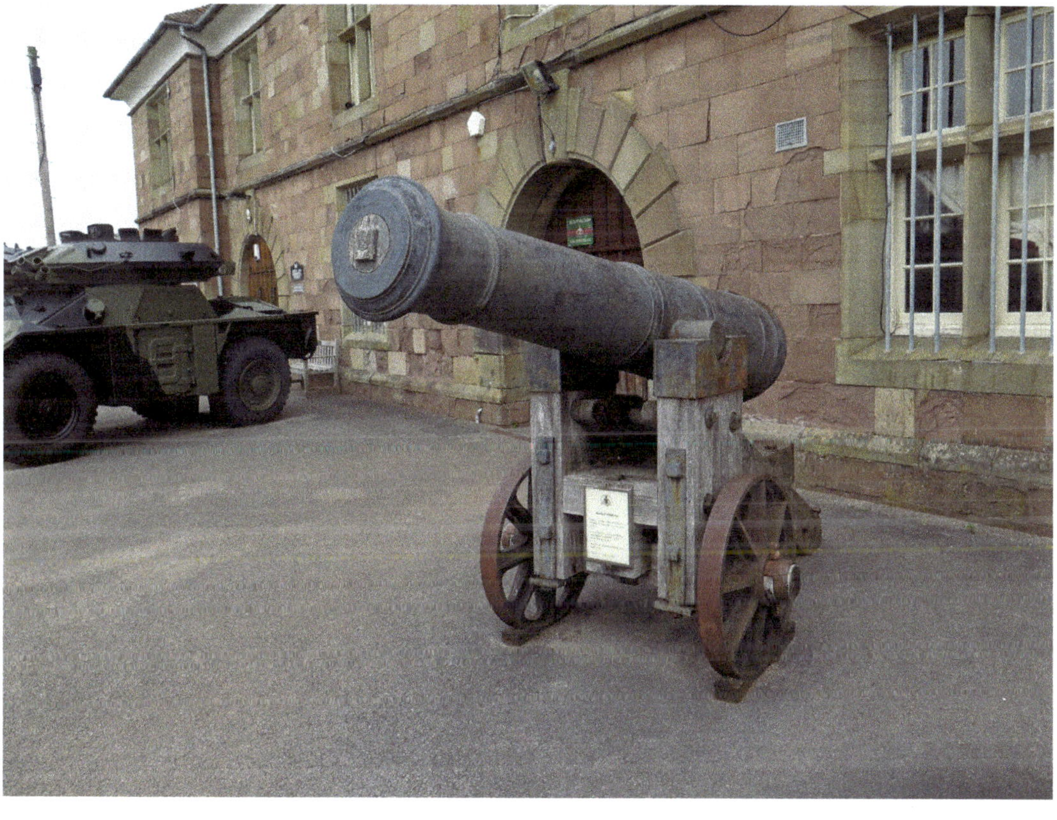

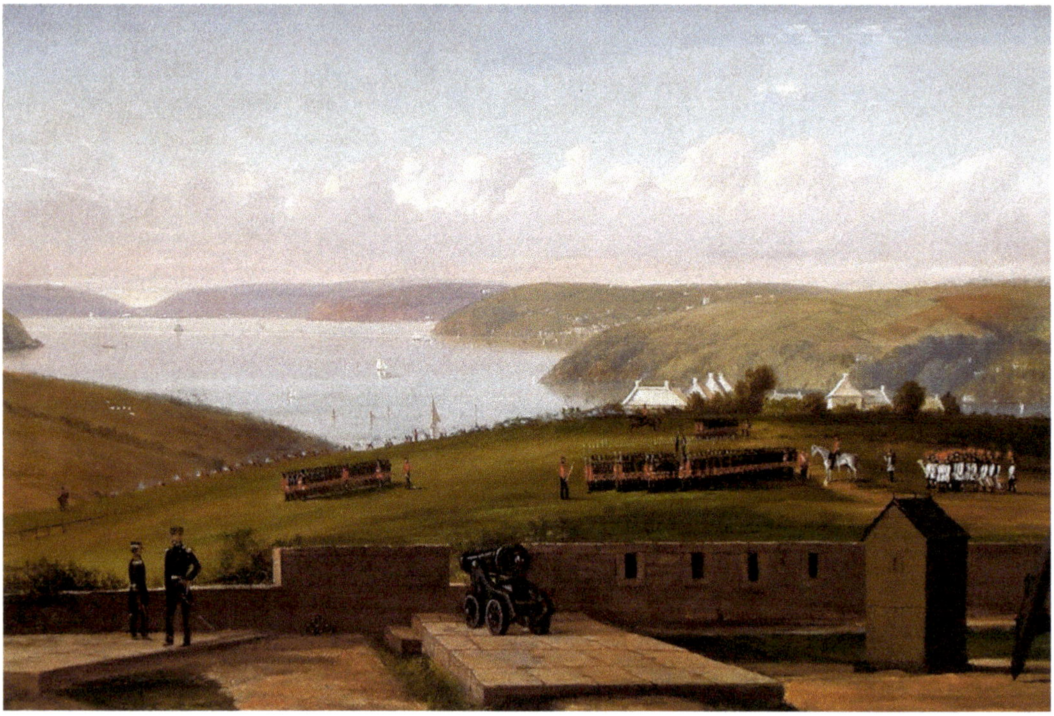

The Royal Monmouthshire Royal Engineers (Militia)
A painting and sketch of the regiment serving at Pembroke Dock in 1855.

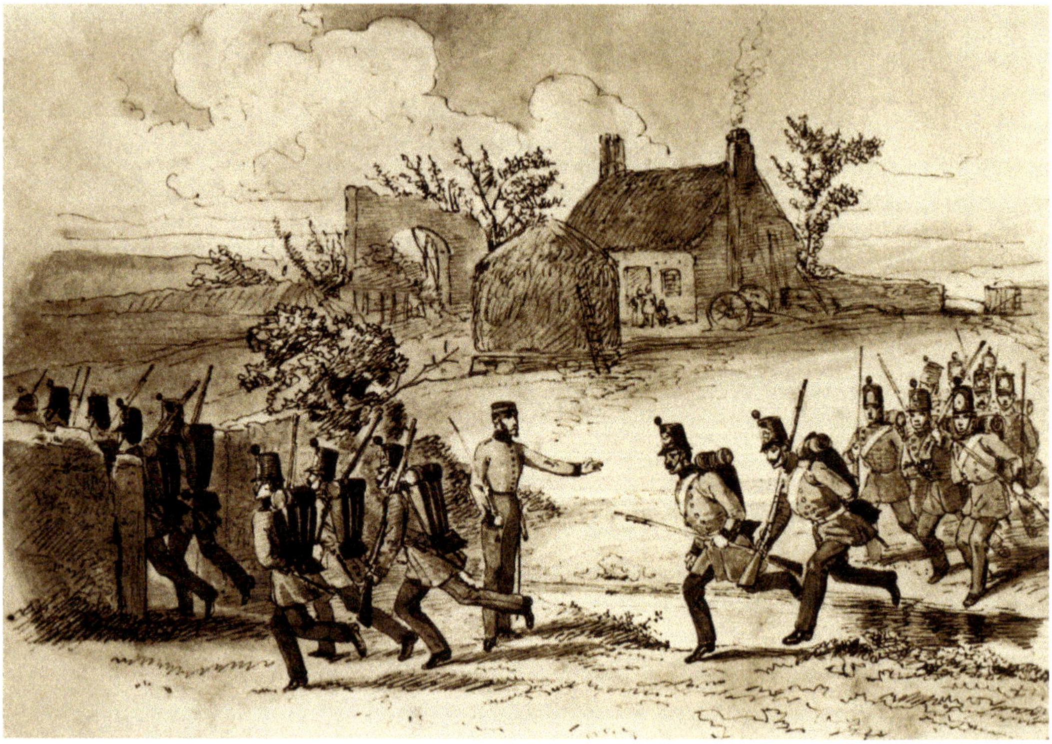

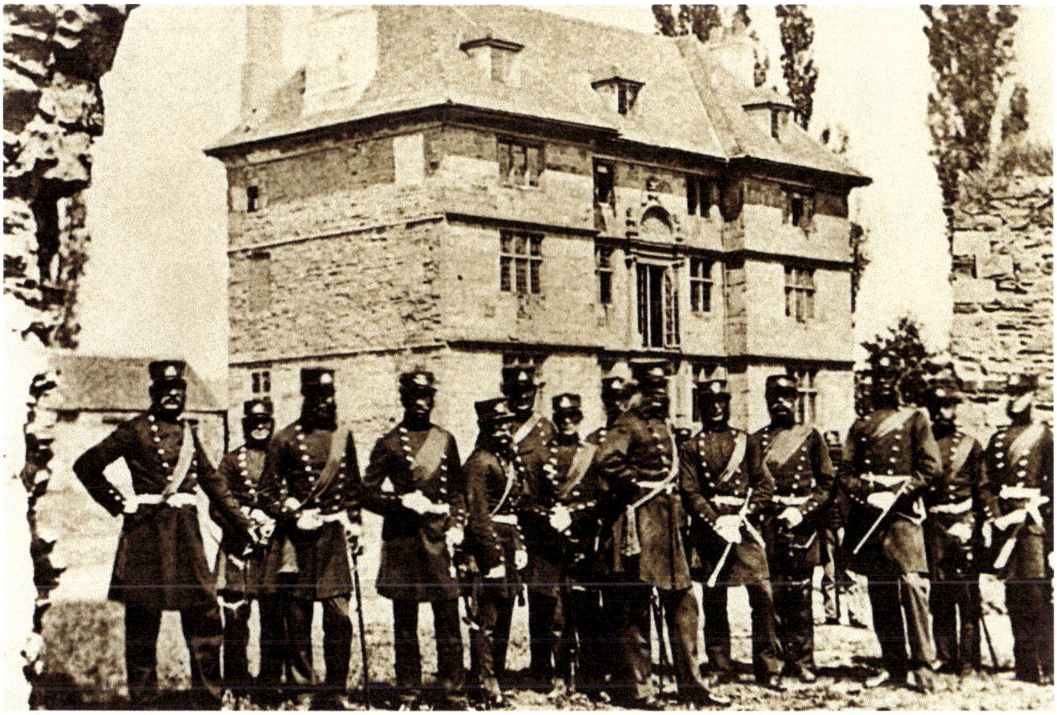

The Royal Monmouthshire Royal Engineers (Militia)

The militia officers in front of the Great Castle House before and after inspection in 1860.

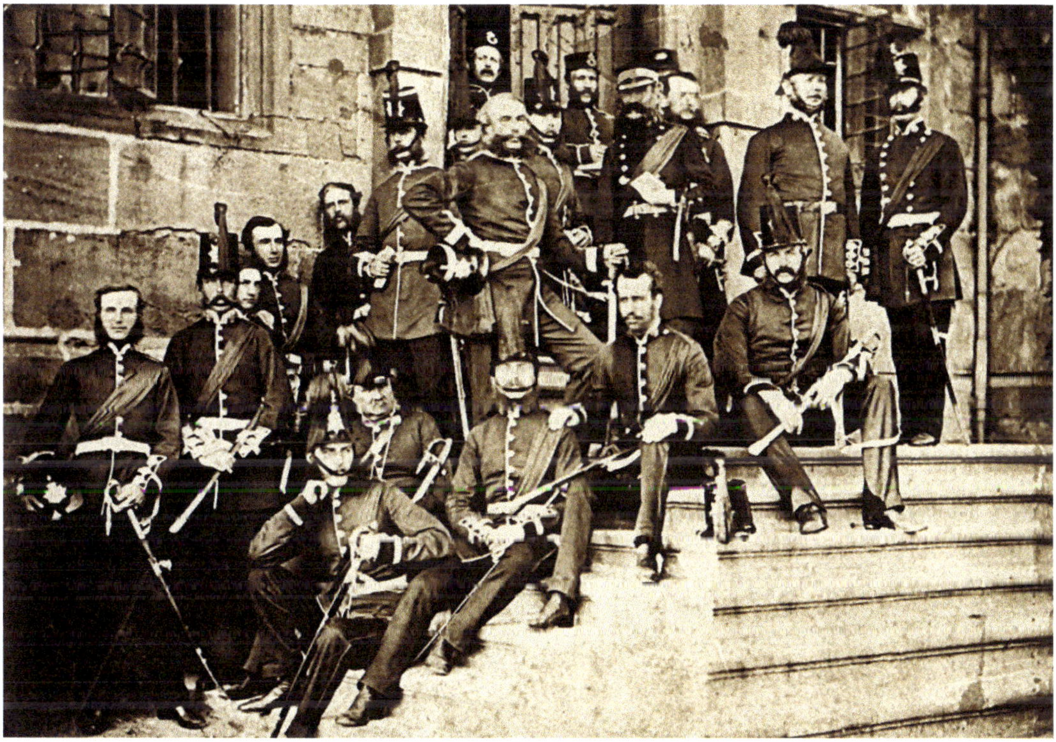

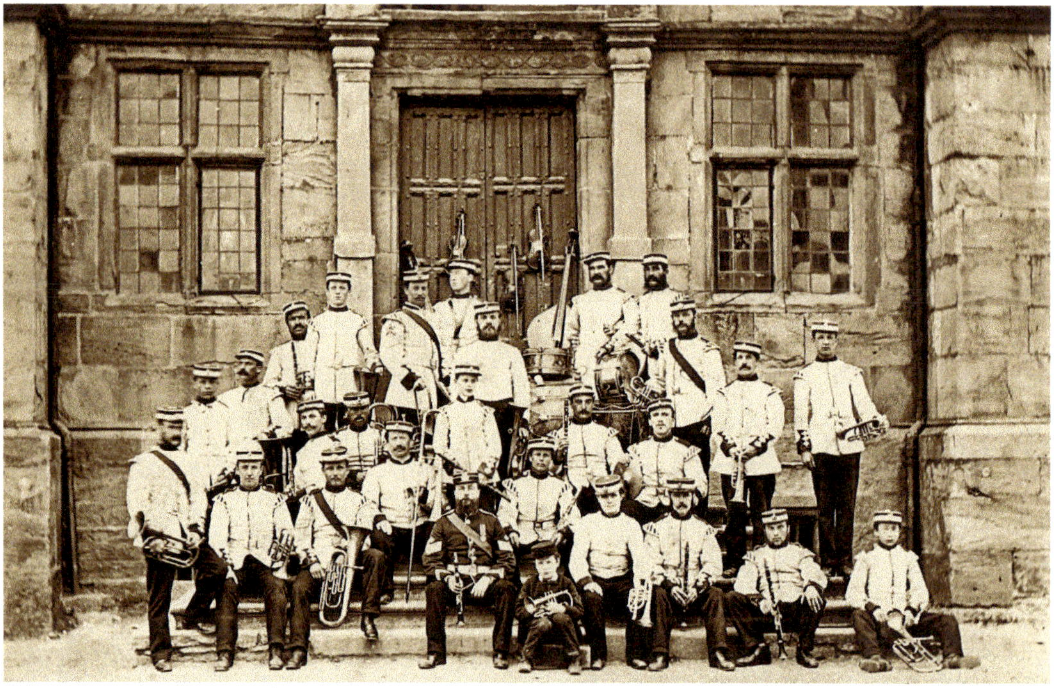

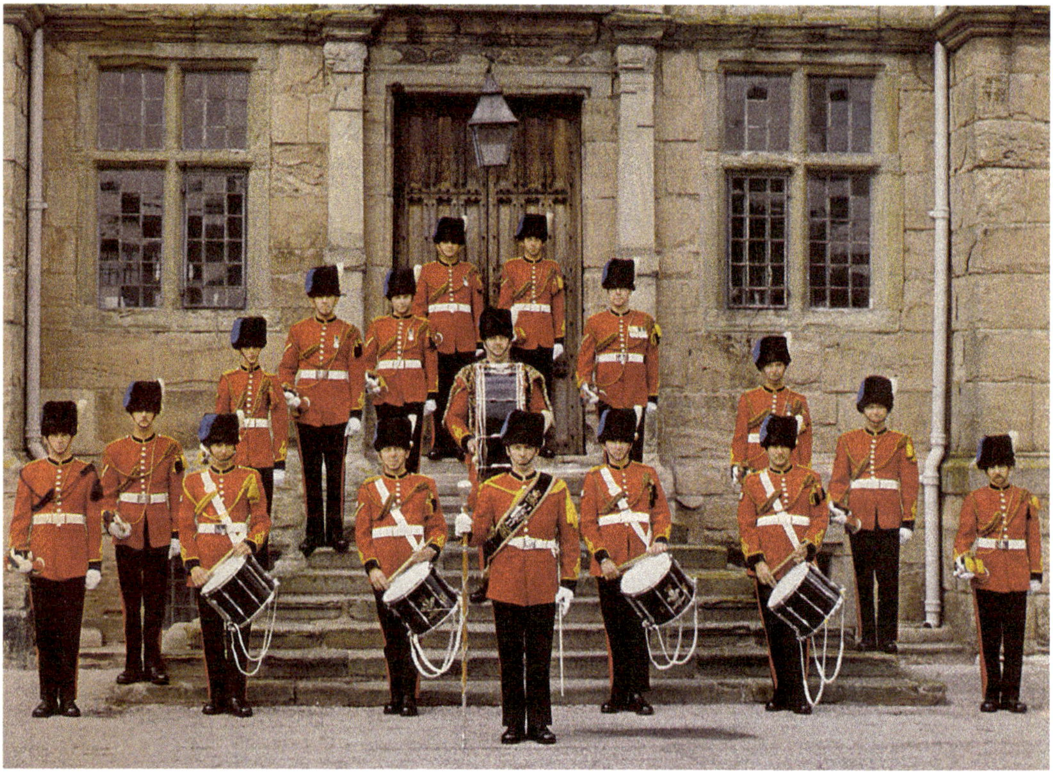

The Royal Monmouthshire Royal Engineers (Militia)
The Militia Band in 1868 and the Nottinghamshire Band of the Royal Engineers in 2010.

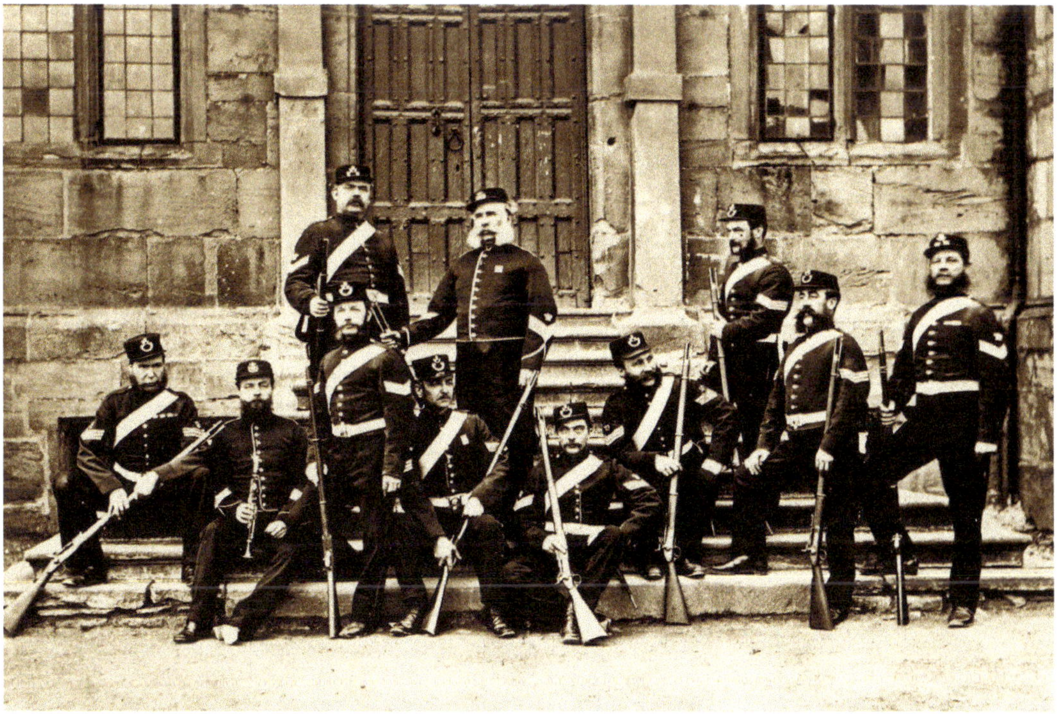

The Royal Monmouthshire Royal Engineers (Militia)
The militia sergeants outside the Great Castle House in 1869 and the Railway Company in 1906.

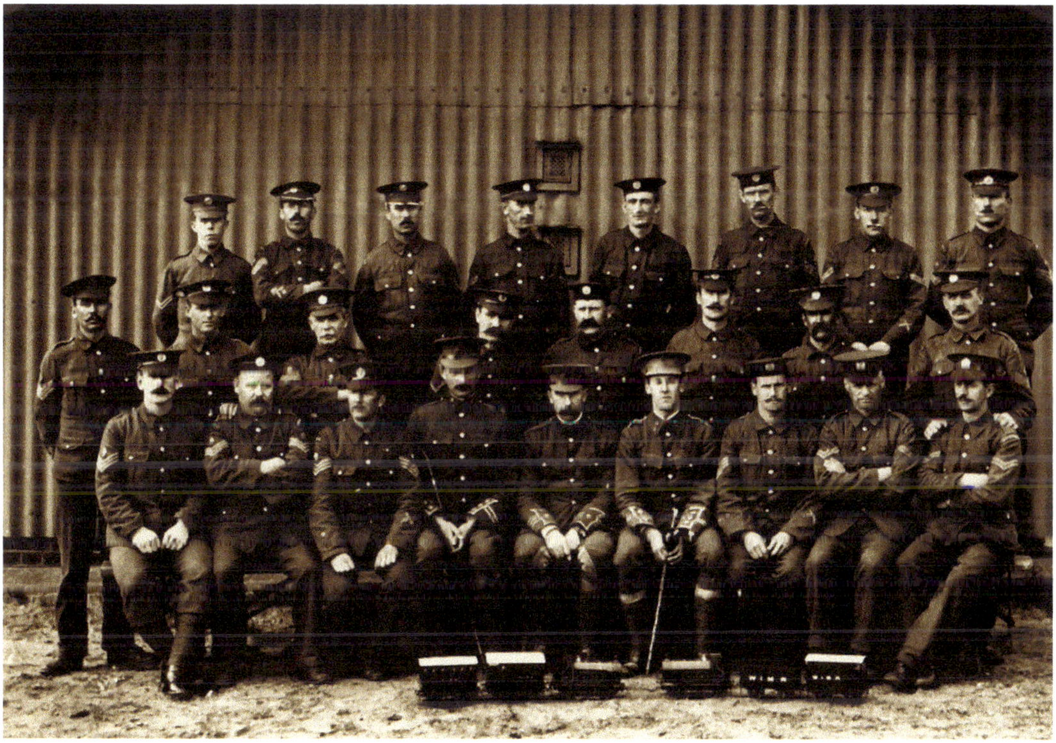

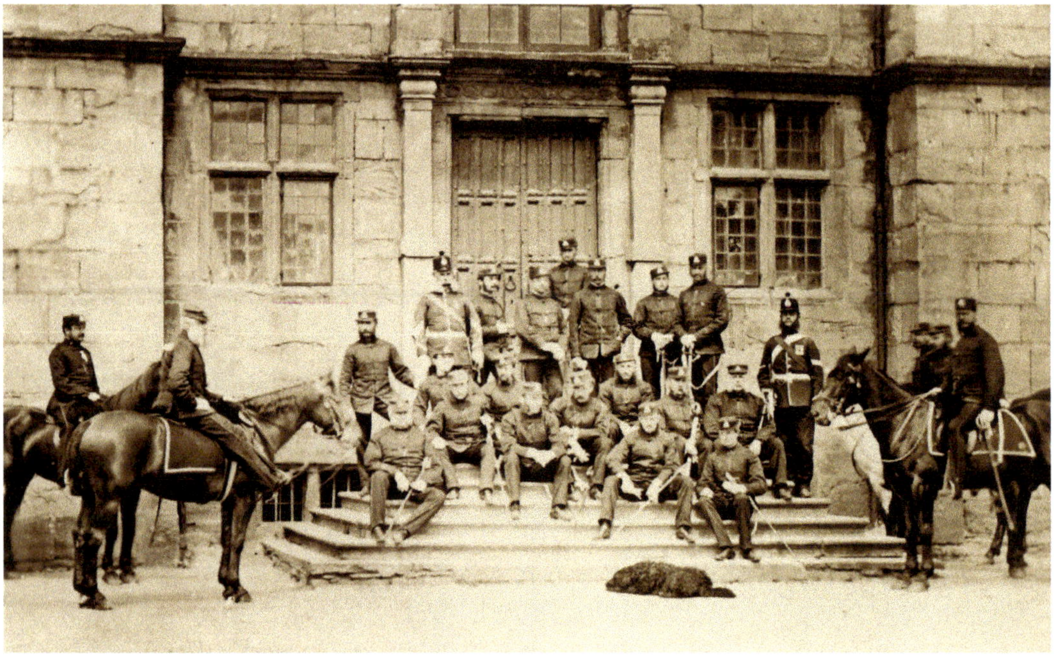

The Royal Monmouthshire Royal Engineers (Militia)

The top photograph shows mounted members of the regiment (presumed to be the officers), with the infantry outside the Great Castle House in 1871. A more leisurely occasion has been captured in the lower photograph taken in 1867 – that of the Presentation of the Shooting Cup after the Regimental Shooting Competition.

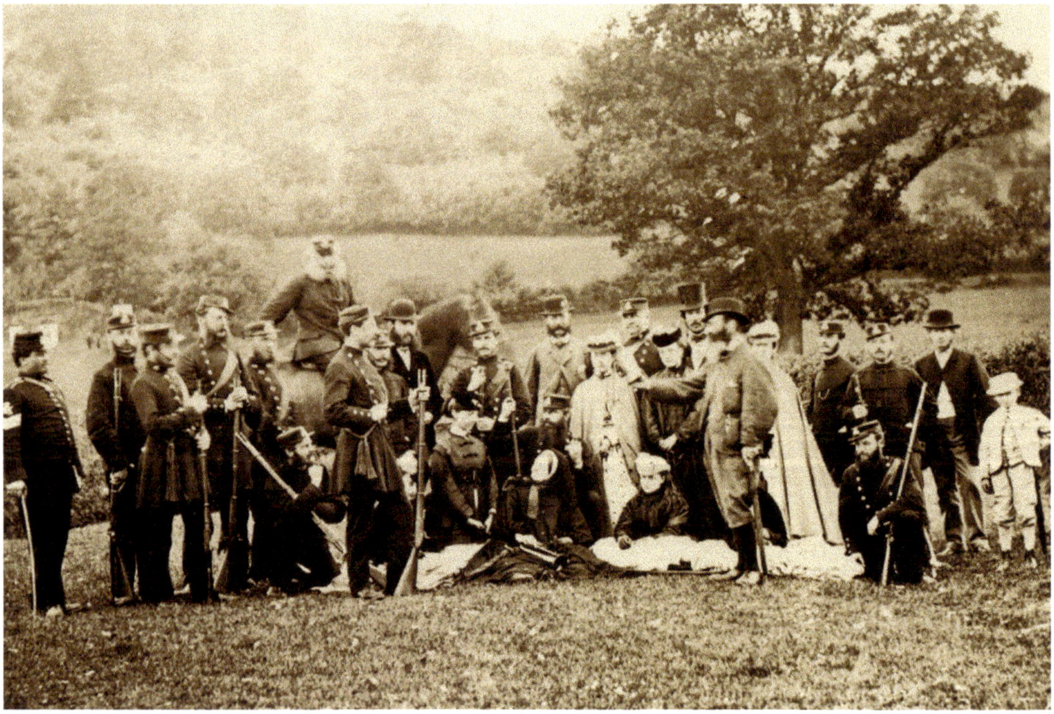

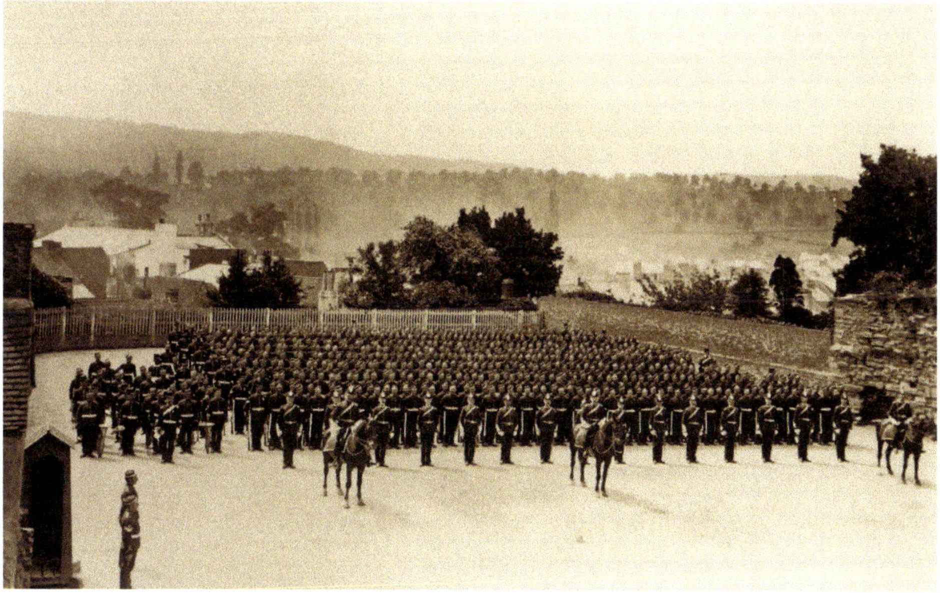

The Royal Monmouthshire Royal Engineers (Militia)

The top photograph shows the regiment on parade in the castle grounds when it switched from an infantry to an engineering role in 1877. The lower photograph was taken in December 2010 in Agincourt Square and is of the Nottinghamshire Band of the Royal Engineers leading the parade of the Royal Monmouthshire Royal Engineers on their return from duty in Helmand Province, Afghanistan. The regiment had taken part in an operation codenamed 'HERRICK 12'.

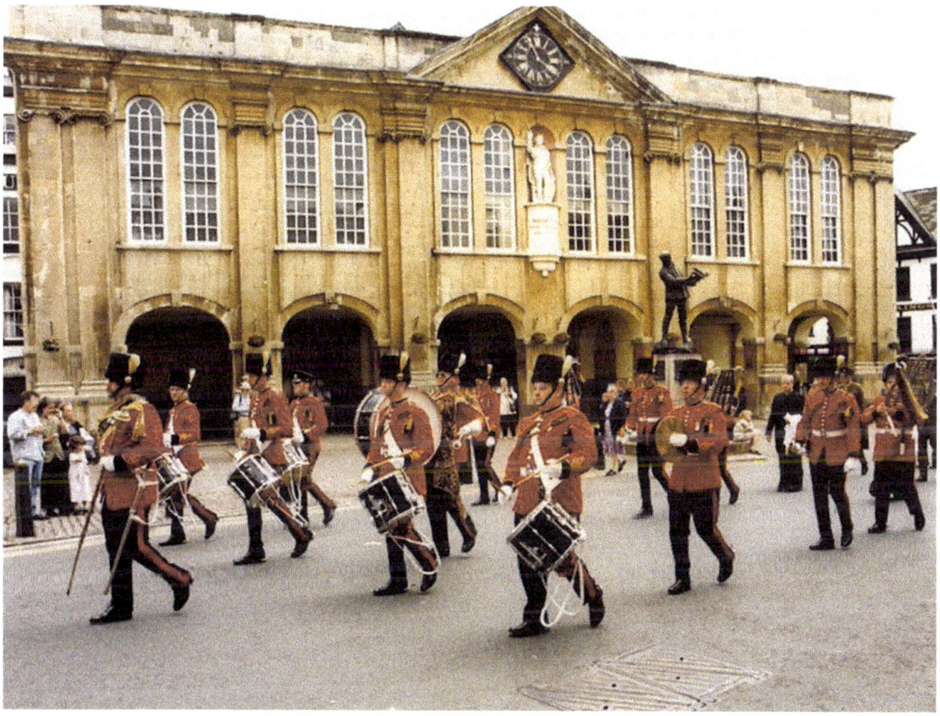

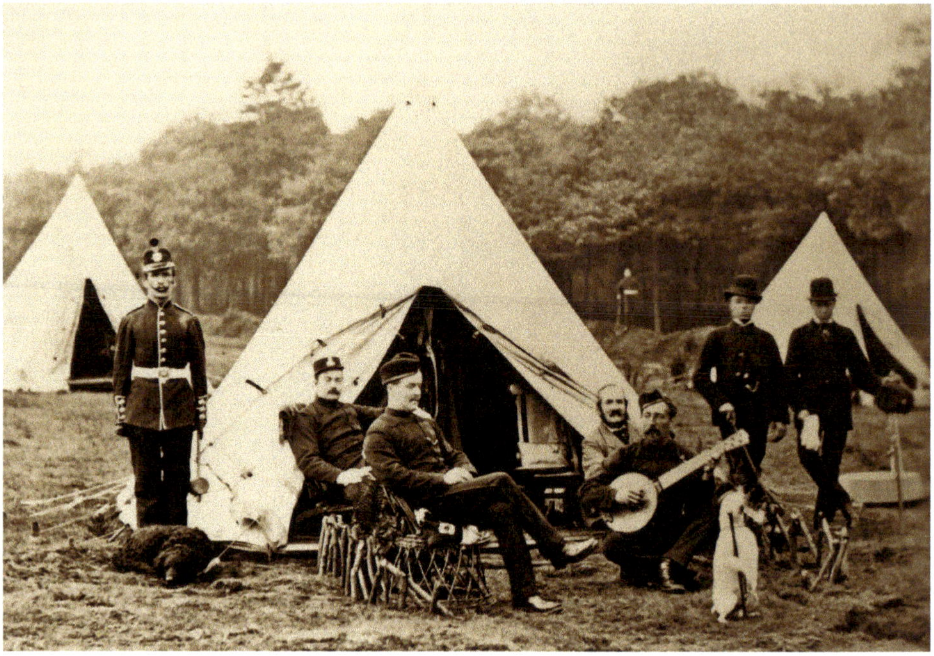

The Royal Monmouthshire Royal Engineers (Militia)

The regiment went on many exercises, including those to the Forest of Dean where they camped in Bell Tents, the stalwart field accommodation for troops in the field that existed well after the end of the Second World War. These two photographs of camping comforts, including a performing dog, were taken in 1873 (top) and 1890 (bottom).

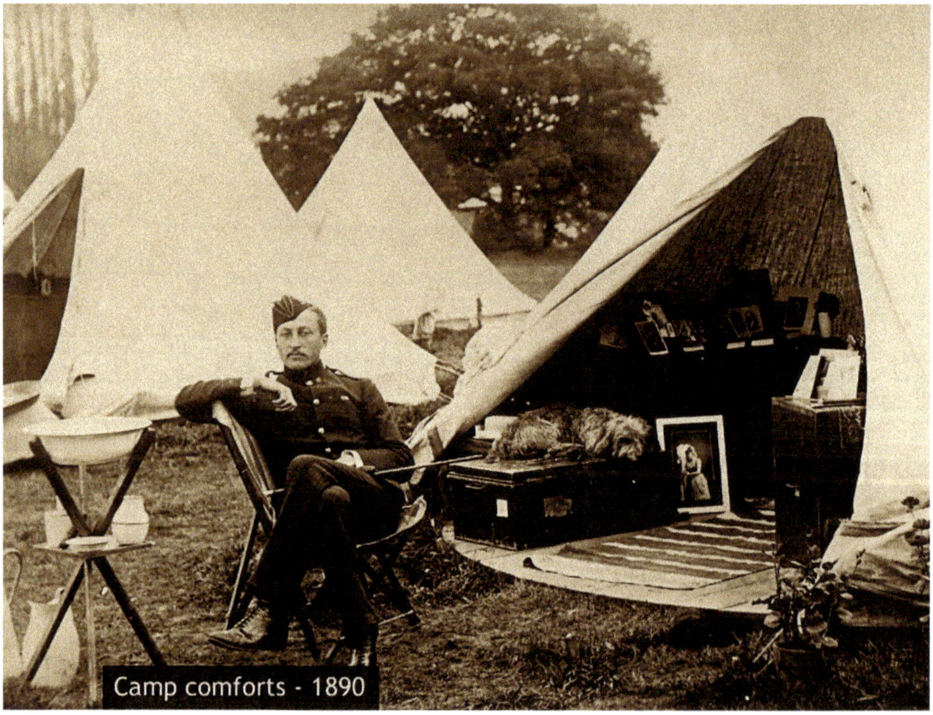

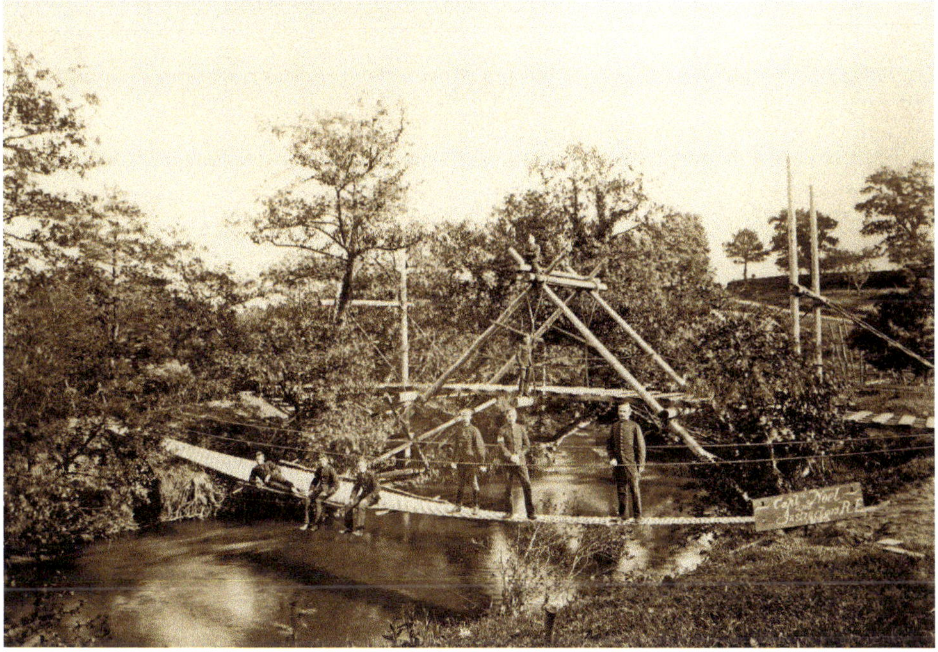

The Royal Monmouthshire Royal Engineers (Militia)

Here the soldiers are building bridges on the River Monnow at Vauxhall Field, where the headquarters of the Royal Monmouthshire Royal Regiment are located. After its conversion to an engineering role, the regiment was keen to keep up to scratch by carrying out many engineering exercises and what better place to do these than on the Monnow River at Vauxhall Field, as evidenced by the two photographs taken in 1883 (top) and 1906 (bottom).

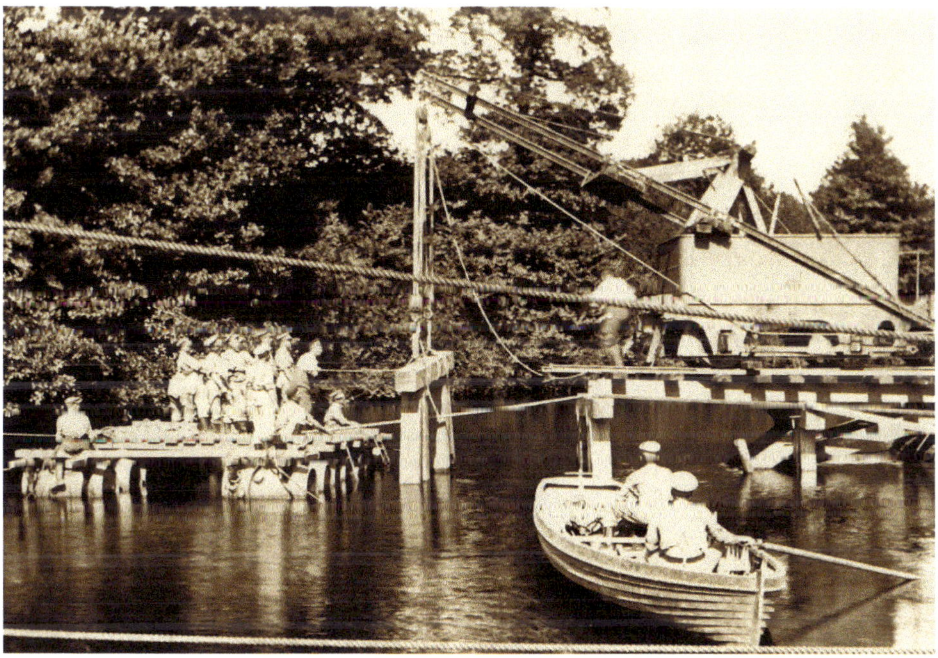

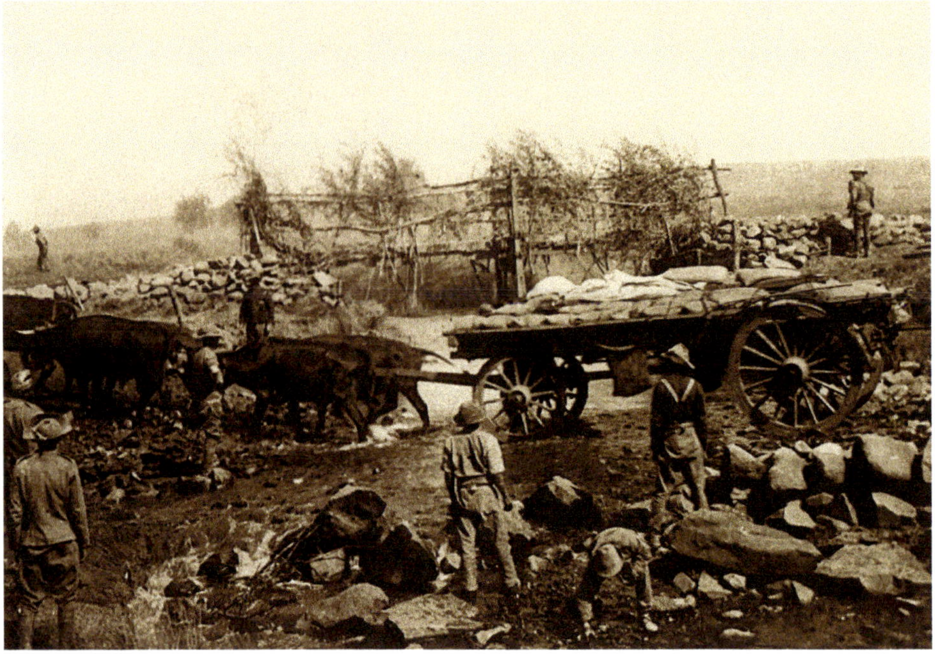

The Royal Monmouthshire Royal Engineers (Militia)

By the time the Second Boer War or South African War (1899–1902) came about, the regiment was allowed to travel overseas and was stationed in the Transvaal, as recorded by the top photograph taken in 1902. Back to Monmouth in 1905, the regiment continued its bridge building and constructed the White Bridge over the River Monnow, giving access to Vauxhall Field from the north end of town. This new bridge replaced an earlier wooden structure that had fallen into decay.

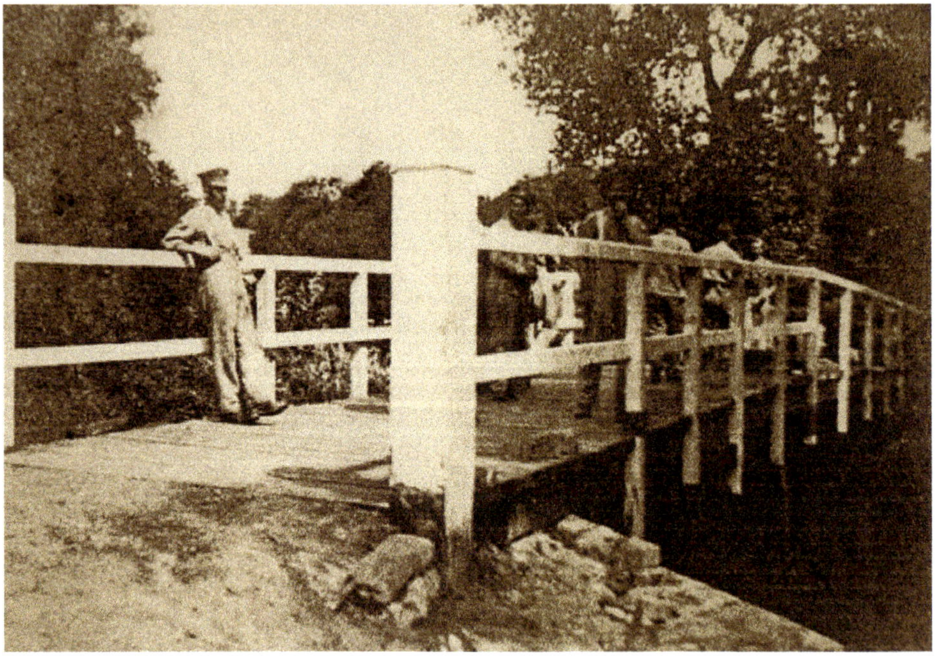

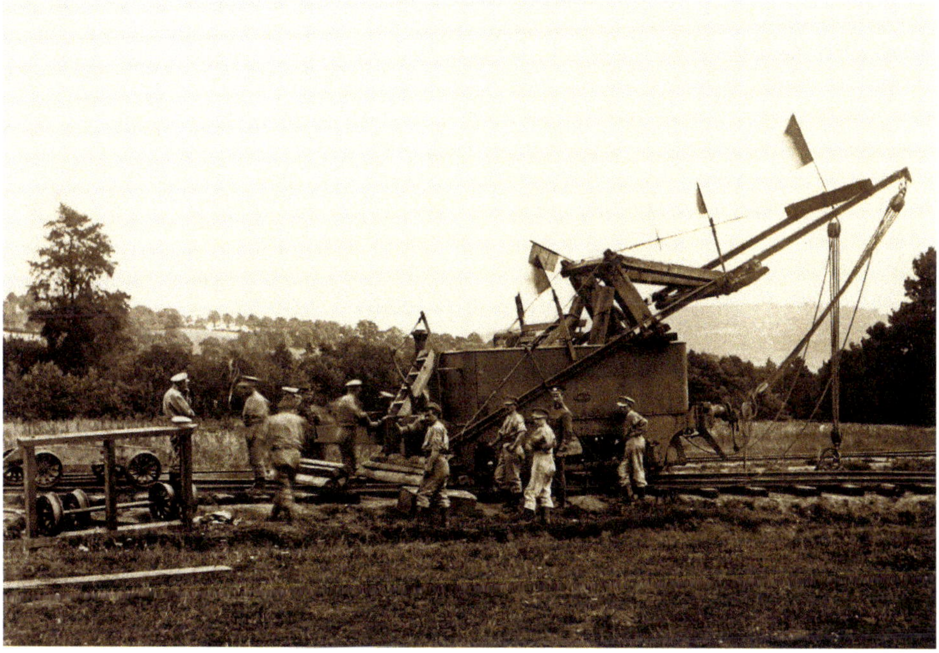

The Royal Monmouthshire Royal Engineers (Militia)

The title given to the top photograph of 1906 was 'The Extemporised Crane', which roughly translates as 'to do something without prior preparation'. The crane probably arrived at regimental headquarters as a flat pack! In comparison, the bottom photograph shows a Combat Engineering Tractor that is preserved outside the Regimental Museum. This huge earth-moving vehicle took part in the 1991 Gulf War and is designed to work near the front line. With a crew of two, it can clear obstacles, dig pits, prepare barriers and rescue vehicles. It is armoured and tracked like a tank and weighs 17 tonnes, yet it can swim and can be transported by air.

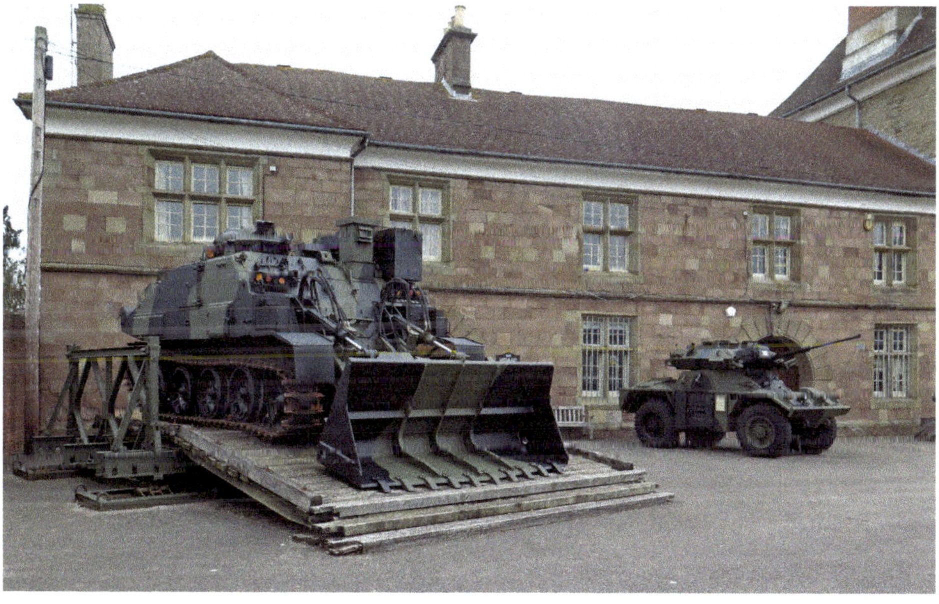

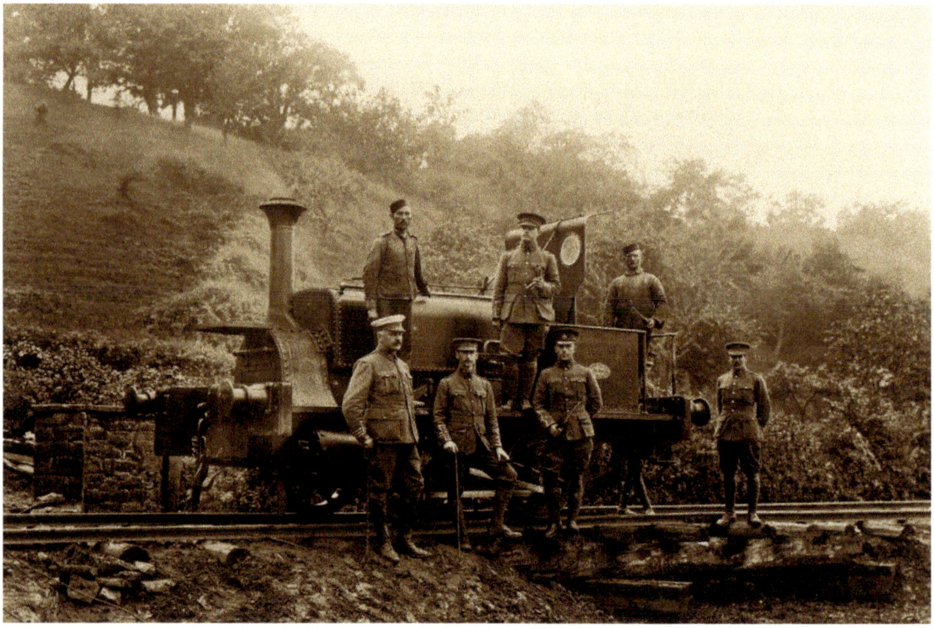

The Royal Monmouthshire Royal Engineers (Militia)

The regiment experienced the use and handling of heavy machinery when it received its own railway locomotive, as shown in the top photograph taken in 1906. The regiment had carried out building, bridging and railway work while in South Africa during the Boer War, by which time railway transportation had become important in warfare. On the regiment's return from abroad, a short section of track with a locomotive was added to the training equipment at Monmouth. The lower modern picture shows members of the regiment building roads using a small bulldozer.

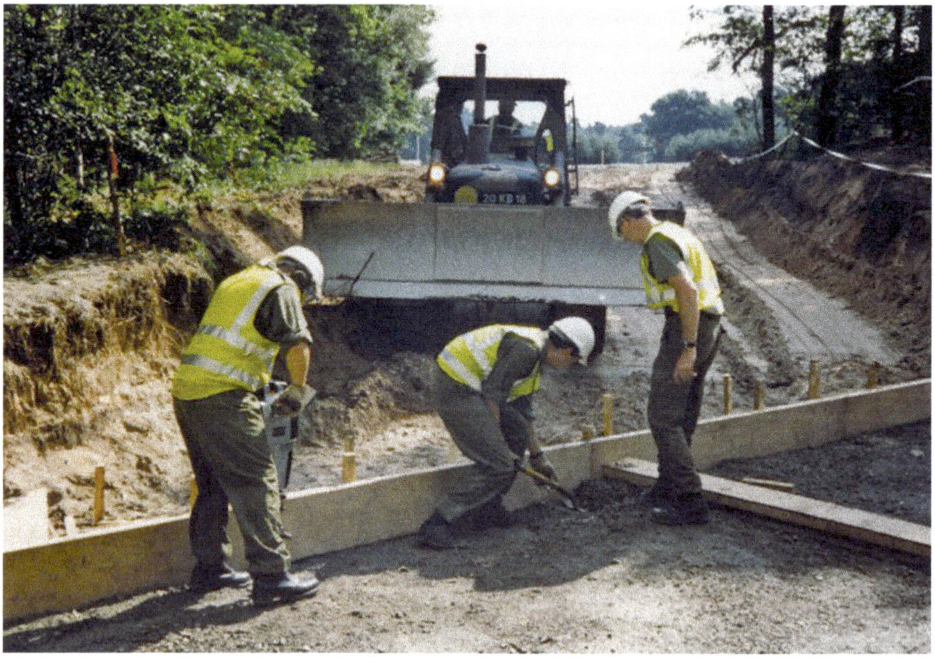

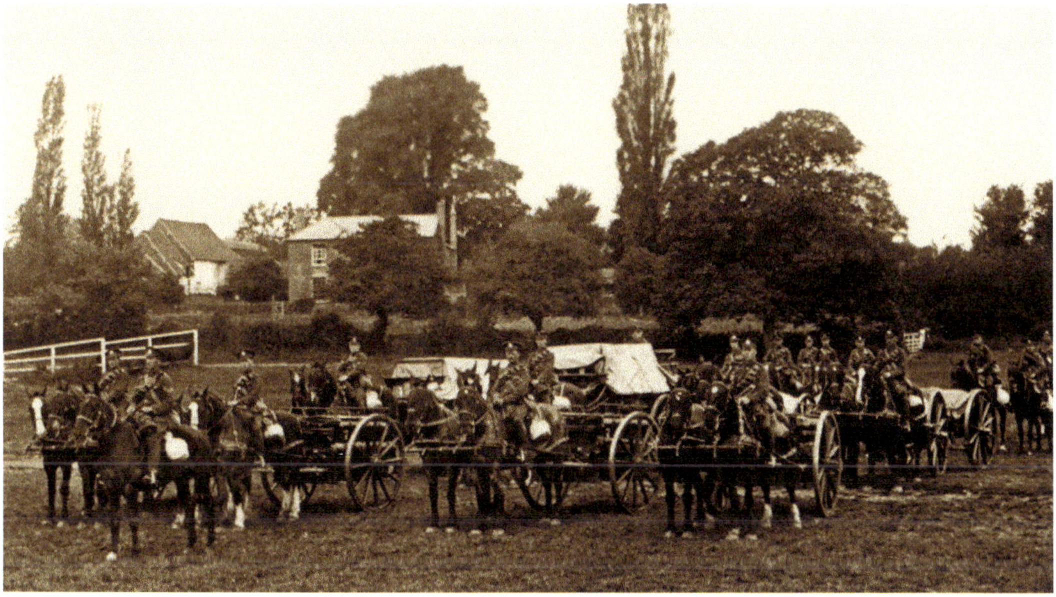

The Royal Monmouthshire Royal Engineers (Militia)
From horse-drawn carriages in 1906 to diesel-engine heavy lorries of today, the regiment has come a long way in its mode and choice of transportation in 116 years.

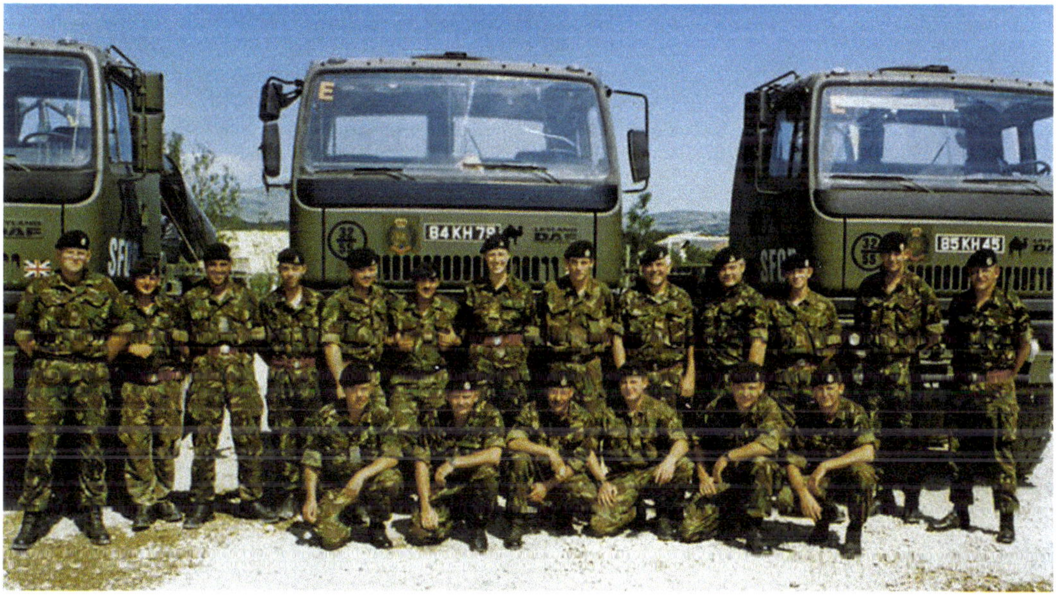

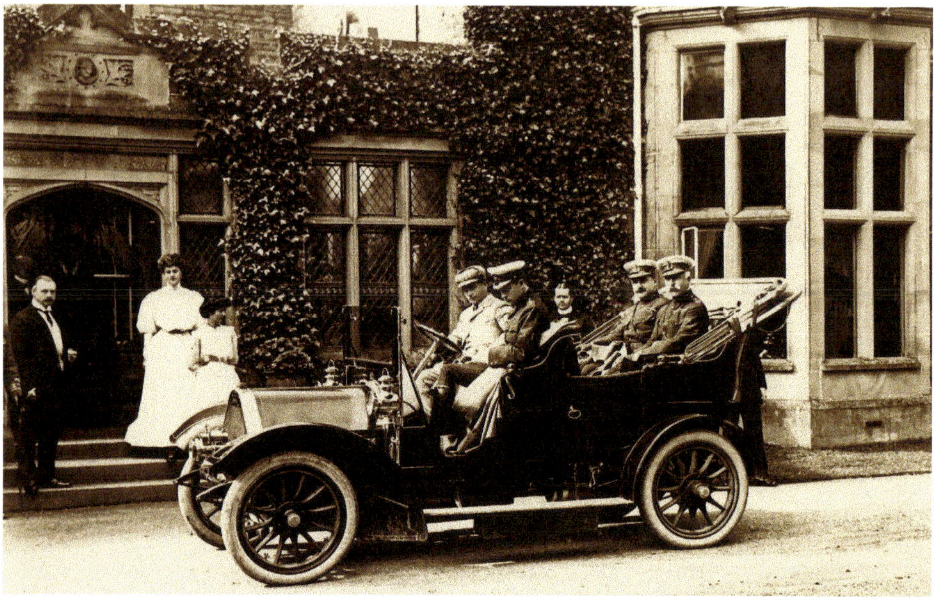

The Royal Monmouthshire Royal Engineers (Militia)

More transport changes. The top photograph has captured the moment when the Duke of Connaught, Edward VII's brother, is leaving the house of the officer commanding the No. 3 company of the Royal Monmouth Royal Engineers, to inspect the regiment in 1906. What a contrast we have in the lower photograph with the Prime Minister, Winston Churchill, with his trademark cigar, sitting in an American Jeep at the Draghunt Bridge in March 1945. The regiment had put a pontoon-style bridge across the Rhine in a day and the Top Man was there to witness the event.

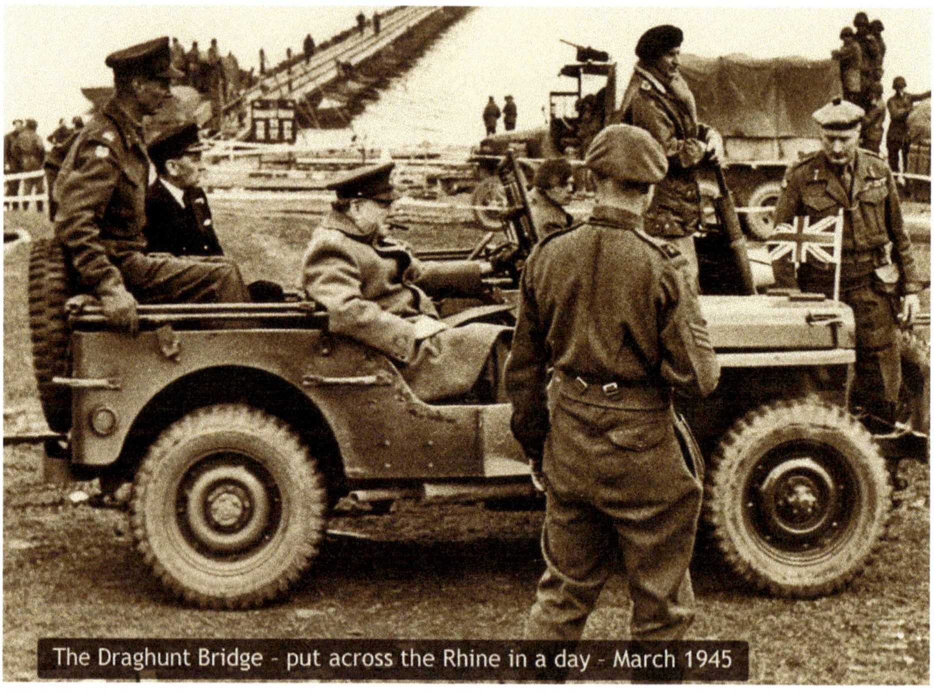

The Draghunt Bridge - put across the Rhine in a day - March 1945

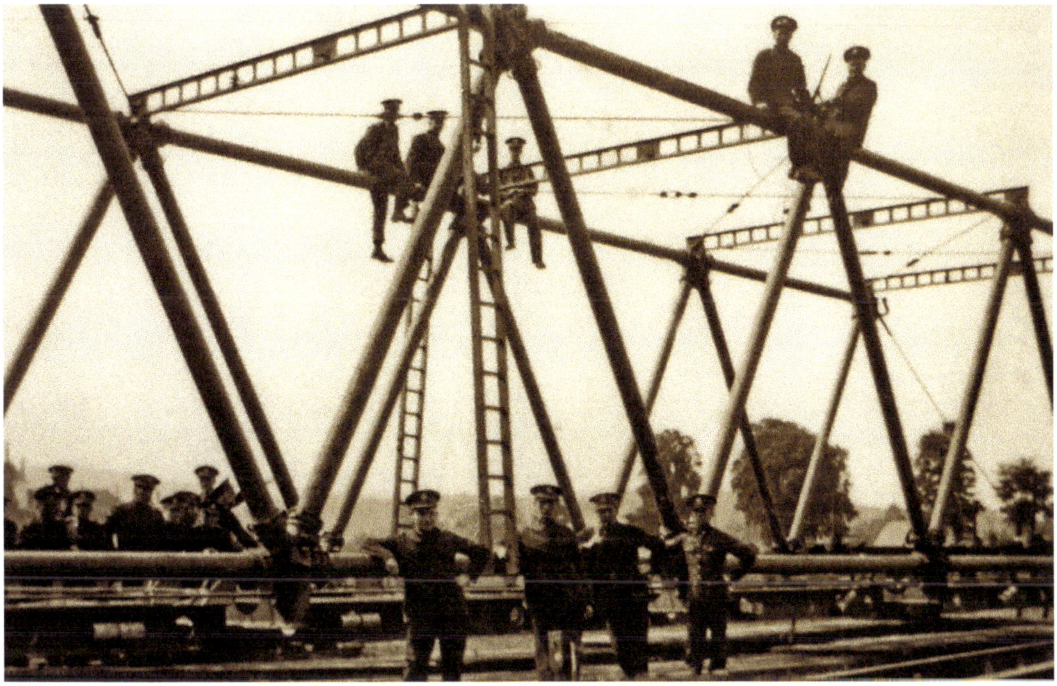

The Royal Monmouthshire Royal Engineers (Militia)

By 1931 the wooden White Bridge, which the regiment had built in 1905 to give access to Vauxhall Field, was itself in need of replacement. The top photograph shows the engineers in the process of erecting an Inglis Mark II prefabricated bridge across the River Monnow. This bridge is still in use today, as shown in the bottom photograph, and is the only one of its kind left in existence. The Inglis range of prefabricated bridges were invented by Charles Edward Inglis and are the forerunners of the famous Bailey Bridge.

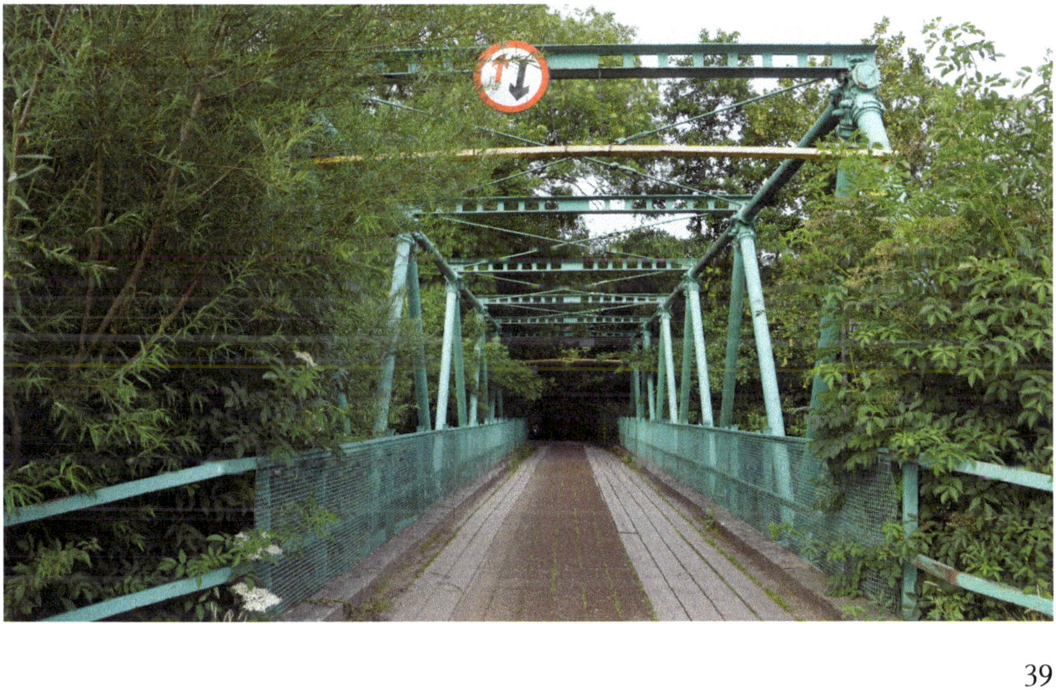

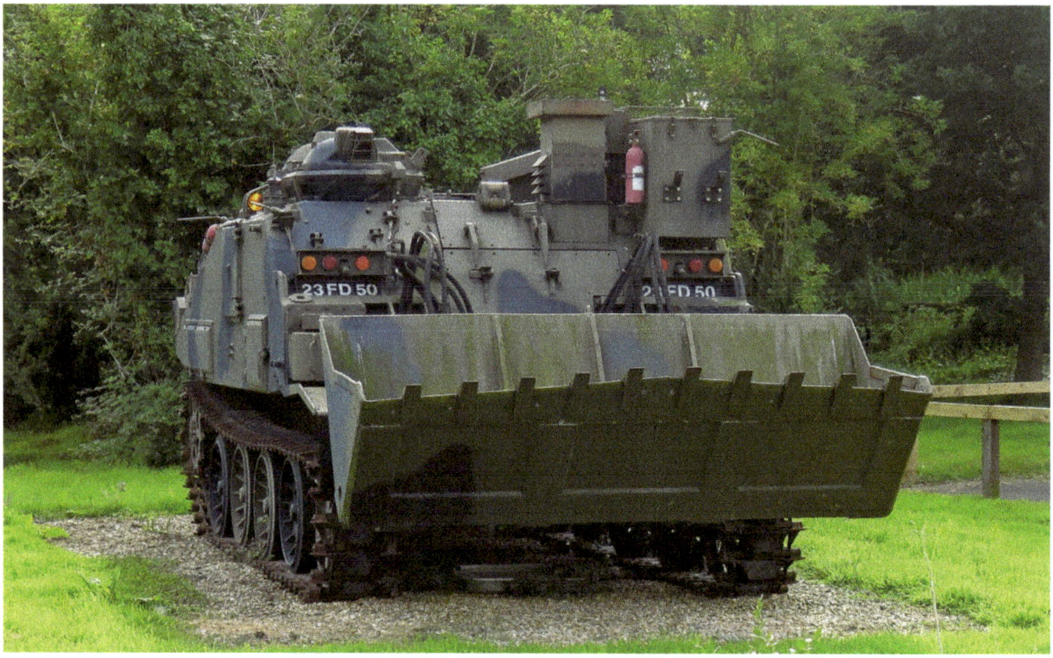

The Royal Monmouthshire Royal Engineers (Militia)

Two Combat Engineer Tractors belonging to the regiment. The tractor in the top picture is housed in the regiment's headquarters at Vauxhall Field, and the machine depicted in the lower photograph is located outside the Regimental Museum at the castle. The significance of this photograph is that it shows the tractor on a section of Bailey Bridge.

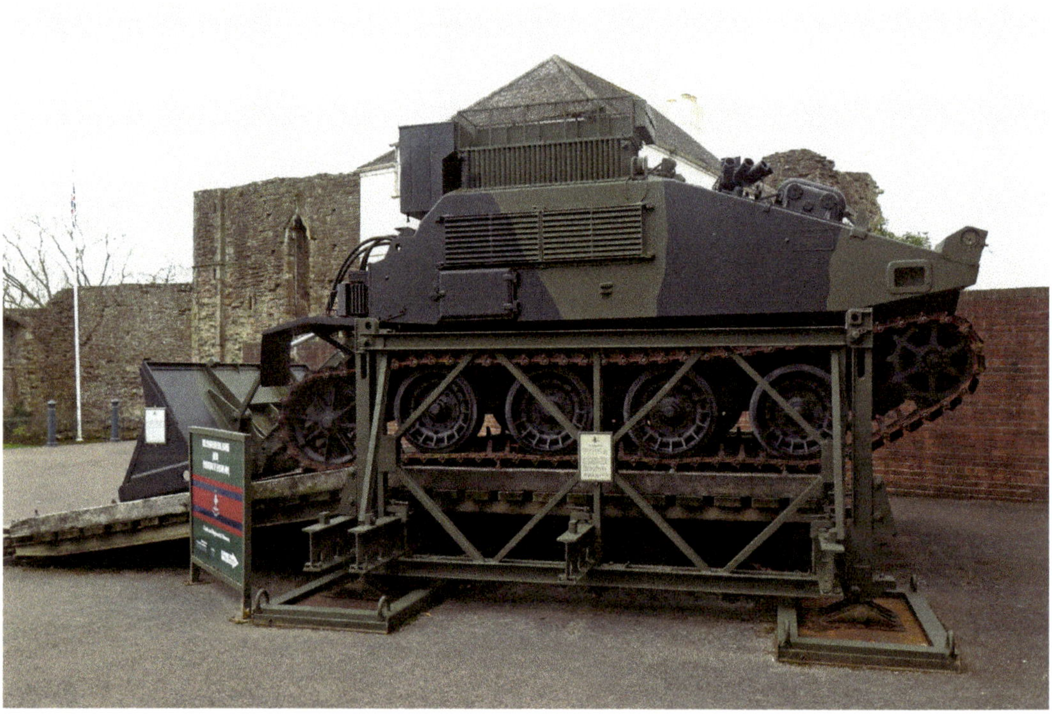

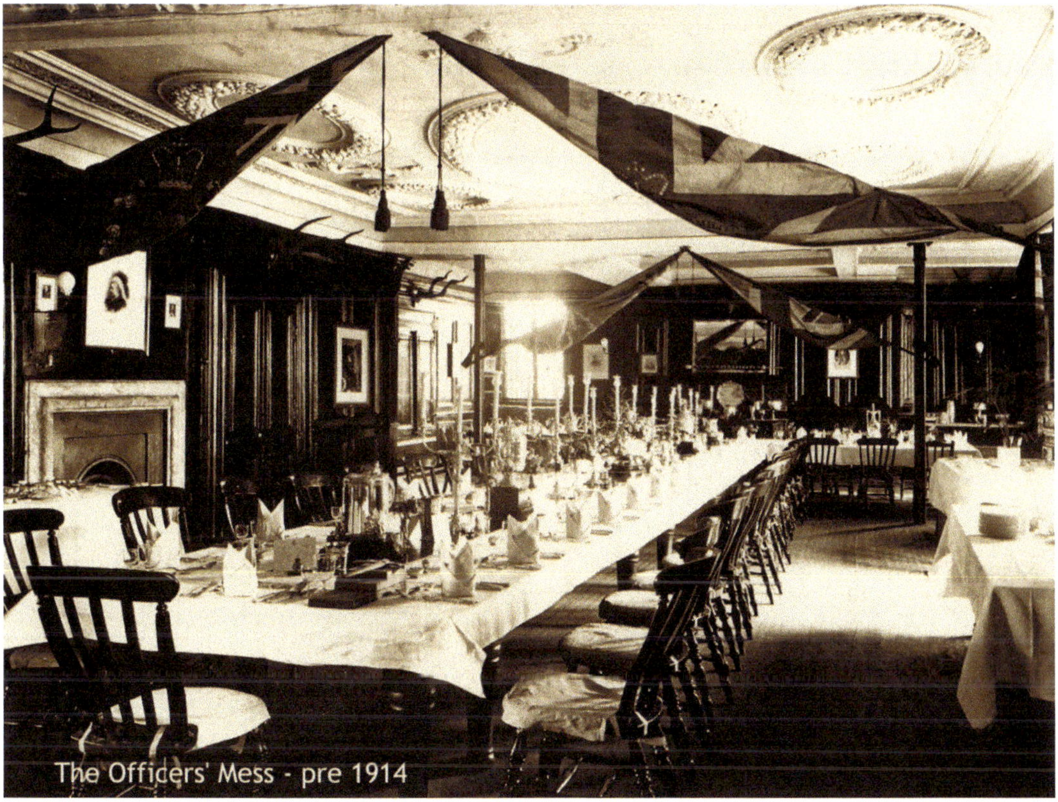

The Royal Monmouthshire Royal Engineers (Militia)
The Officers' Mess in the Great Castle House pre-1914 and today.

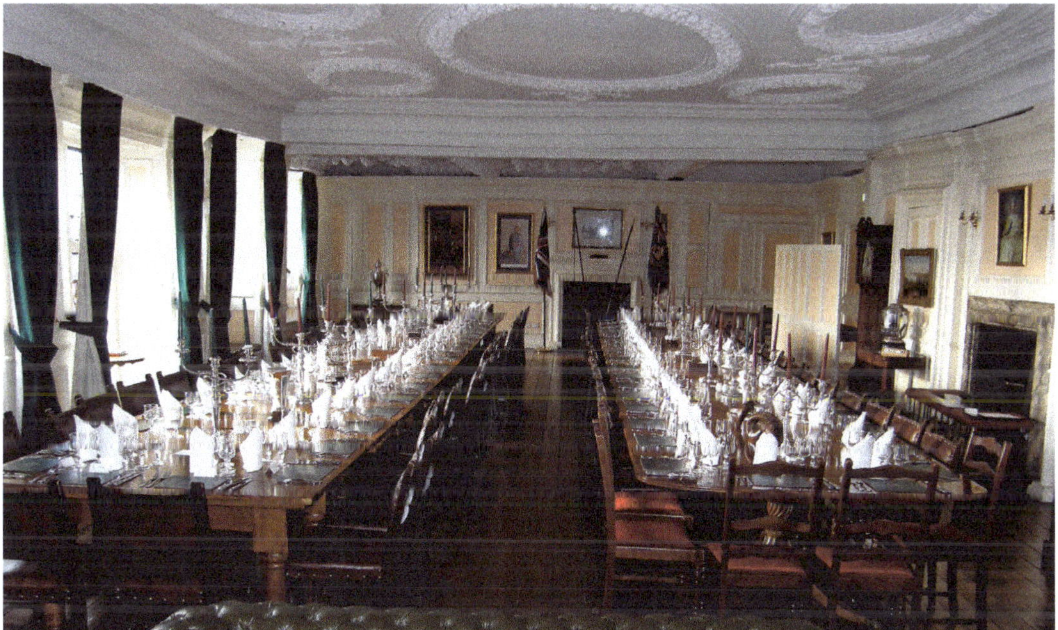

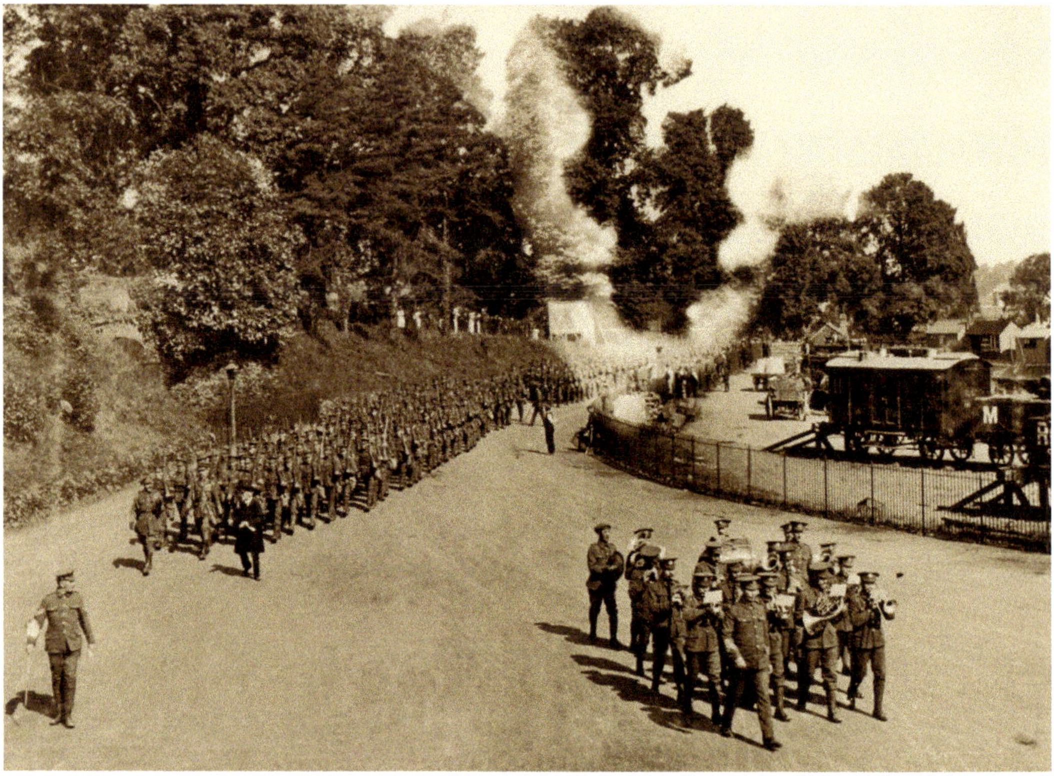

The Royal Monmouthshire Royal Engineers (Militia)

Off to war! Led by the band, the Royal Monmouth Royal Engineers march to the Railway Station in 1914. Of the four sappers shown in the lower photograph, the first three on the left were to be killed in 1916. Left to right, these men were Sapper Williams, Sapper Tyler, Staff Sergeant Ronald Smith (Heavyweight Boxing Champion) and Corporal Frank Jones.

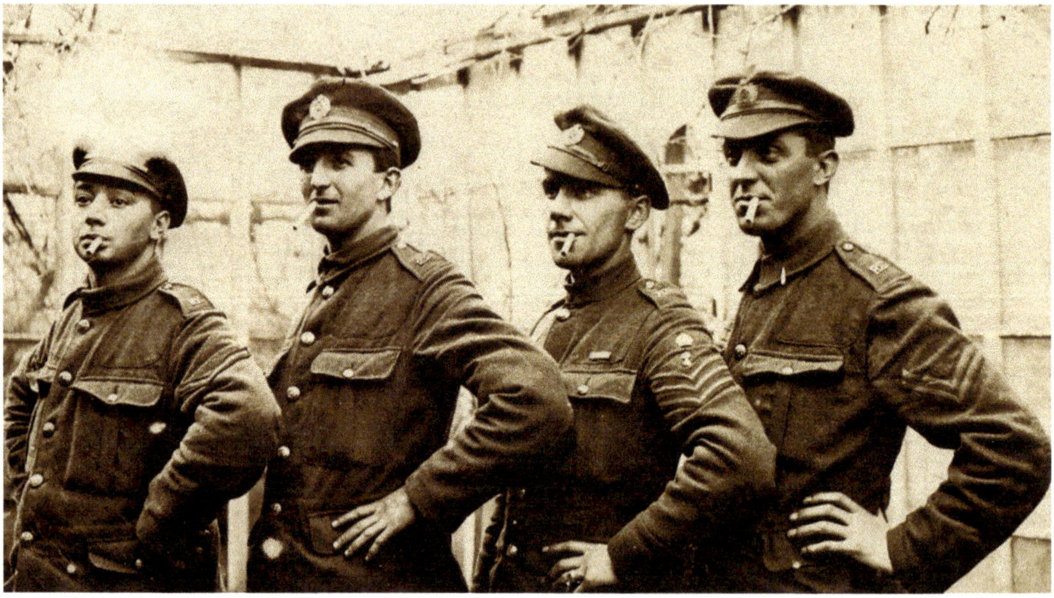

The Royal Monmouthshire Royal Engineers (Militia)

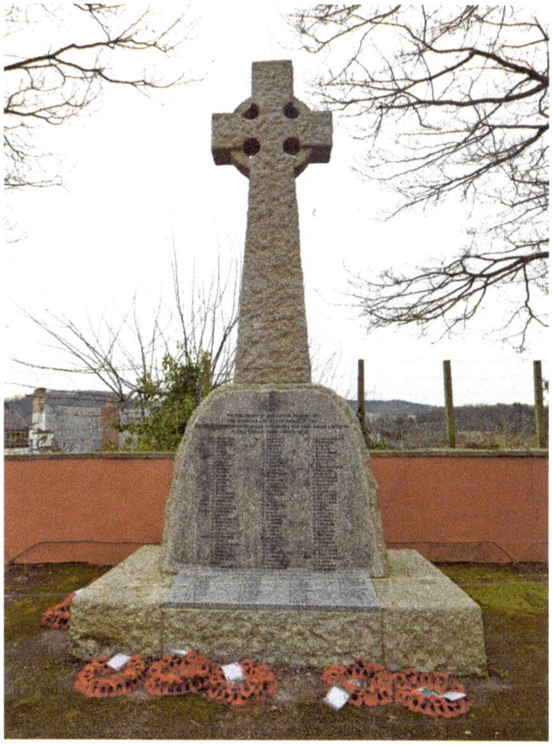

A war memorial in the Castle Parade Ground records the names of all those from the Royal Monmouth Royal Engineers who gave their lives in two world wars, while the plaque on the wall nearby records the opening, by the Duke of Gloucester on 6 September 2008, of a Garden of Remembrance in the ground alongside the Castle Hall. This garden is also featured on page 14, and commemorates 100 years of Reserve Service.

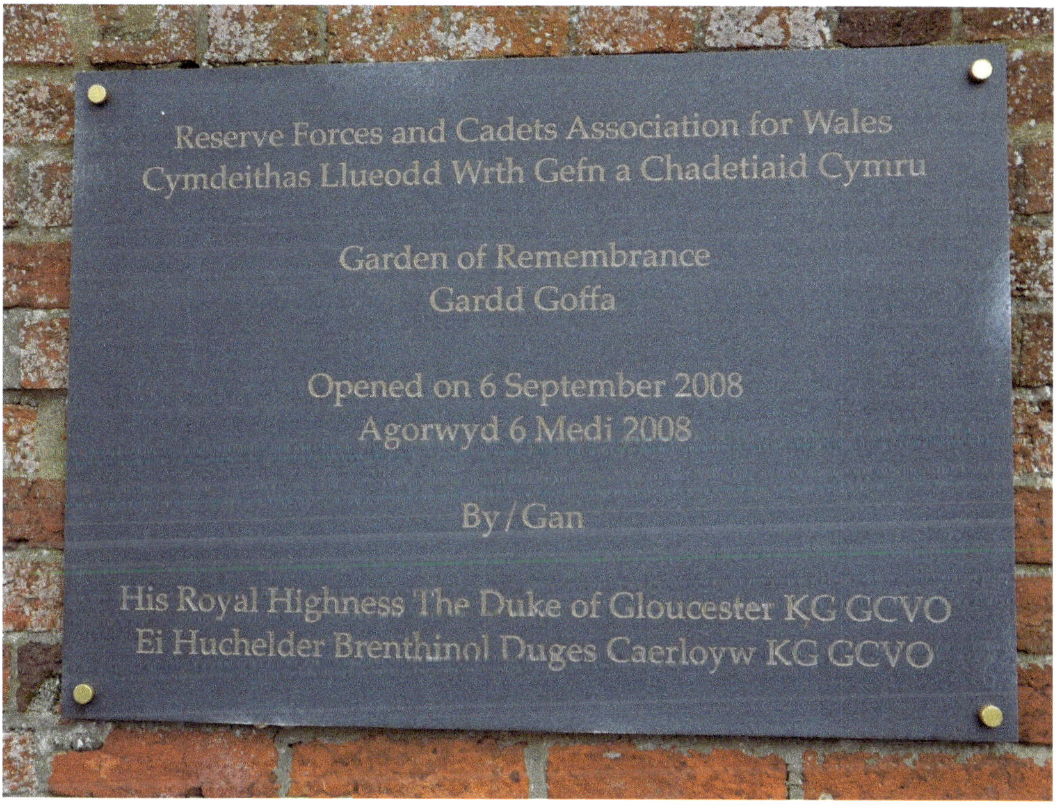

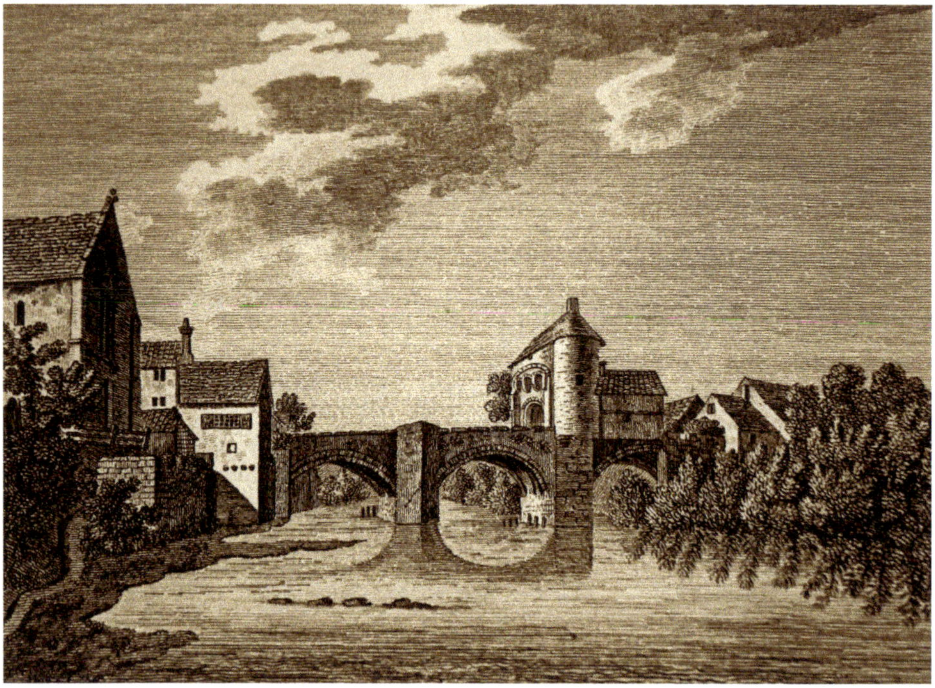

The Monnow Bridge and Gatehouse

The Monnow Bridge and Gatehouse form part of the Monmouth town walls and defences. The caption that accompanied the top print of 1775 stated:

> This plate presents the south aspect of Monnow Gate and Bridge, so called from the river over which it is constructed. Both are mentioned in Leland's Itinerary, and indeed have undoubted marks of antiquity; but neither history not tradition afford any lights respecting the date of their erection. As a picturesque object they have long been noticed by connoisseurs.

Little appears to have changed over the years, except that the building on the left nearside of the bridge appears to have been demolished. St. Thomas' Church is hidden behind the trees on the left in the lower photograph.

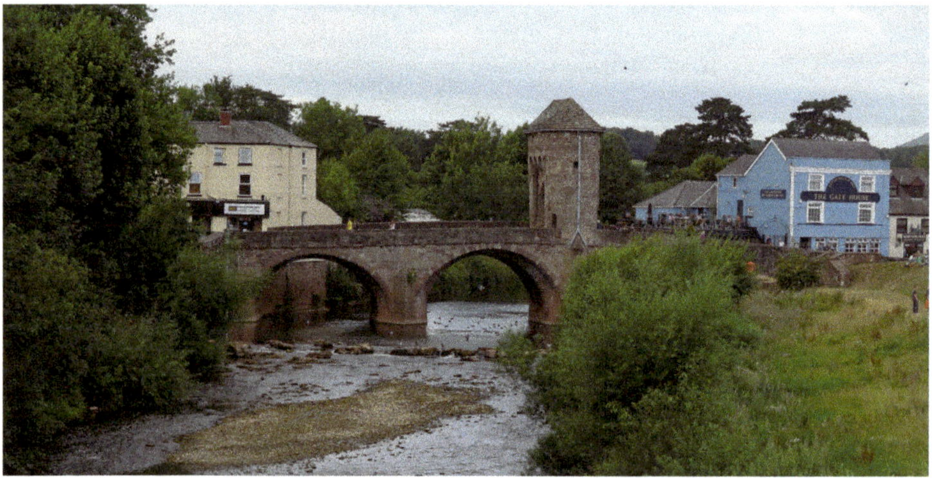

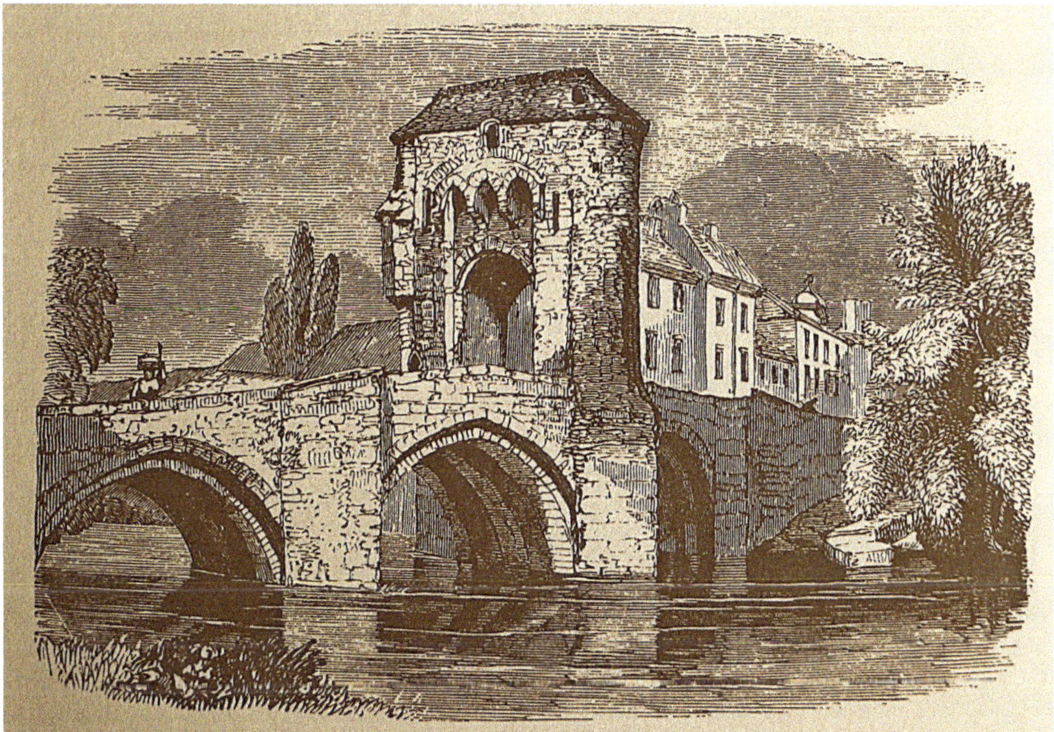

MONNOW BRIDGE.

The Monnow Bridge and Gatehouse

In comparing the print of the bridge and gatehouse on this page with that on the preceding page, little change appeared to have taken place between 1775 and 1861 when the second engraving was published. The Monmouth town walls and defences comprise the defensive system of walls and gates that were built between 1297 and the early part of the next century. Of these defences, only the Monnow Bridge Gatehouse survives intact, albeit in a substantially modified form to that of the original building.

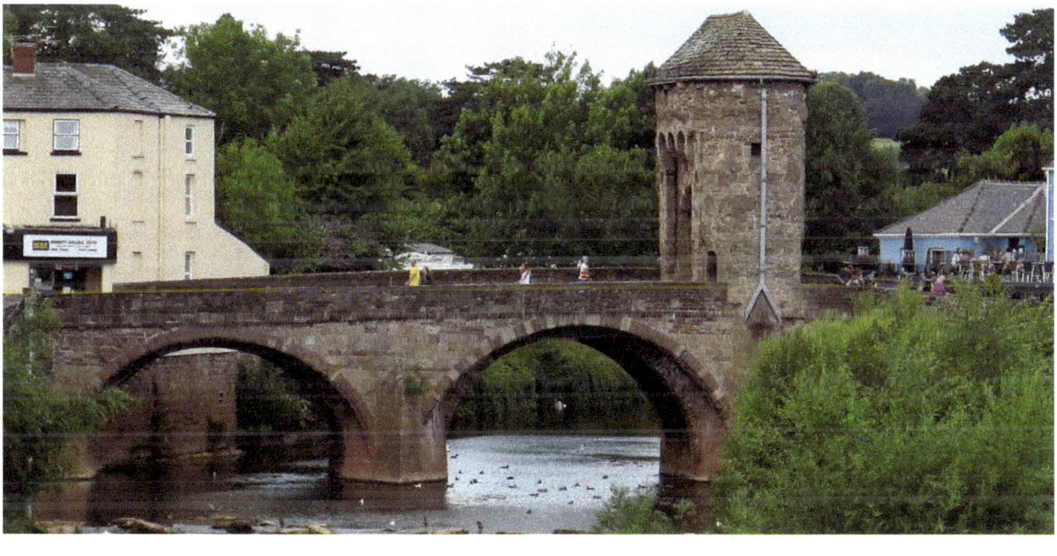

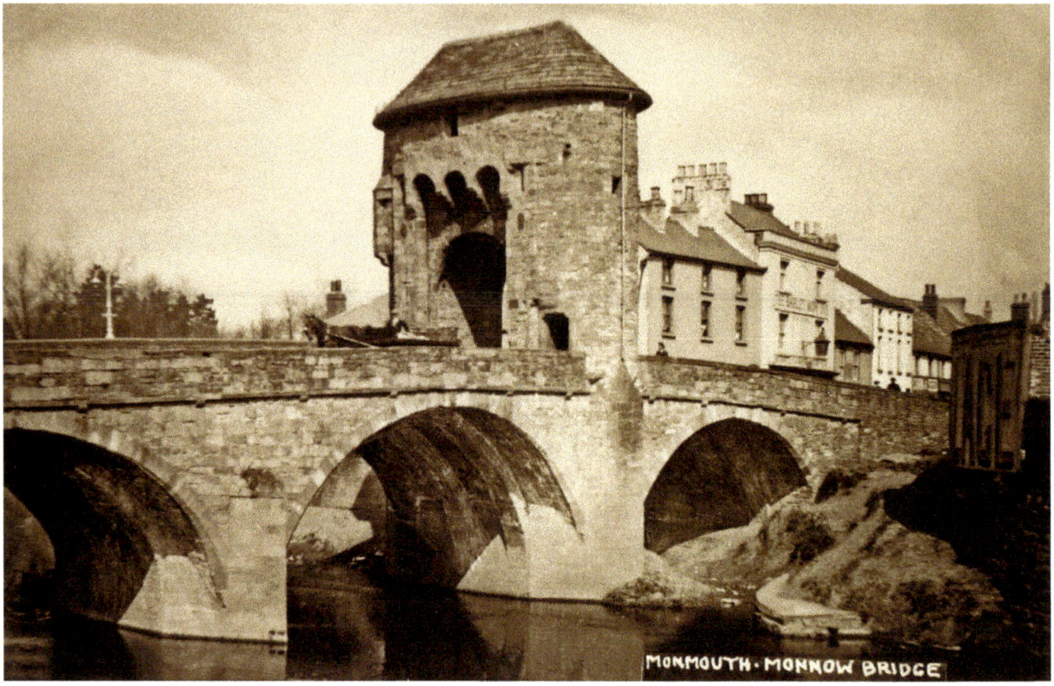

The Monnow Bridge and Gatehouse
In addition to the Monnow Bridge Gatehouse, there were four other gates around the perimeter of the town walls giving access to Monmouth – the Wye Bridge Gate, East Gate (Dixton Gate) and Monk's Gate. There was also a west gate (possibly St Stephen's Gate) across the top end of Monnow Street, which was a further internal access point.

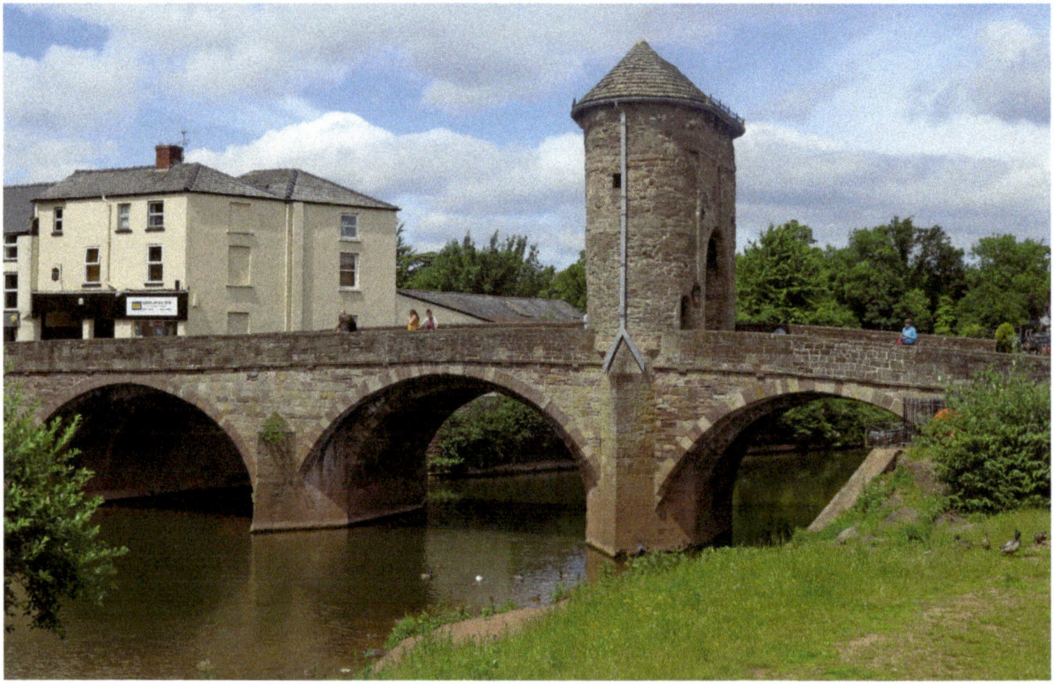

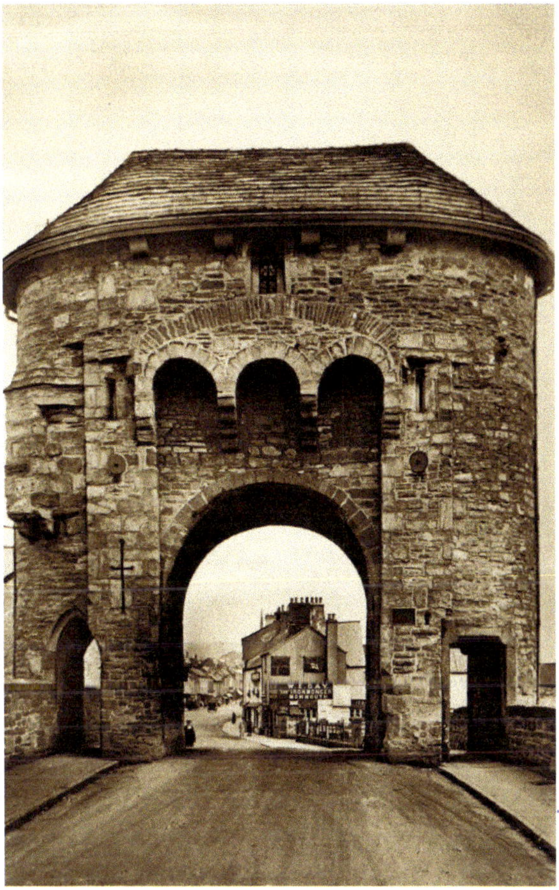

The Monnow Bridge and Gatehouse

Monmouth's town walls were regarded as necessary for several reasons. Firstly, they provided defensive protection for the Anglo-Norman dwellers of the town against the sometimes hostile Welsh inhabitants of the nearby countryside. Secondly, they allowed the policing of the market and thirdly they allowed the easier collection of taxes and dues. The walls and gates also served as a status symbol and, in addition to their defensive use, the town gates were used for hundreds of years to collect tolls.

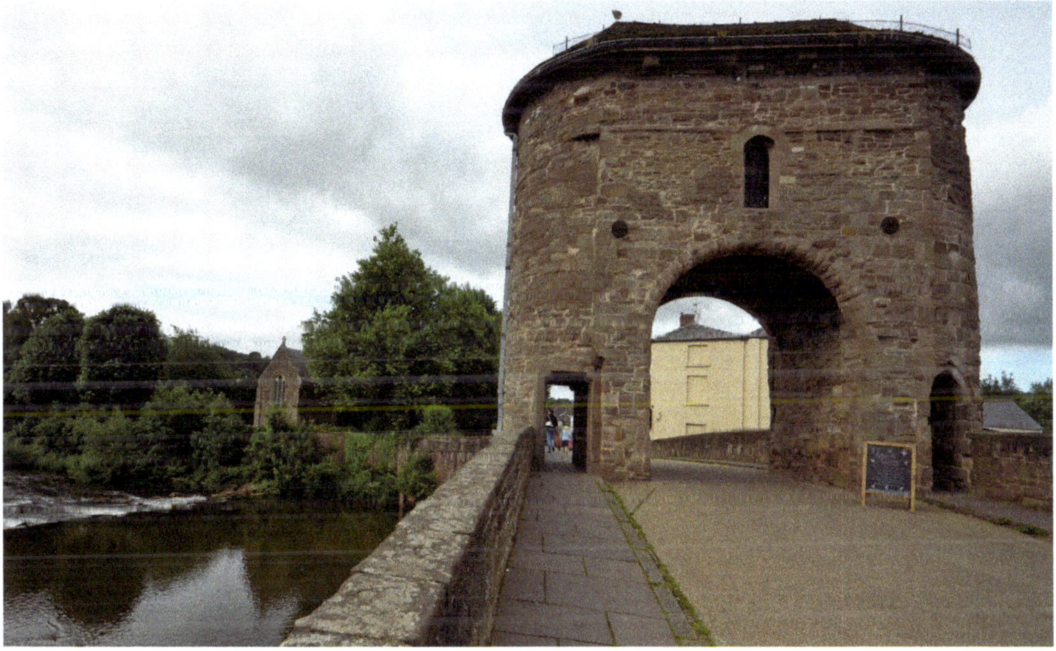

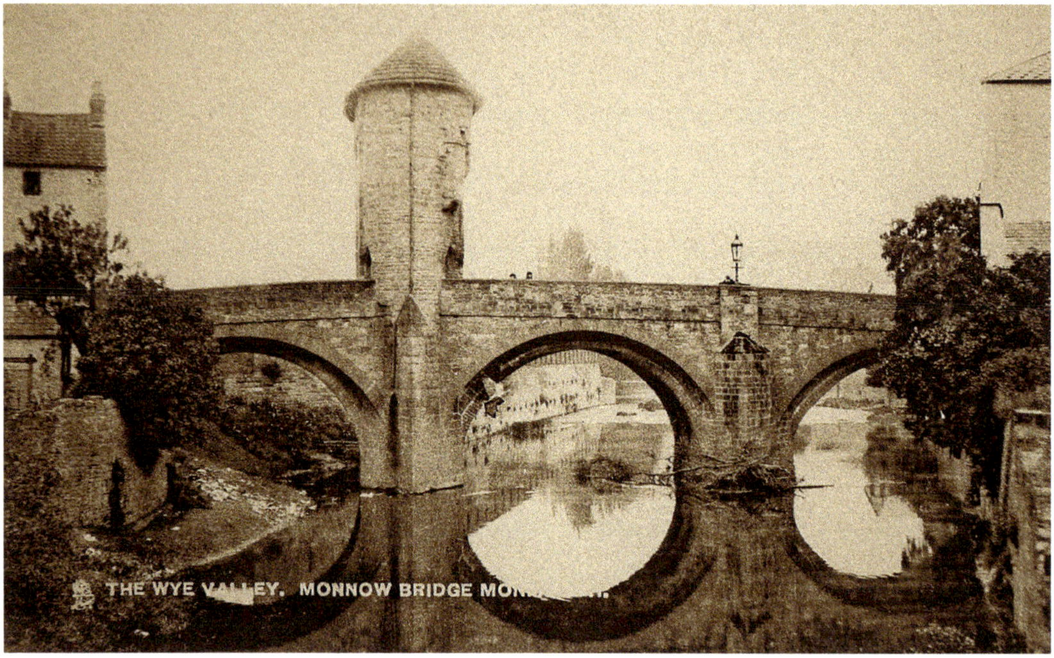

The Monnow Bridge and Gatehouse

The Monnow Bridge Gatehouse is the most renowned and visible portion of the town walls and defences and is now the only surviving medieval fortified bridge in Britain with a stone gatehouse that is positioned on the bridge itself.

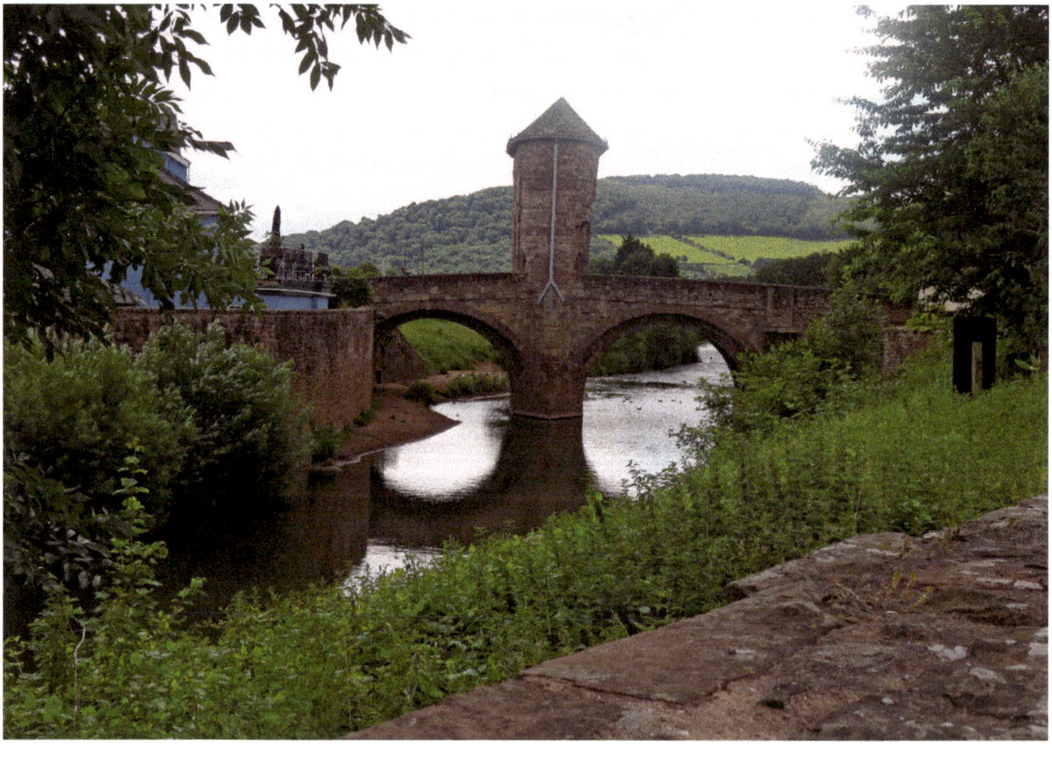

Church of St Thomas the Martyr, Overmonnow

The Church of St Thomas the Martyr at Overmonnow is located beside the medieval Monnow Bridge across the River Monnow in St Thomas's Square. Part of the building dates from around 1180 and it has a fine twelfth-century Norman chancel arch. The west entrance also has a similar Norman-style arch, but this might date from when the exterior was largely rebuilt in the nineteenth century.

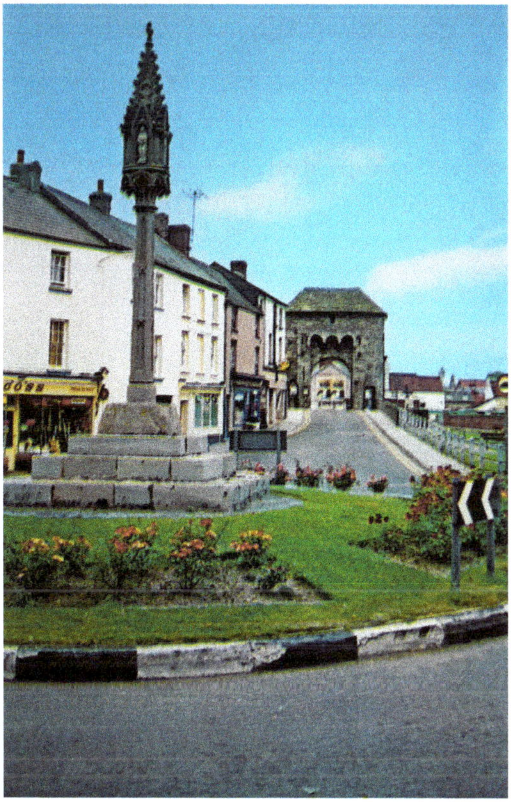

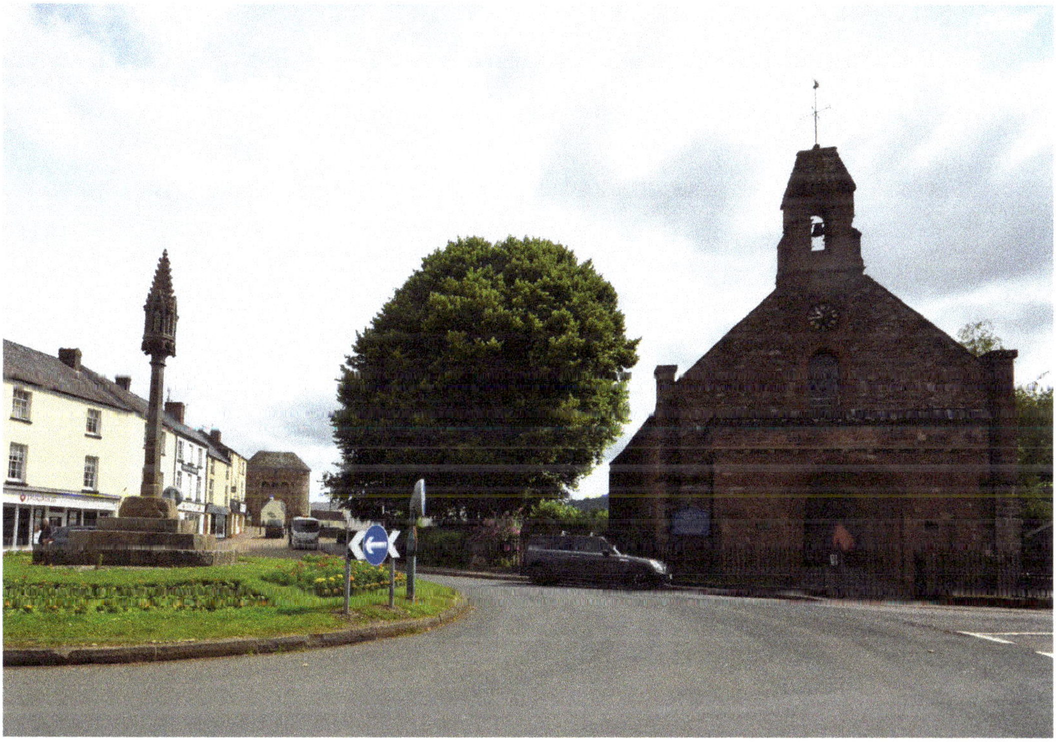

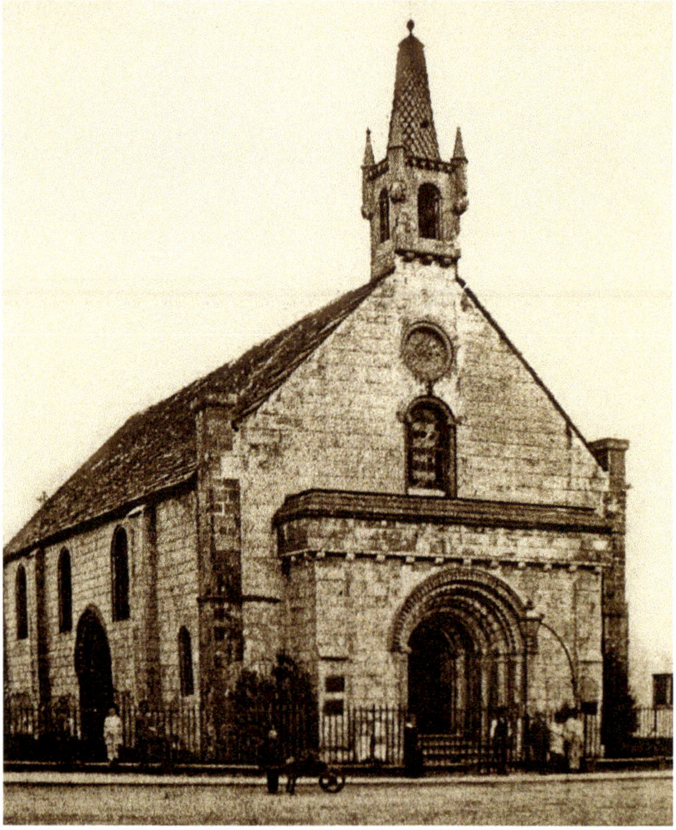

Church of St Thomas the Martyr, Overmonnow
The building is constructed of old red sandstone and it is dedicated to St Thomas à Becket. It is one of twenty-four buildings on the Monmouth Heritage Trail and is a Grade II-listed building.

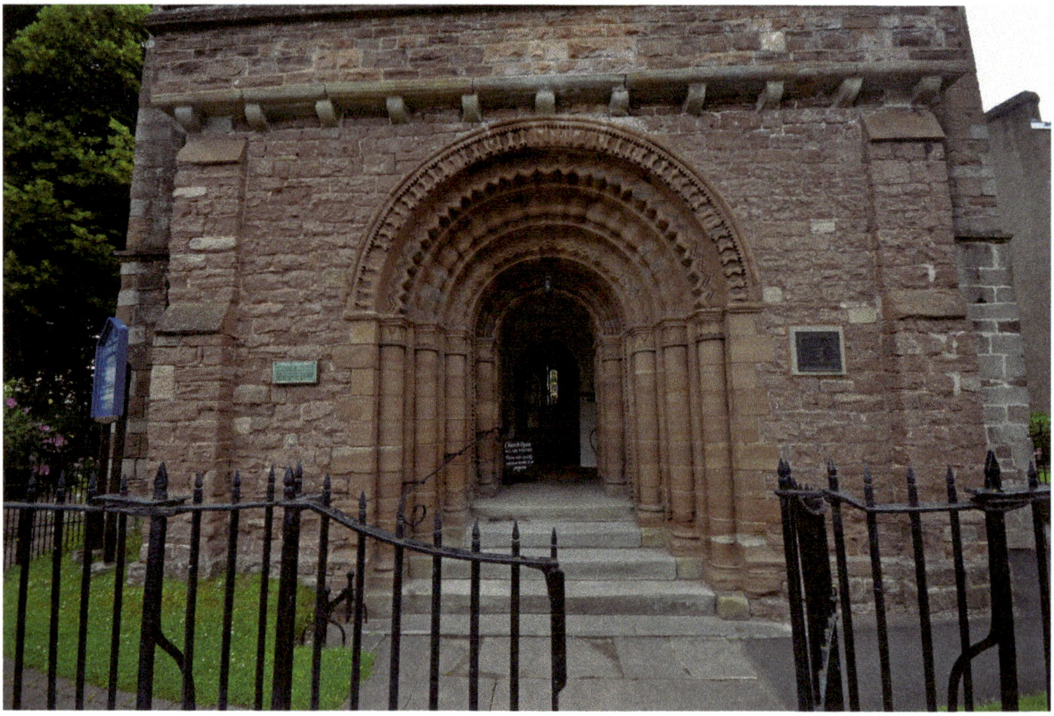

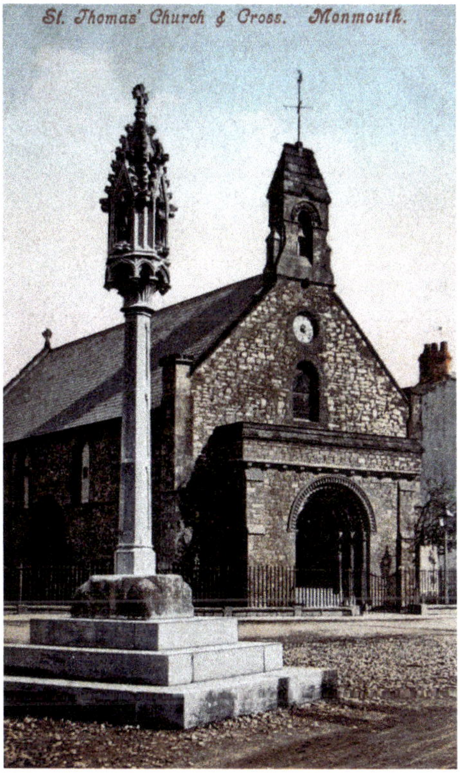

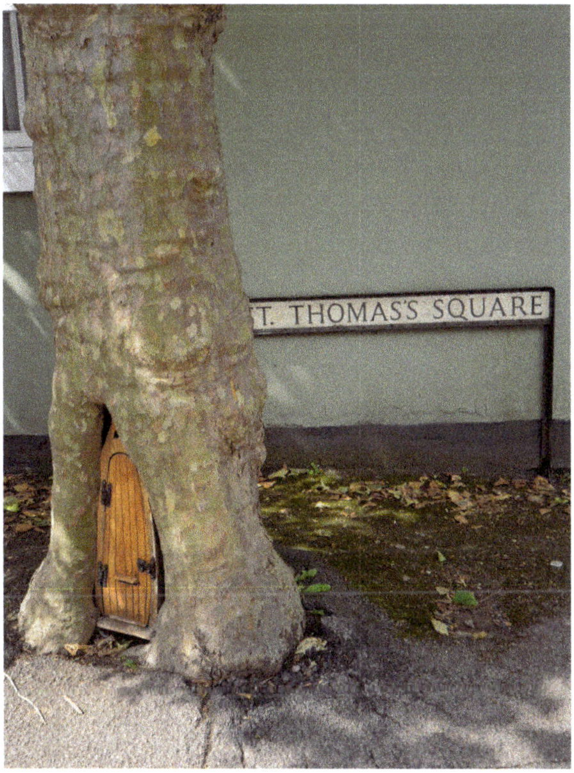

Church of St Thomas the Martyr, Overmonnow

The top left-hand photograph dates from about 1904 and highlights the very elaborate cross that dominates St Thomas's Square as also captured in the lower picture. The tree show in the right-hand top photograph must have been home to the 'little people' at one time!

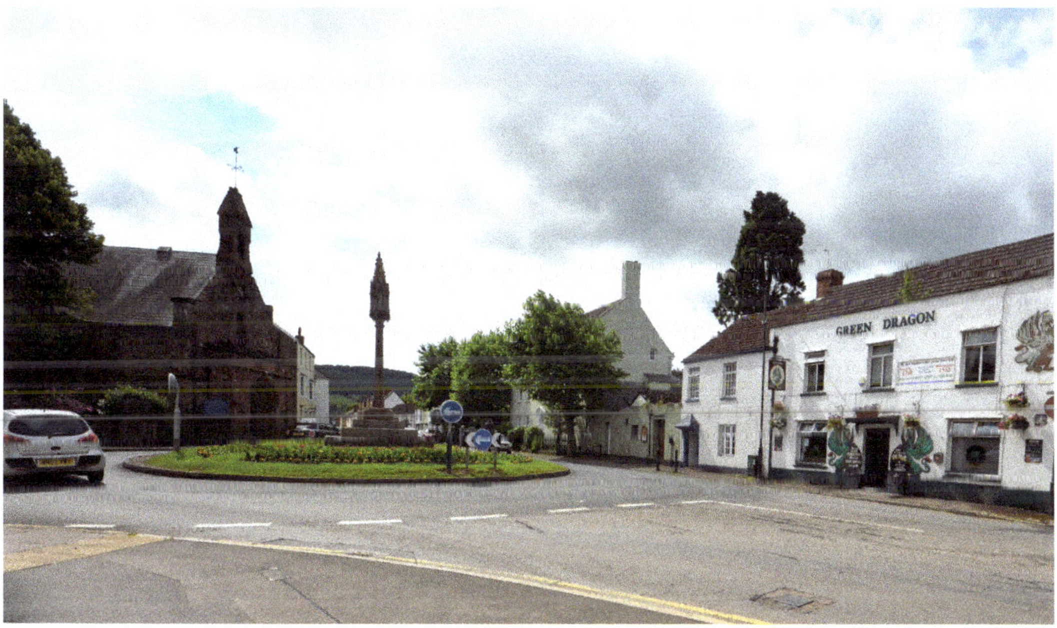

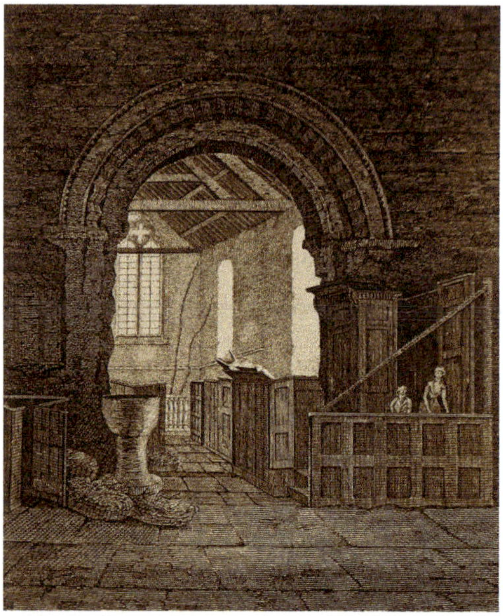

Church of St Thomas the Martyr, Overmonnow

Inside the church, the fine dog-tooth Norman chancel arch is still largely untouched; the piscine in the south wall and the two doorways opposite also appear to be original. There is a very unusual font in the church decorated with crude images of faces, birds and a serpent in what appears to be a Garden of Eden theme. Thought initially to date from the twelfth century, historians are now of the opinion it is of the nineteenth century.

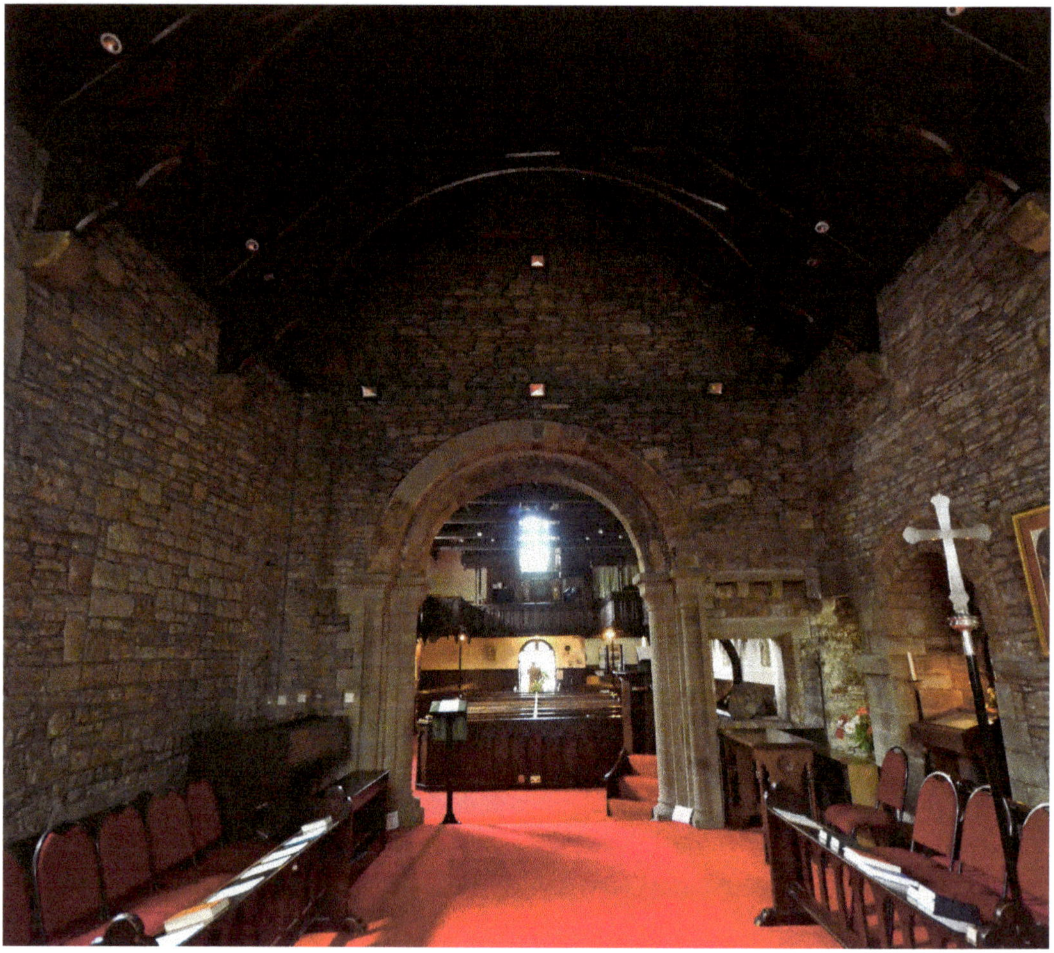

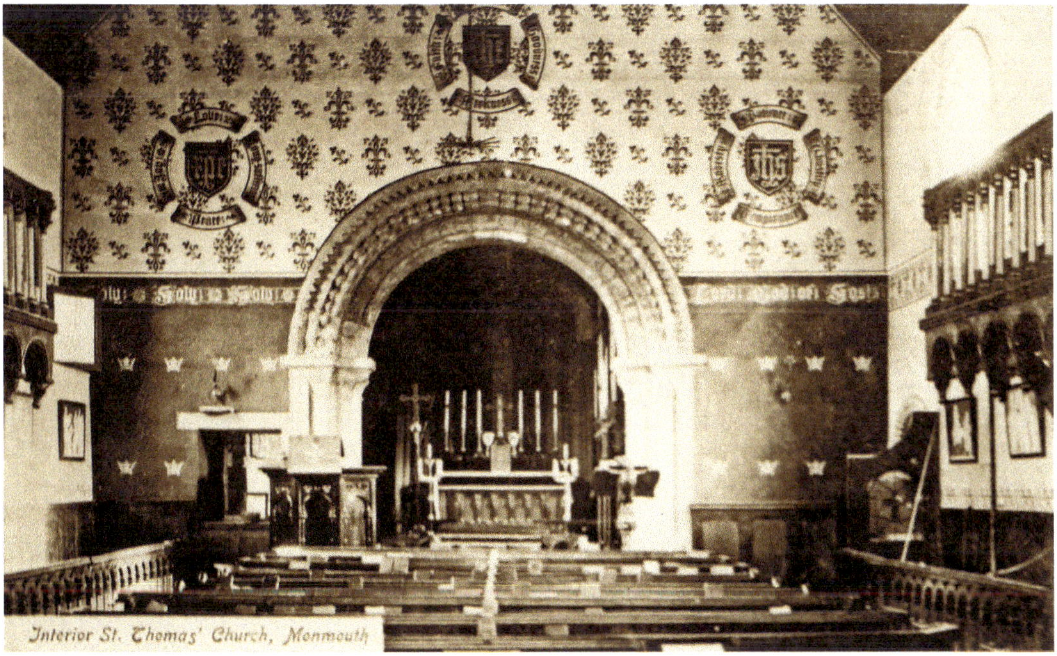

Church of St Thomas the Martyr, Overmonnow

A major restoration of St Thomas's Church was carried out before 1880 by the distinguished London architect Thomas Henry Wyatt. He added box pews and oak galleries on both sides of the church, which are still in existence today.

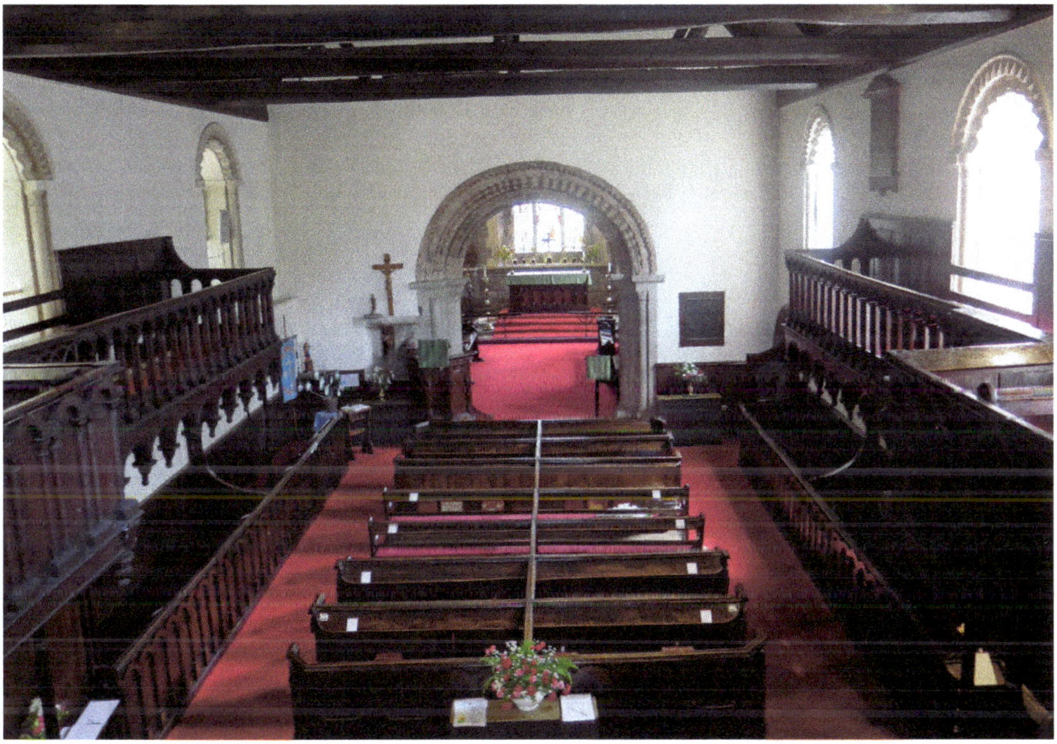

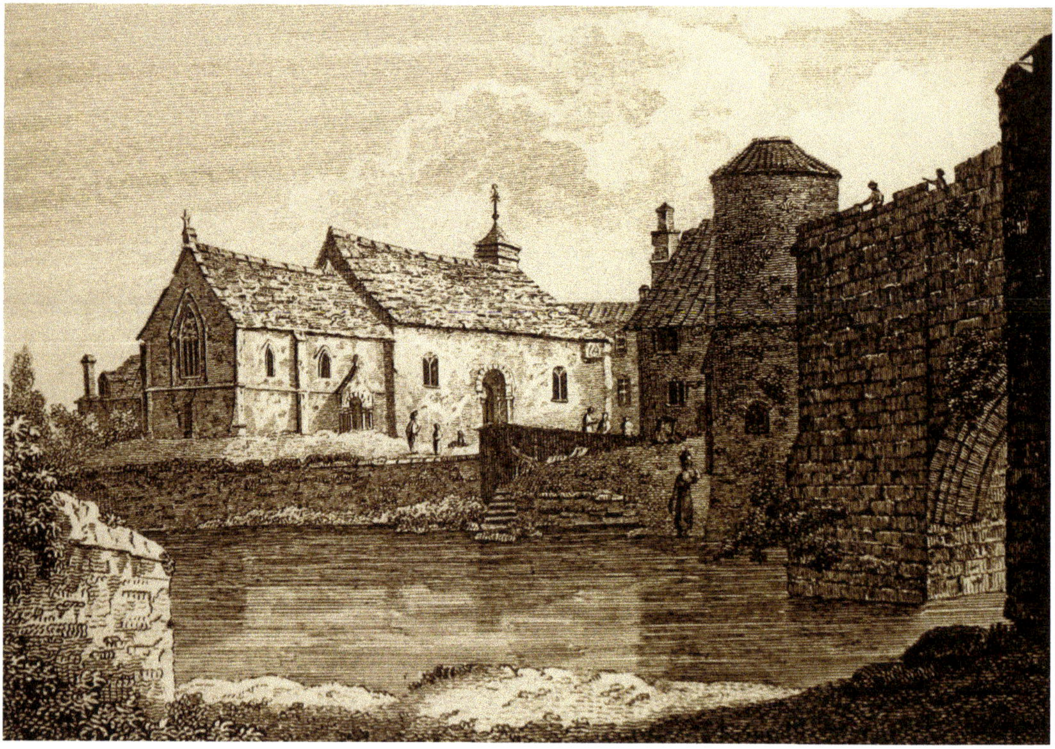

Church of St Thomas the Martyr, Overmonnow

Today, it is not possible to fully replicate with a photograph the engraving that William Coxe made in 1801 of the Church of St Thomas the Martyr at Overmonnow because of tree growth.

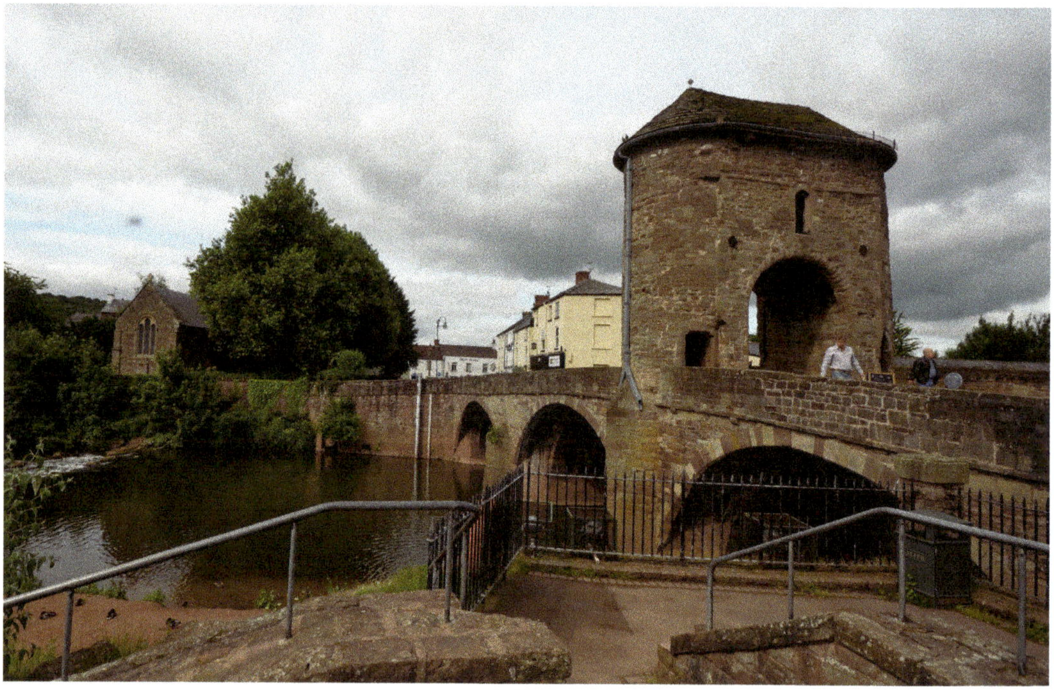

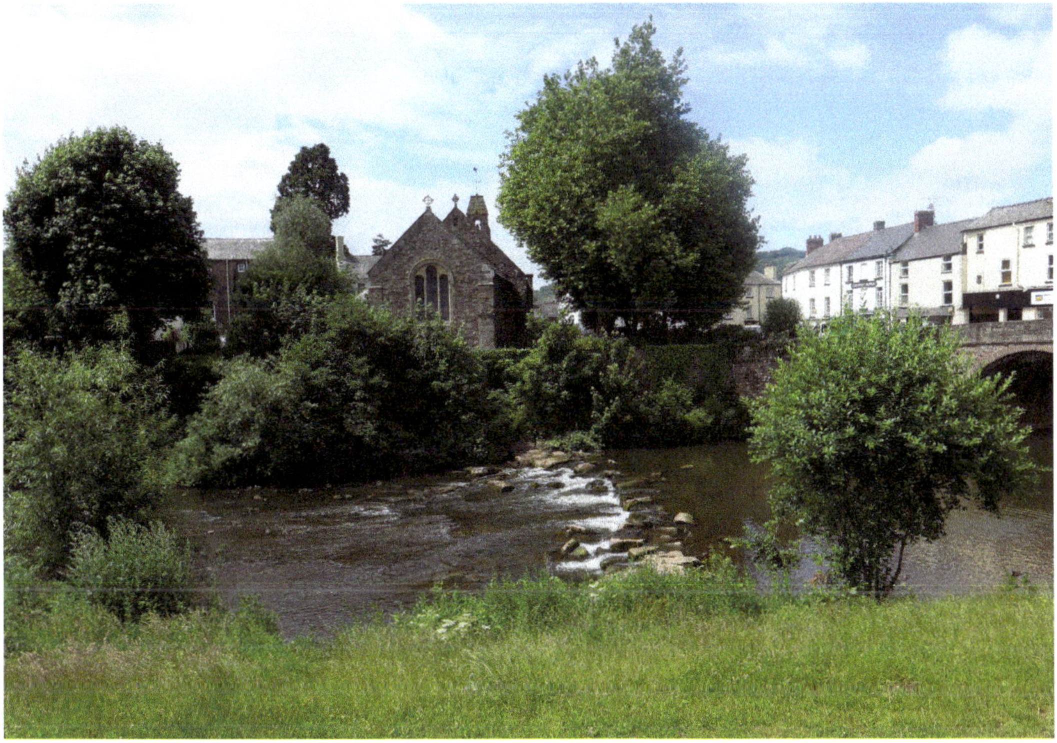

Church of St Thomas the Martyr, Overmonnow
Night and day views of the Church of St Thomas the Martyr from across the River Monnow.

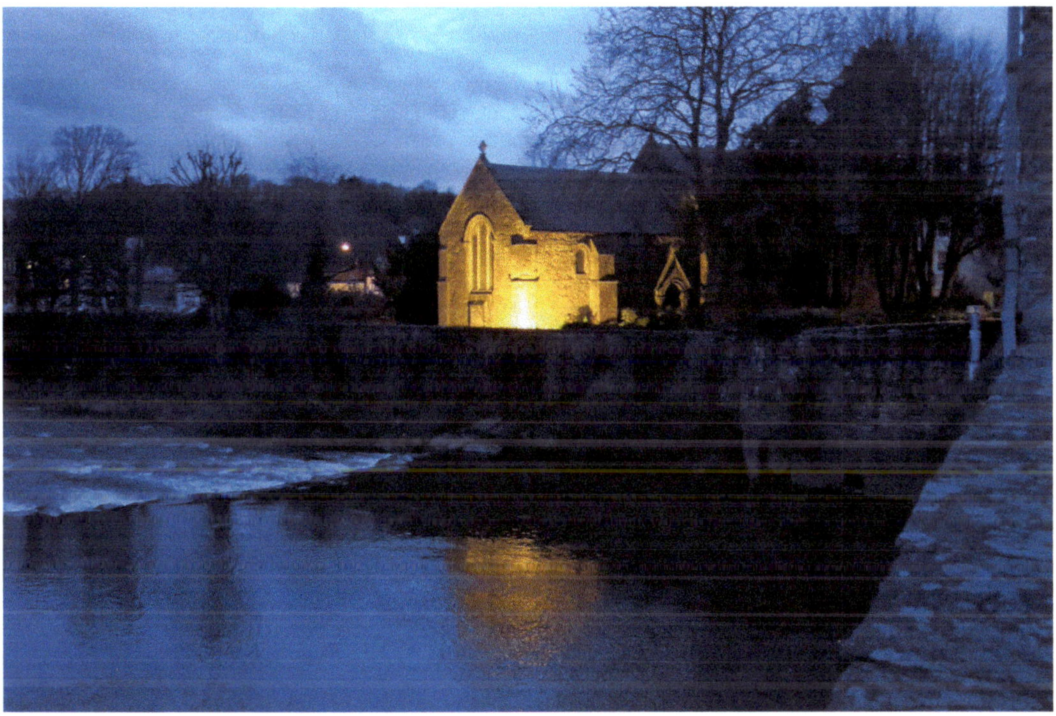

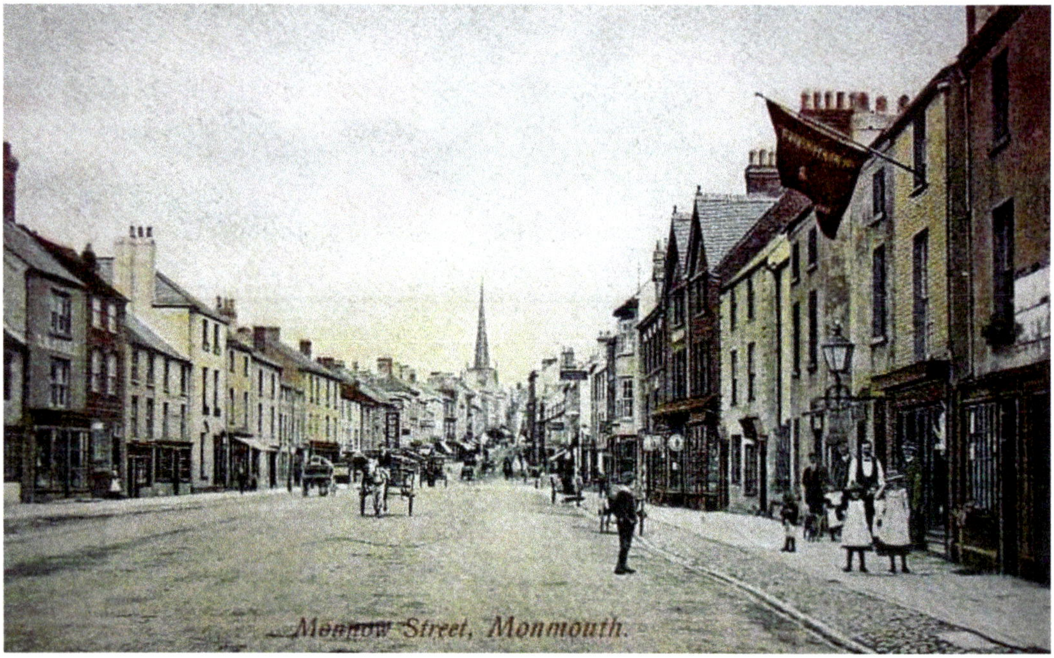

Monnow Street

A postcard view of Monnow Street taken in the early 1900s and looking north-east towards Agincourt Square and St Mary's Church. Designed as a market town, the centre of the street would have been wide to accommodate livestock as well as stalls, but narrow at both ends to control the movement of animals. The Robin Hood Inn at the Monnow Bridge end of Monnow Street is one of Monmouth's oldest buildings.

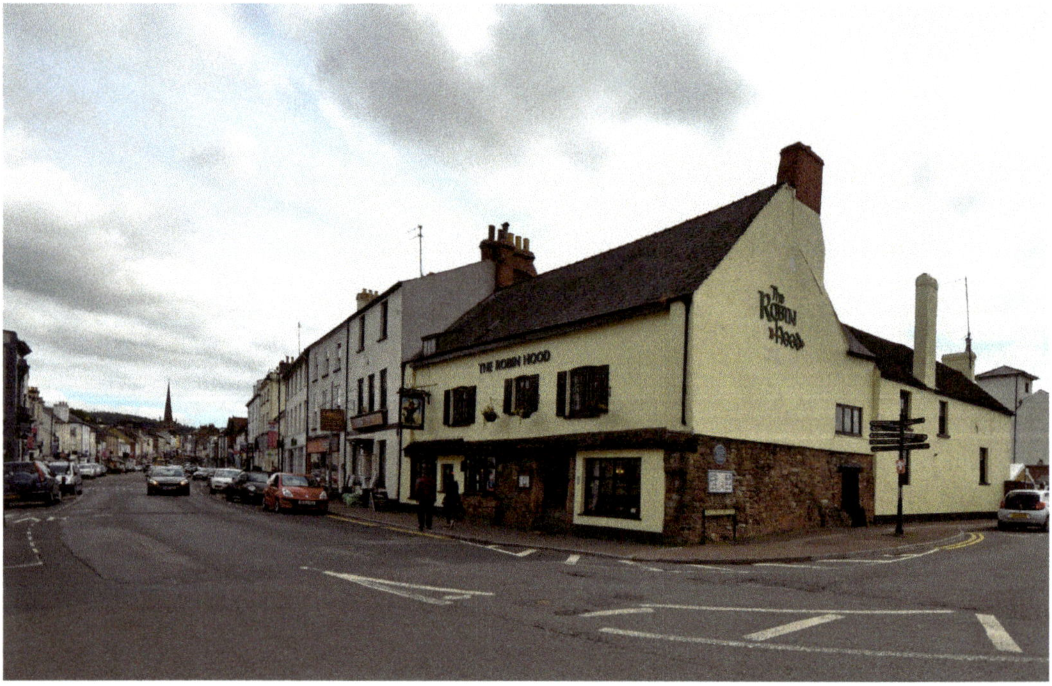

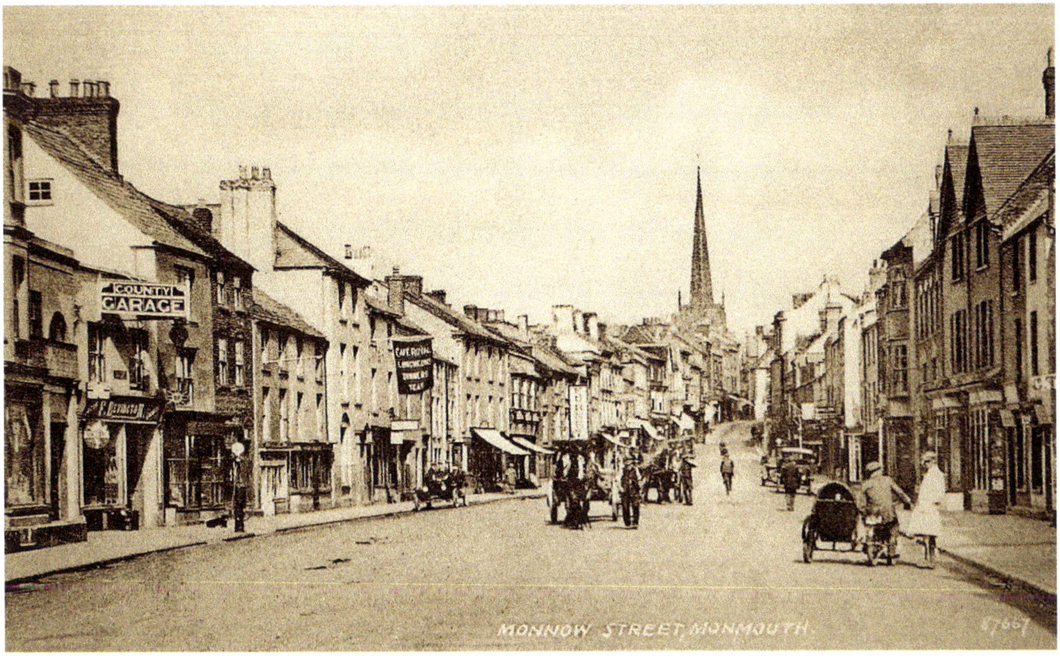

Monnow Street

Two more views of Monnow Street with the top postcard again dating to the early 1900s, but this time showing mechanised transport in the form of a motorbike and sidecar in the bottom right-hand corner of the image. In comparing the old with the new, very little change has appeared to have taken place over the last century.

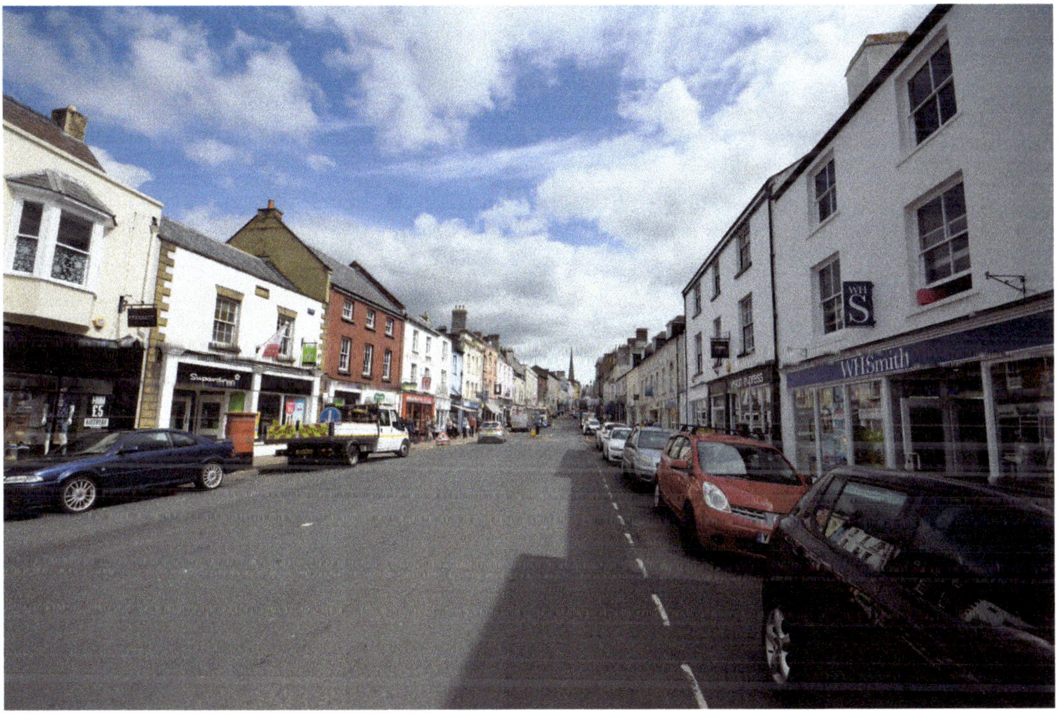

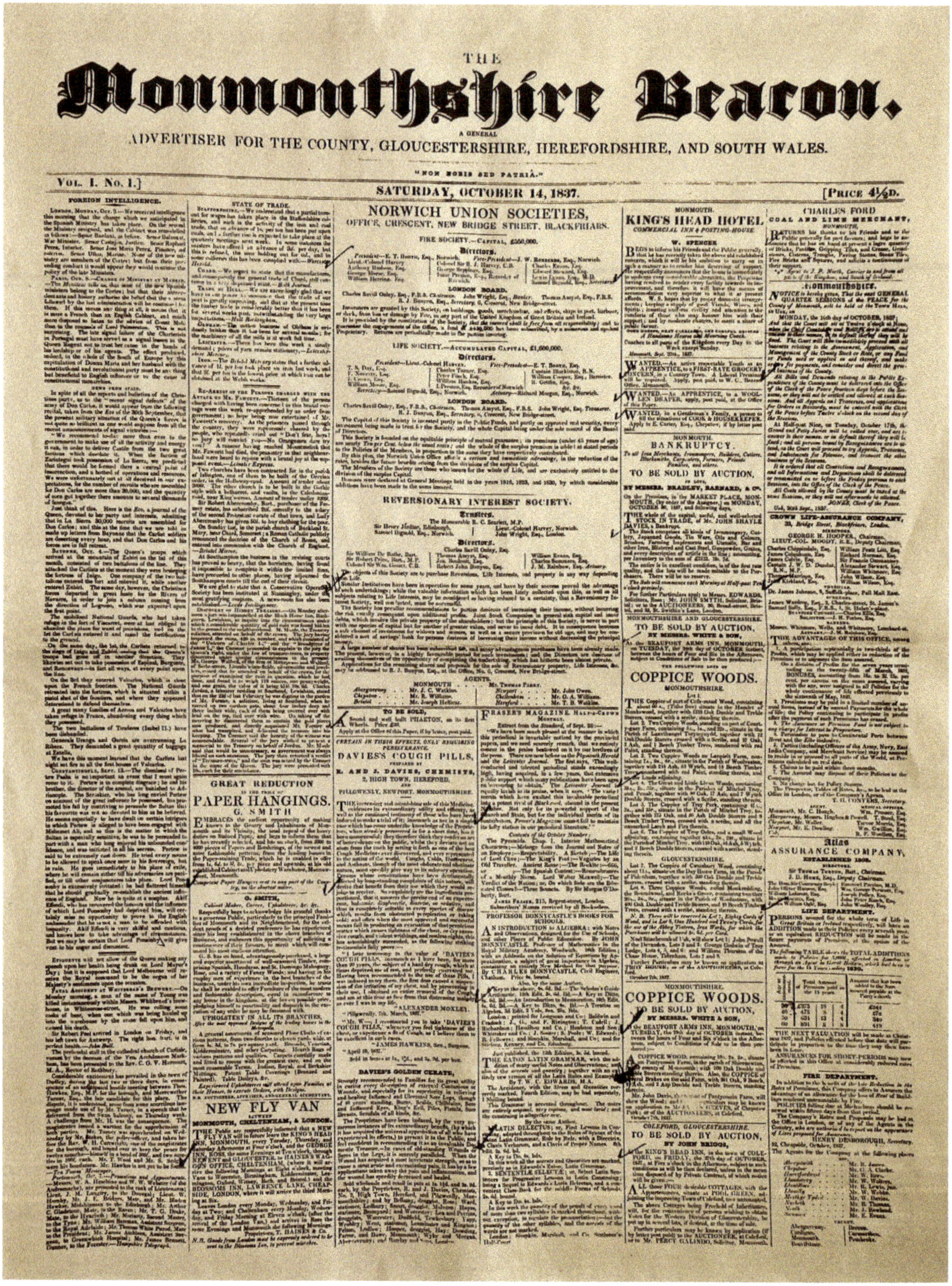

THE

Monmouthshire Beacon.

A GENERAL

ADVERTISER FOR THE COUNTY, GLOUCESTERSHIRE, HEREFORDSHIRE, AND SOUTH WALES.

"NON SORIS SED PATRIÆ."

VOL. I. No. I.] SATURDAY, OCTOBER 14, 1837. [PRICE 4½D.

FOREIGN INTELLIGENCE.

STATE OF TRADE.

NORWICH UNION SOCIETIES,

OFFICE, CRESCENT, NEW BRIDGE STREET, BLACKFRIARS.

REVERSIONARY INTEREST SOCIETY.

DAVIES'S COUGH PILLS,

GREAT REDUCTION IN THE PRICE OF PAPER HANGINGS.

G. SMITH

NEW FLY VAN

FRASER'S MAGAZINE

KING'S HEAD HOTEL

BANKRUPTCY.

TO BE SOLD BY AUCTION,

COPPICE WOODS.

CHARLES FORD

COAL AND LIME MERCHANT,

Monmouthshire.

ASSURANCE COMPANY,

FIRE DEPARTMENT.

Monnow Street – The *Monmouthshire Beacon*

The first edition of the *Monmouthshire Beacon* was printed on Friday 18 October 1837. It is still growing strong and continues to cover all the main towns and areas in the county of Monmouthshire.

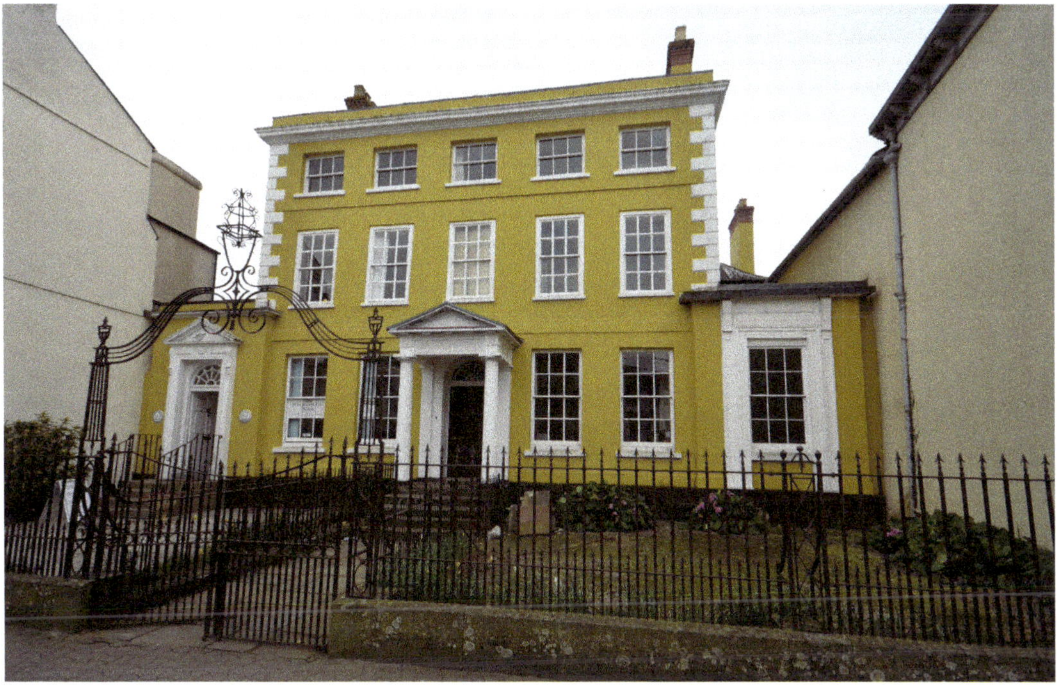

Monnow Street – the *Monmouthshire Beacon* and Cornwall House

The offices of the *Monmouthshire Beacon* are accommodated in part of Cornwall House, a property dating to 1753. Veronica Halifax, the editor of the *Monmouthshire Beacon*, is standing on the steps leading to the Beacon offices.

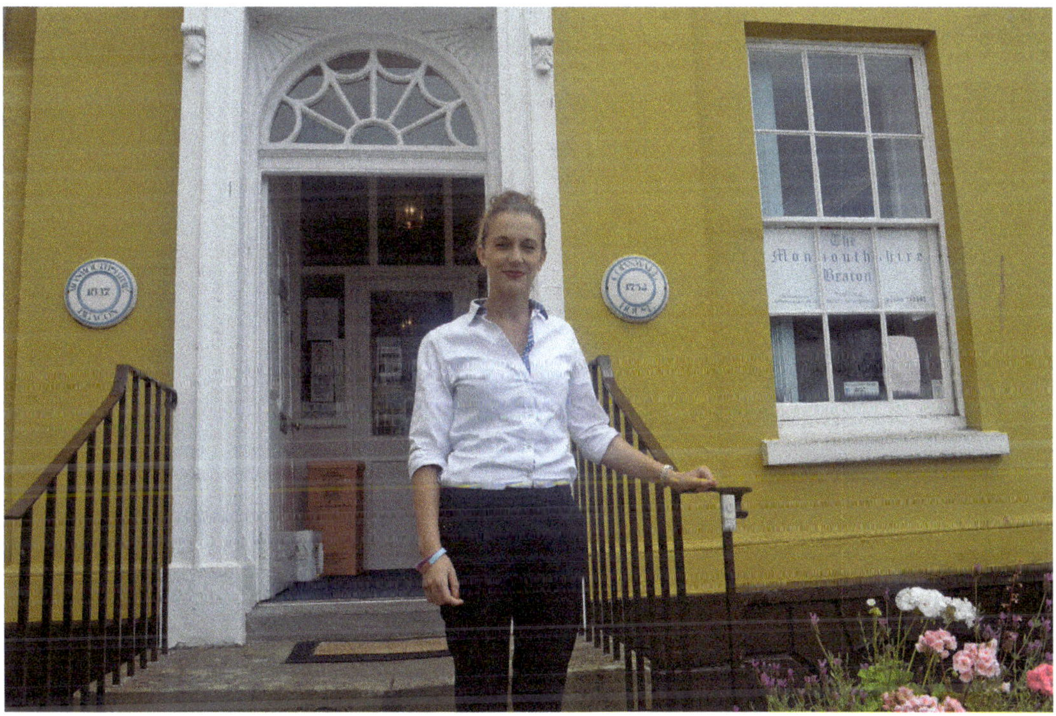

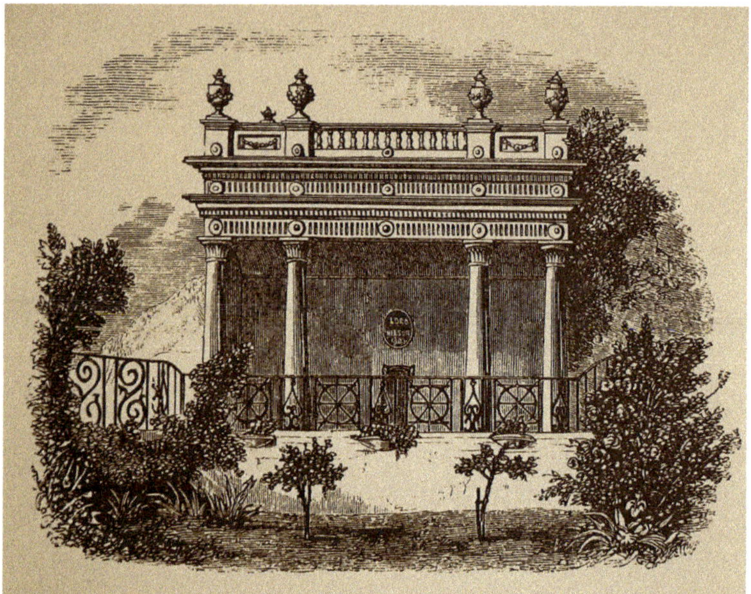

NELSON'S SUMMER-HOUSE.

Nelson's Garden

The Nelson Garden at No. 13 Chippenhamgate Street, at the rear of No. 18 Monnow Street, is a nineteenth-century garden that was the scene of a tea party held to honour Lord Nelson in 1802. The garden is one of twenty-four sites on the Monmouth Heritage Trail and commemorates the visit of Lord Nelson, with Sir William and Lady Emma Hamilton to Monmouth on 19 August 1802, three years before he was killed at the Battle of Trafalgar. Although the original summerhouse, referred to as the charming retreat, has vanished, the present Memorial Pavilion, shown in the lower photograph, was erected in around 1840 to commemorate Nelson's visit. The top engraving, from *The Book of the Wye*, shows the Pavilion in 1861, but with the incorrect caption of 'Nelson's Summer-House'.

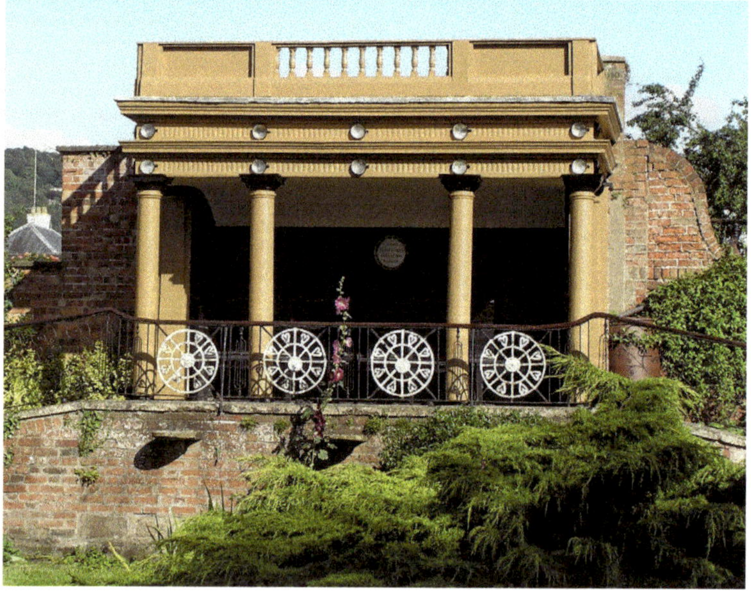

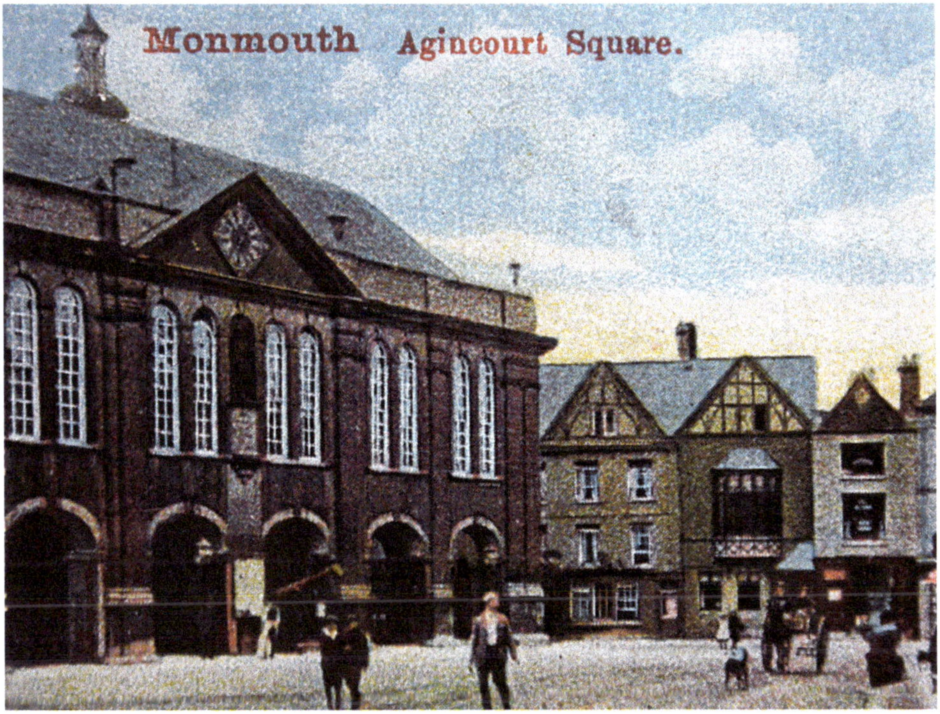

Shire Hall

The top postcard must date to the early 1900s as the statue of Charles Rolls, who died in 1910, is yet to be erected. Note the Crimean or Boer War gun sticking out from one of the arches under Shire Hall. By 1916 or 1917, the lower photograph shows the statue in position with a First World War tank behind it, partially obscured by the crowd. The tank, which was first introduced at the Battle of Flers in September 1916, was either there to drum up volunteers to join the fight or to raise cash.

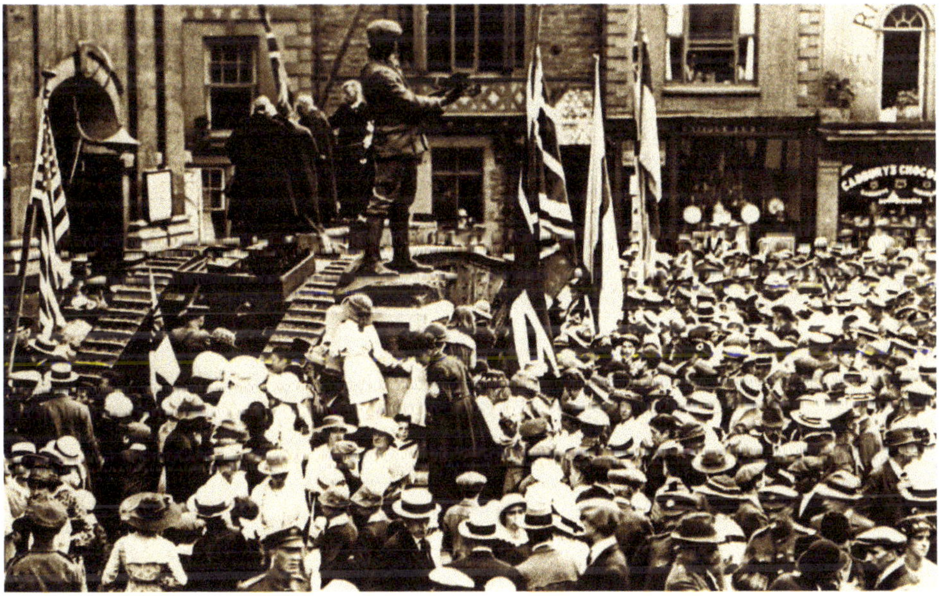

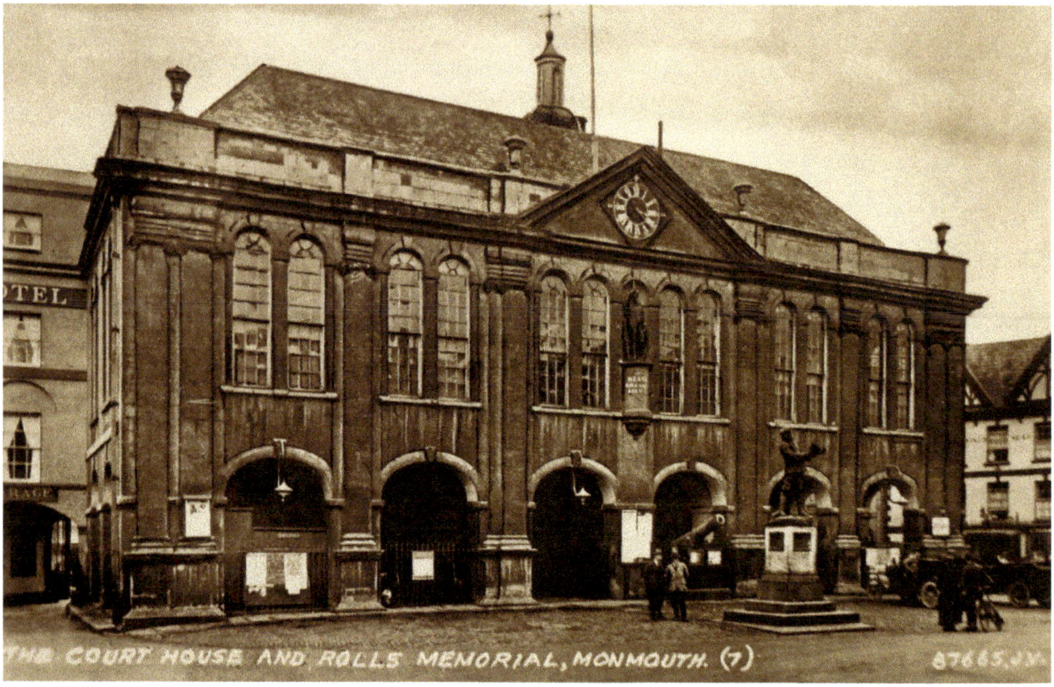

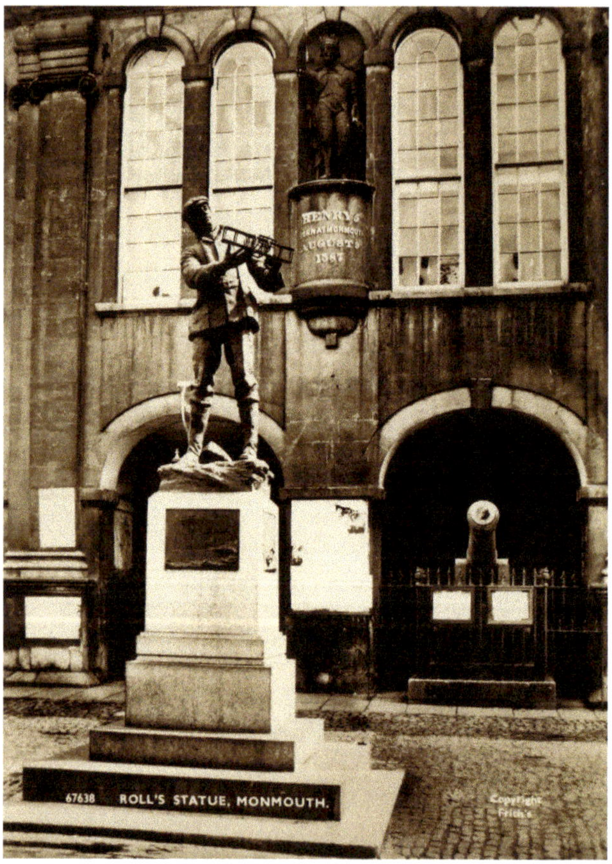

Shire Hall

Two photographs of Shire Hall and the Charles Rolls memorial statue that probably date to the late 1920s or early 1930s. The gun is still present under one of the archways of the building. The Shire Hall itself was built in 1792 and the statue of Henry V was erected in the niche at the front of the building in the same year.

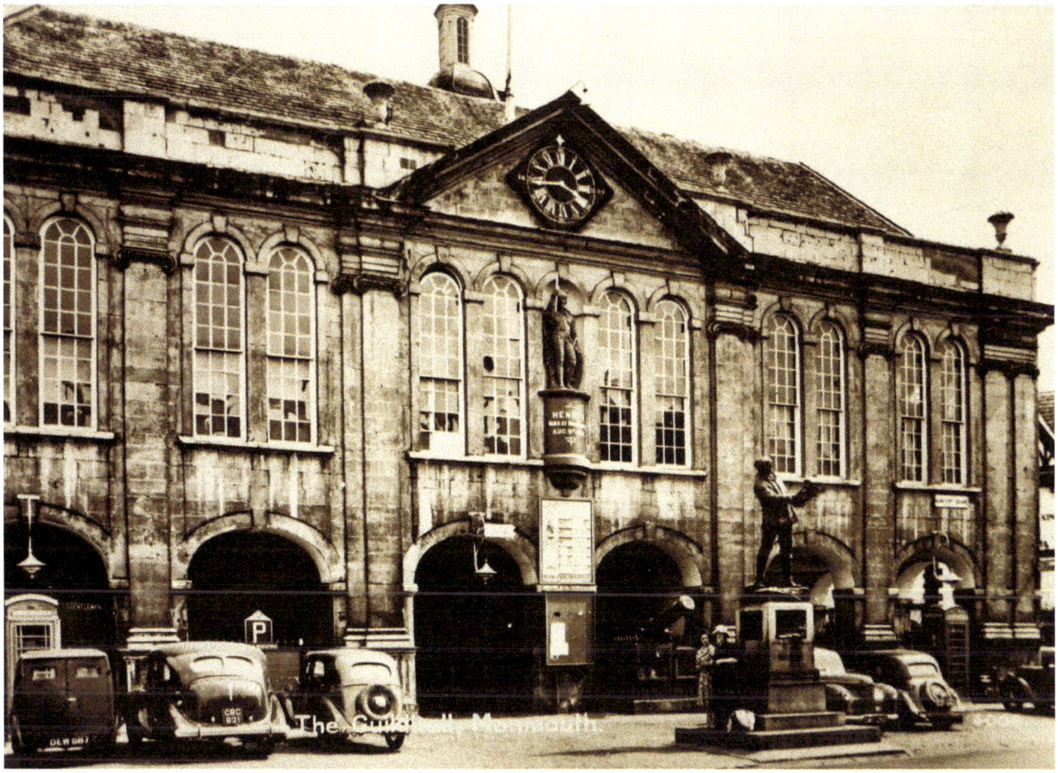

Shire Hall and Agincourt Square

The top postcard of the Shire Hall probably just pre-dates the start of the Second World War as the gun is still in position. The lower photograph captures the scene of Agincourt Square as well as the Shire Hall.

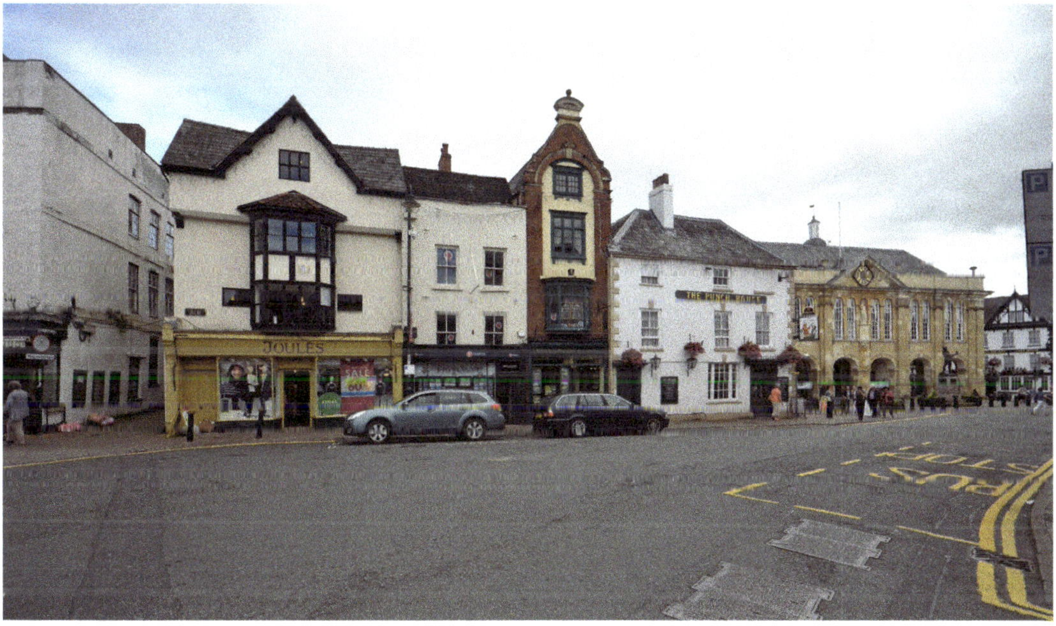

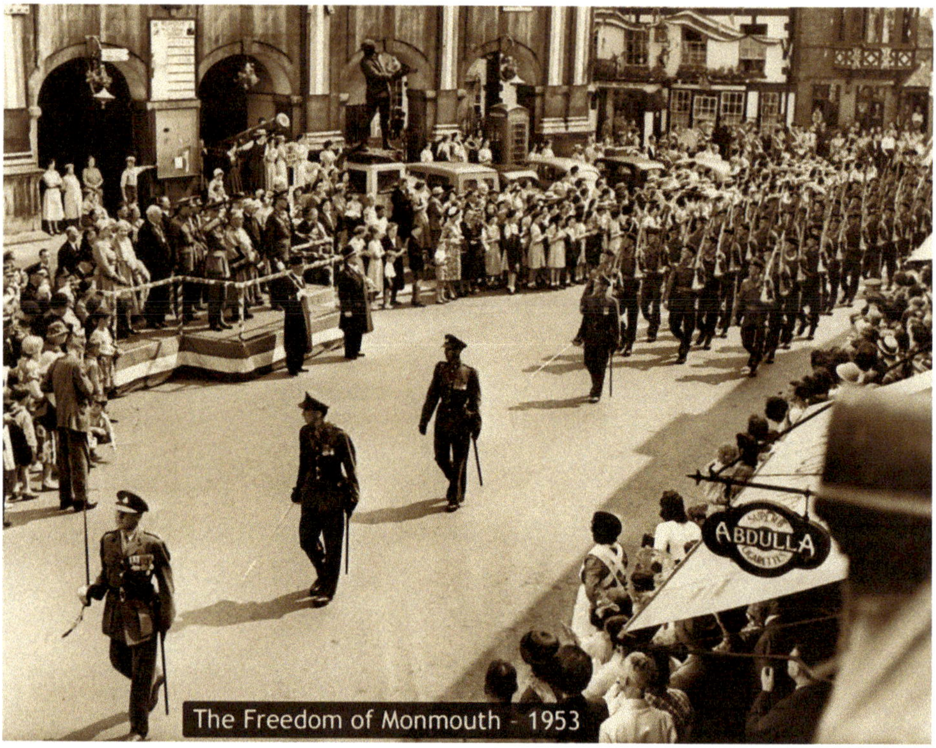

Shire Hall

The parade marking the Freedom of Monmouth the town given to the Royal Monmouth Royal Engineers Regiment in 1953.

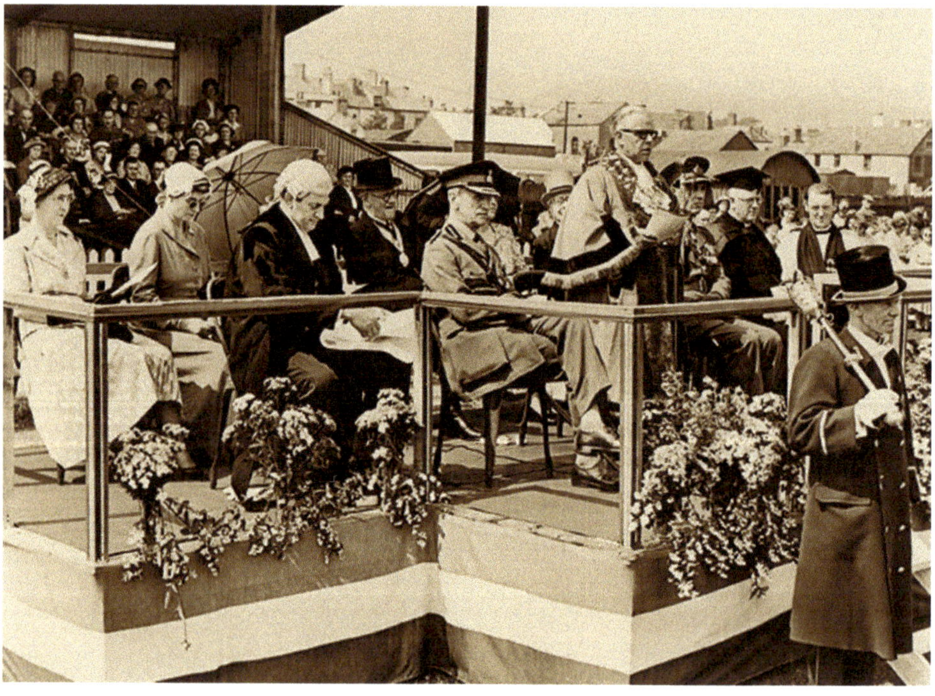

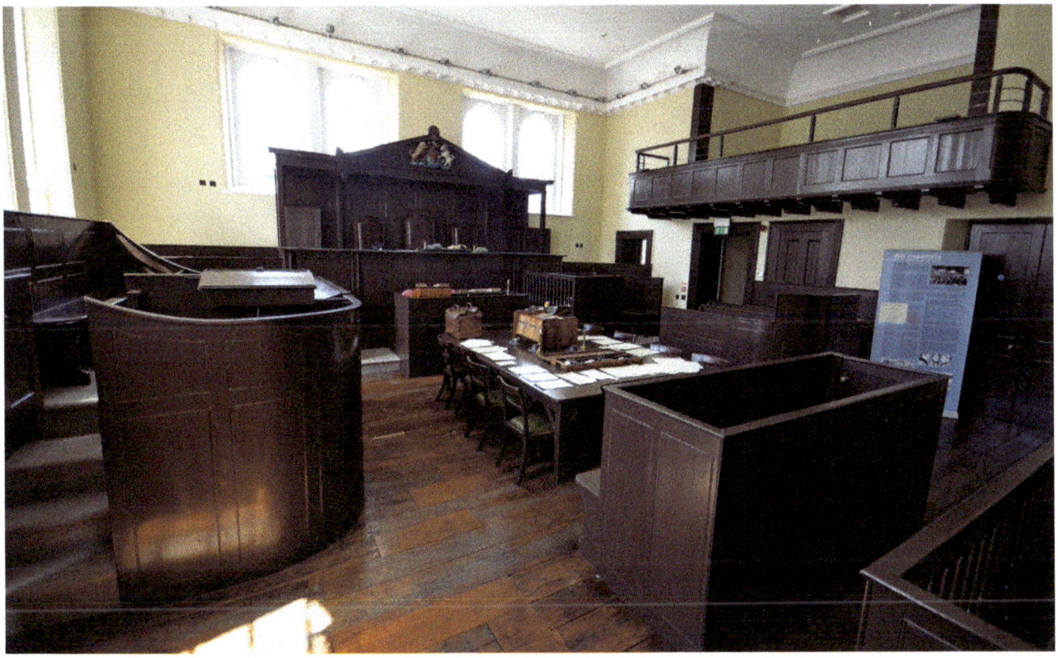

The Old Court House, Shire Hall

The Old Court House and cells have been restored and set up as a museum recording the trial of the Newport Chartists held here in 1839. The three Chartist leaders on trial were John Frost, Zephaniah Williams and William Jones. All three were found guilty as traitors and condemned to death by being hanged, drawn and quartered. This was the last time that such a sentence was given in a British court of law.

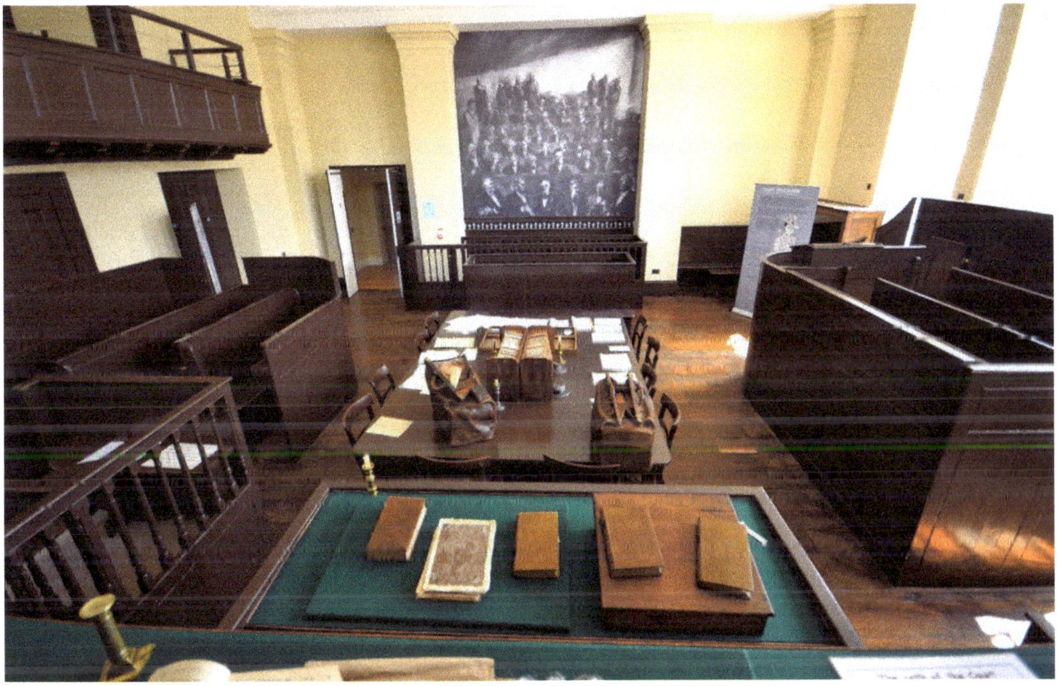

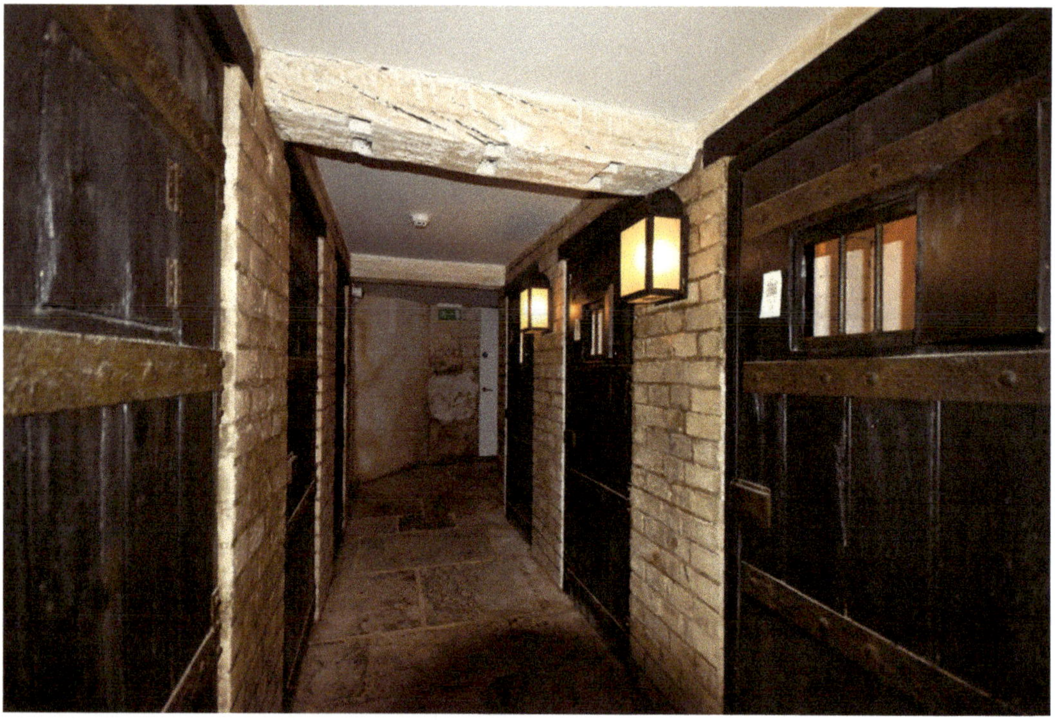

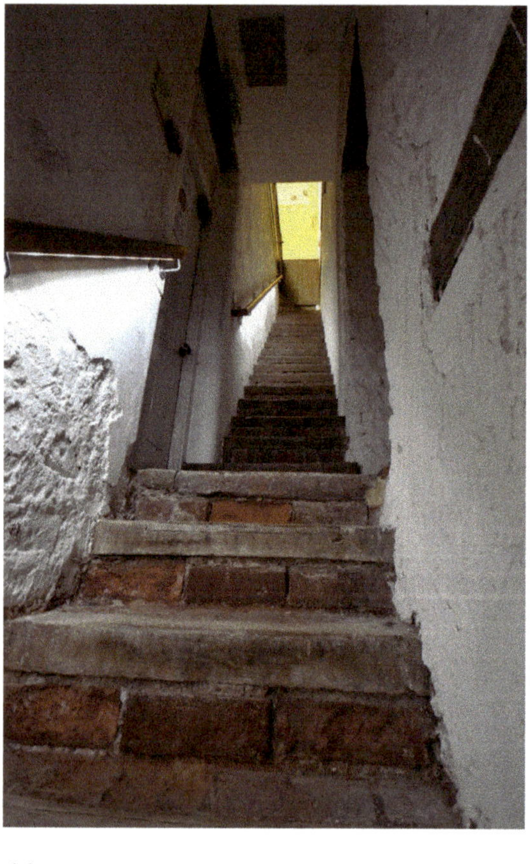

The Old Court House, Shire Hall

The photographs on this page are of the cells below the courtroom and the long staircase the prisoners would have had to climb to get to the dock. The sentences on the three Chartist leaders were eventually commuted to transportation to Van Diemen's Land, now Tasmania.

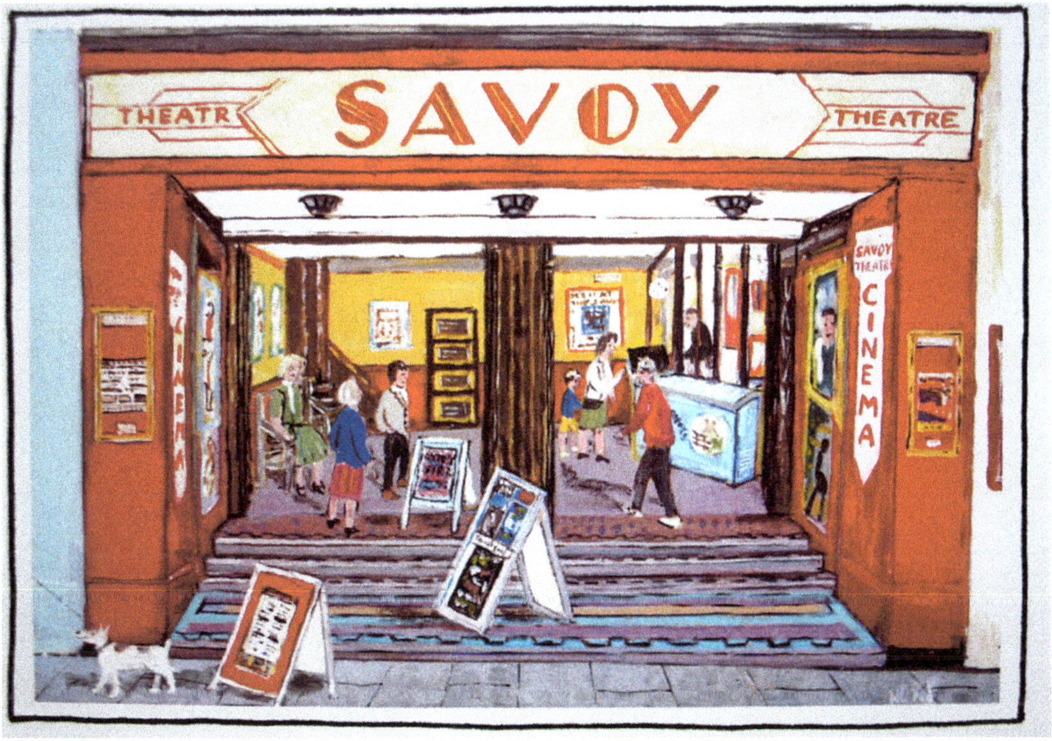

The Savoy Theatre

The Savoy Theatre occupies the oldest known theatre site in Wales. It was extensively refurbished in 1927, but as it retained the basic structure of the previous Victorian building, it can claim to be one of, if not the oldest, working cinema in Wales. The Savoy Theatre is managed by the Monmouth Savoy Trust. The lower photograph shows Chris Ryde, manager and director, and Paul Halpin, technical director, outside the Savoy Theatre in July 2016.

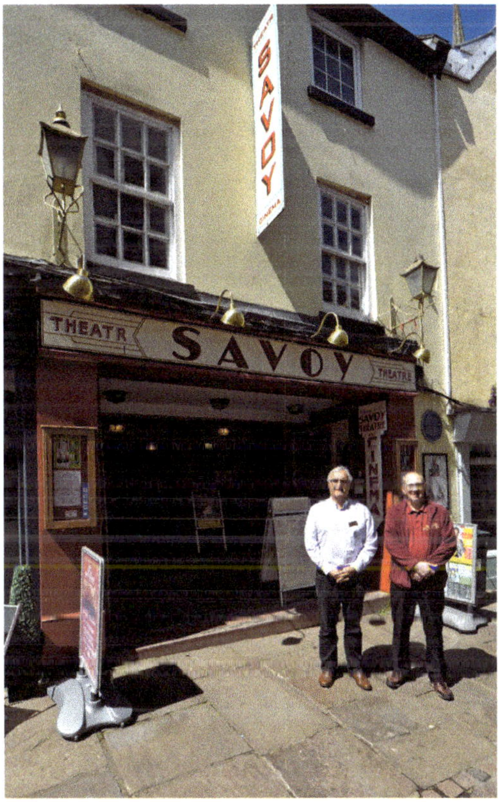

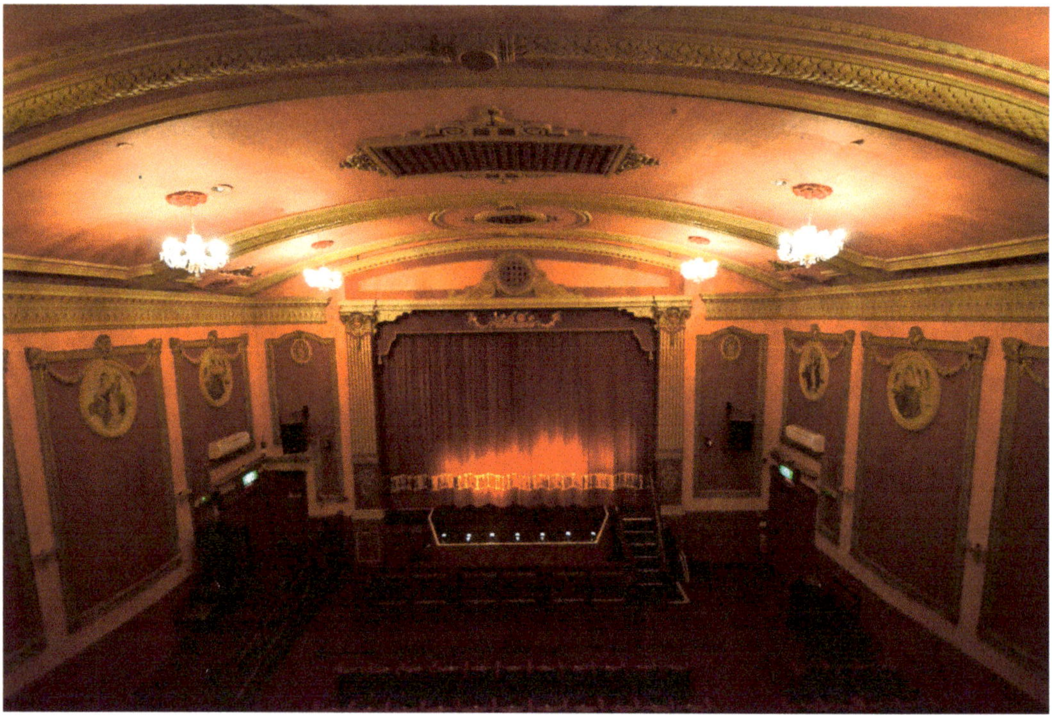

The Savoy Theatre

The top photograph captures the magic of the Victorian auditorium of the Savoy Theatre while the lower picture takes in the theatre entrance lobby and box office desk, behind which receptionist Georgina Peace is partly hidden.

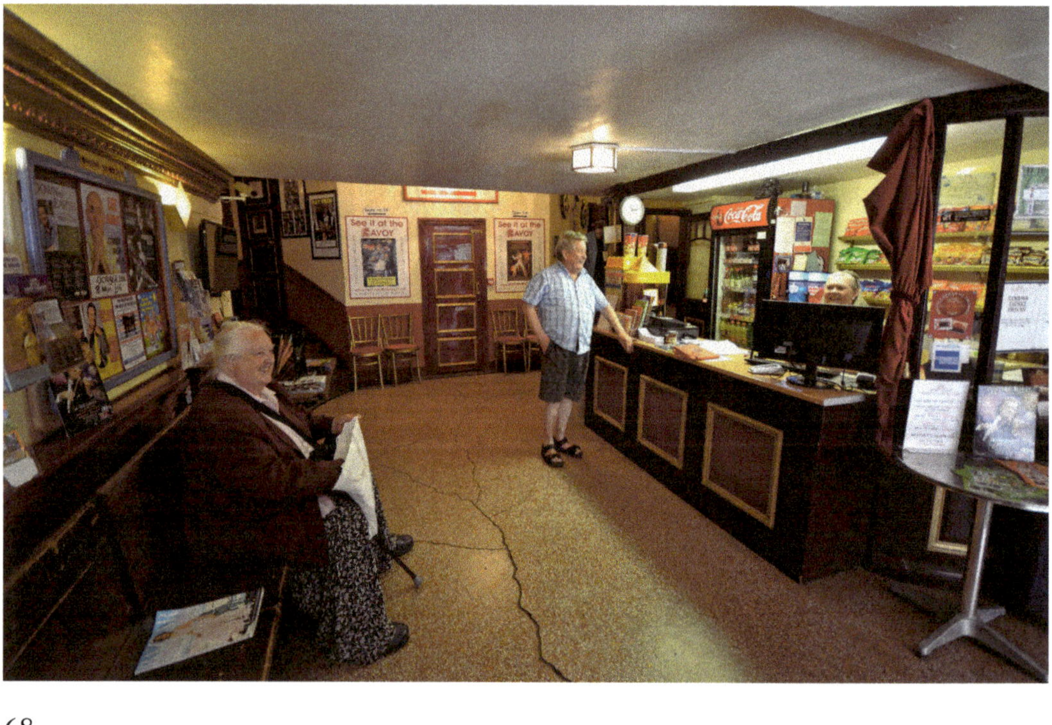

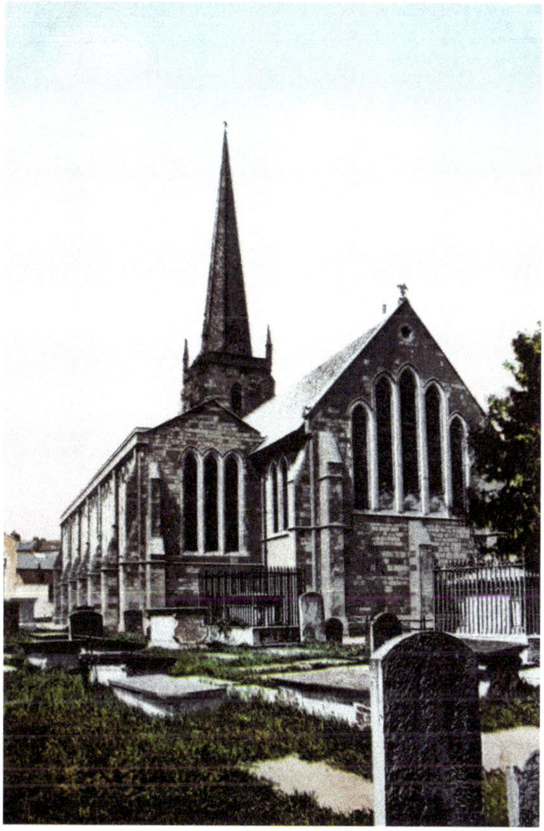

St Mary's Priory Church

St Mary's Priory Church in Whitecross Street is an Anglican church today, but was originally founded as a Benedictine priory in 1075. It is one of the twenty four buildings on the Monmouth Heritage Trail and was designated a Grade II-listed building in 1952. The present church dates mainly from the eighteenth and nineteenth centuries.

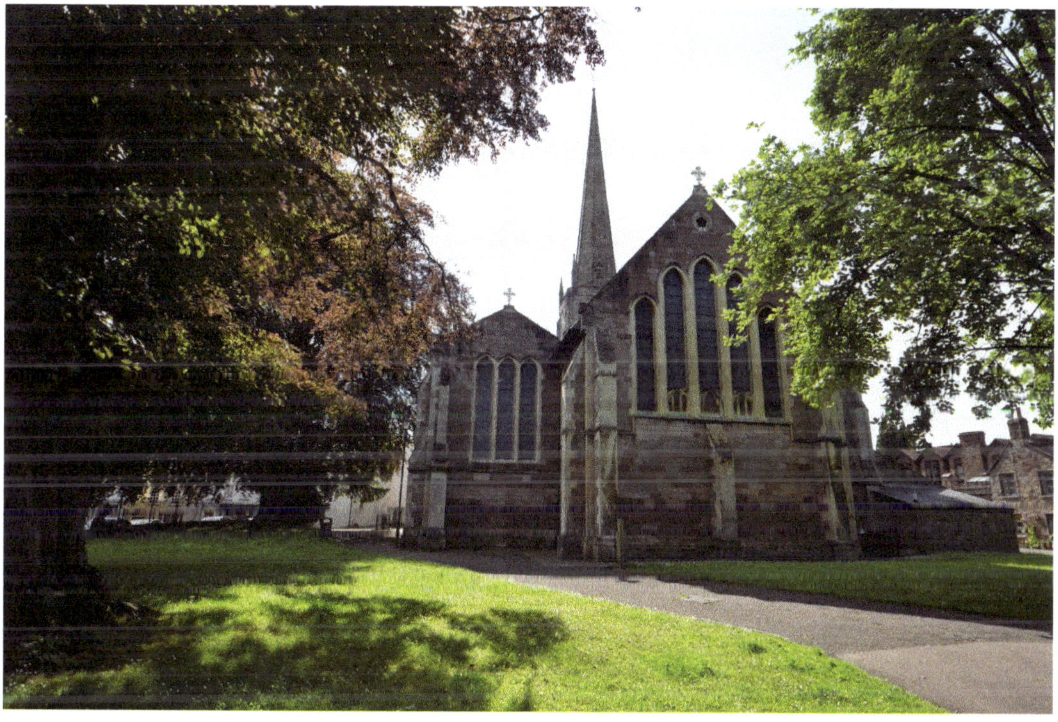

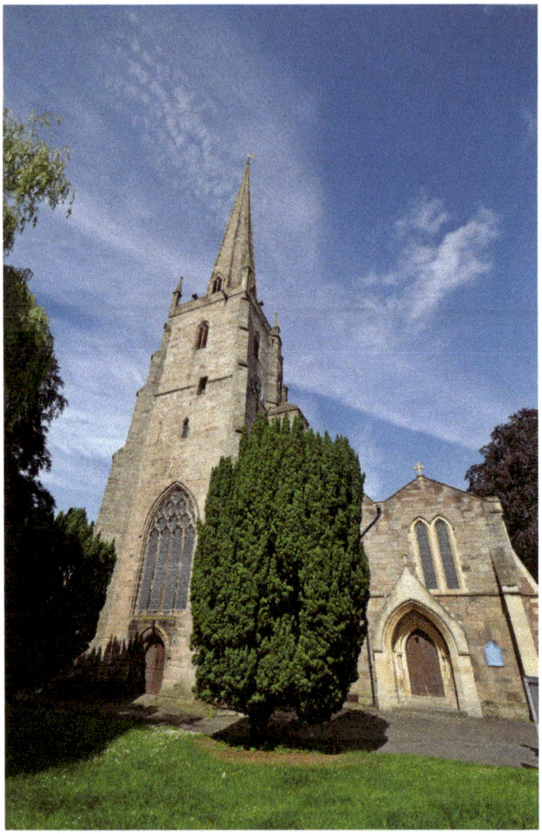

St. Mary's Priory Church

In the late nineteenth century, the church was almost completely rebuilt by George Edmund Street. The church is by far the highest structure in Monmouth, with the gilded cockerel weathervane being some 205 feet above ground. The interior of the church dates from 1882 and was designed to accommodate 1,000 people.

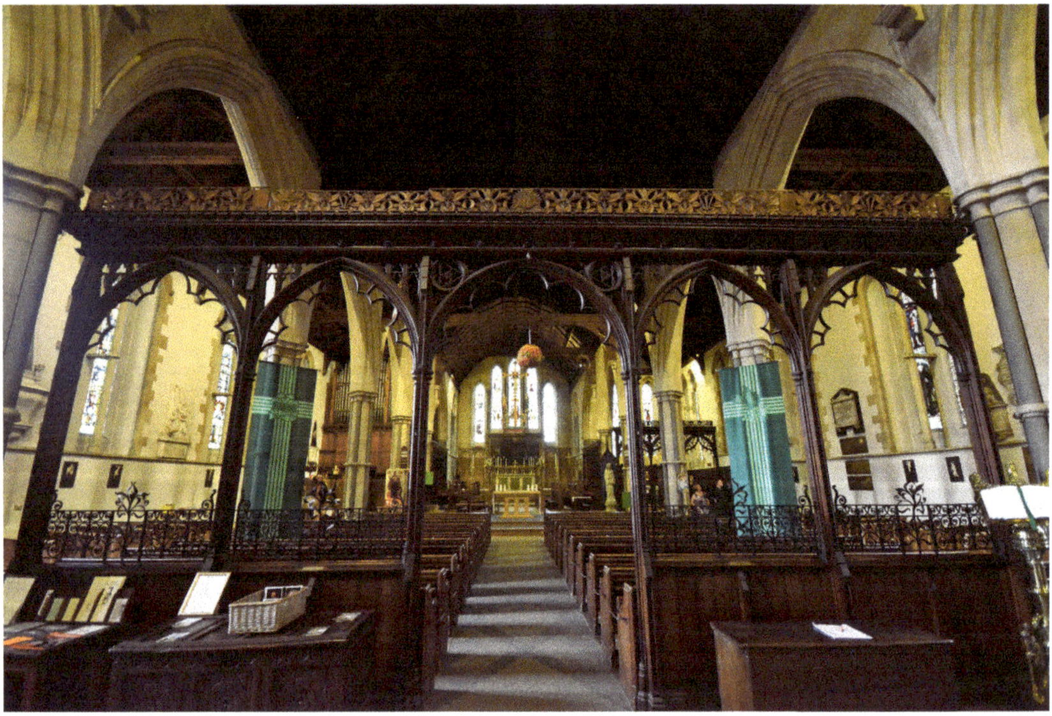

The Priory and Geoffrey of Monmouth

The priory was founded by Withenoc (or Gwethenoc), a Breton who became Lord of Monmouth in 1075. The priory was dissolved in 1536 and the present building incorporates the remains of the prior's lodgings attached to St Mary's Priory Church. The only recognisable surviving medieval feature is the 'sumptuous mid-fifteenth-century oriel window'. This is often erroneously described as being Geoffrey of Monmouth's window, but Geoffrey lived over three centuries earlier. Nevertheless, the legend persists and a tapestry illustrating his life was produced by fourteen volunteers and now hangs in the priory. Geoffrey is famous for his 'stories' of King Arthur, which might now have some truth in them as 'King Arthur's Palace' has supposedly been found by archaeologists at Tintagel in Cornwall.

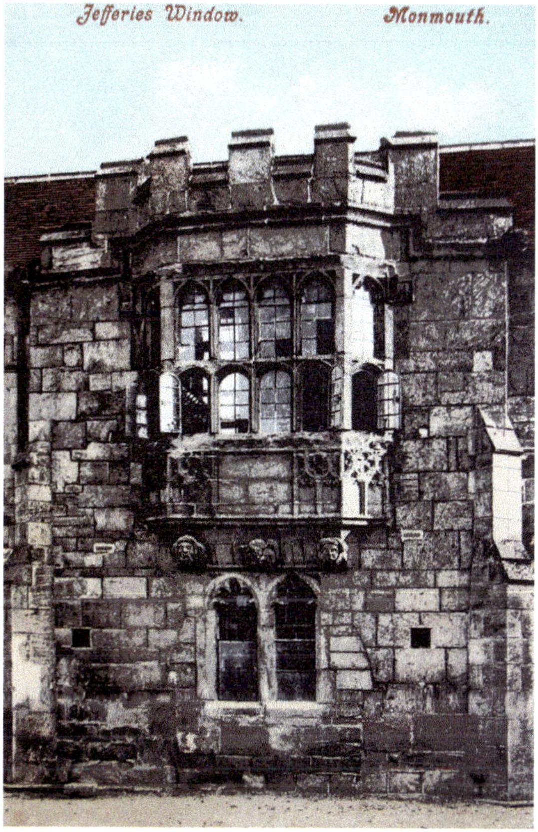

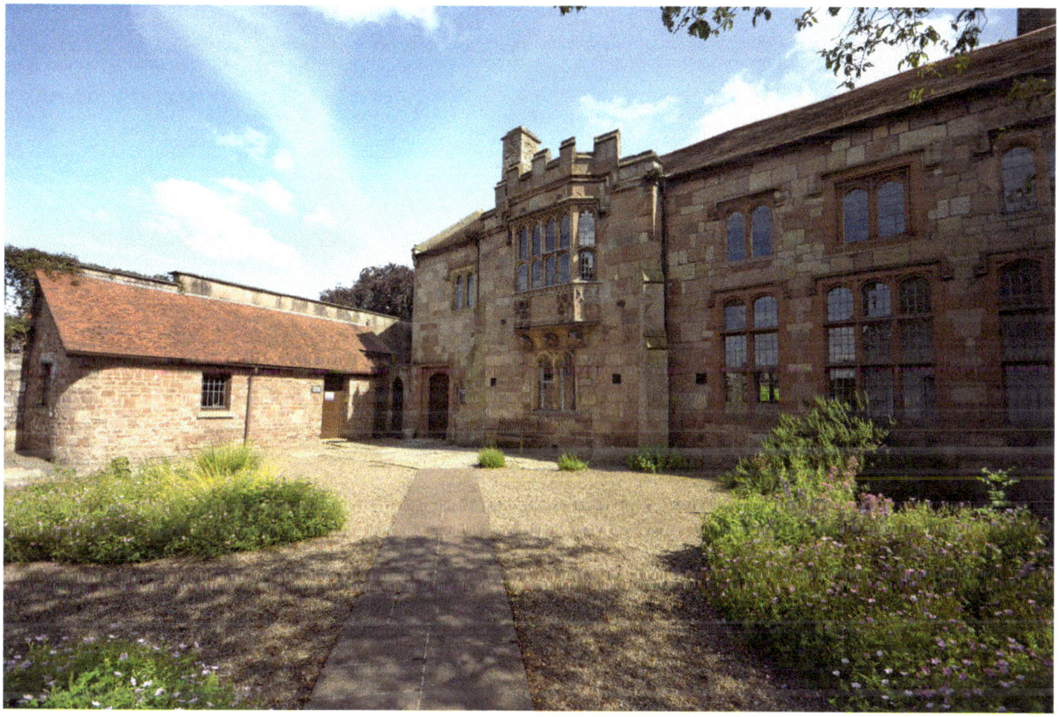

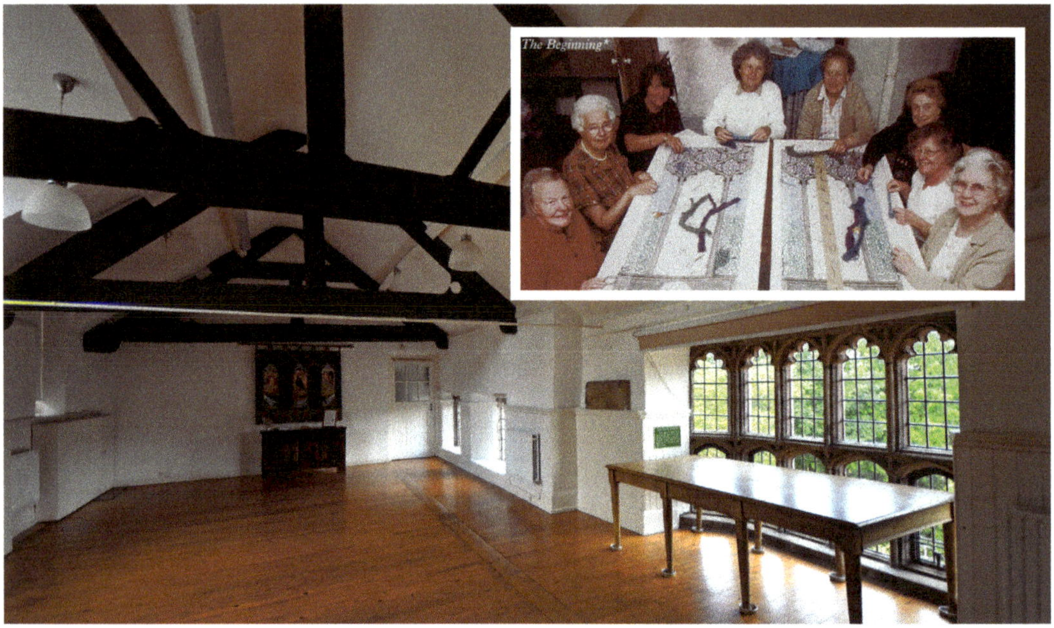

The Priory and Geoffrey of Monmouth

A view of the inside of the prior's lodgings showing Geoffrey of Monmouth's oriel window, the tapestry and, in the insert, some of the volunteers who provided the nimble fingers for the stitch works.

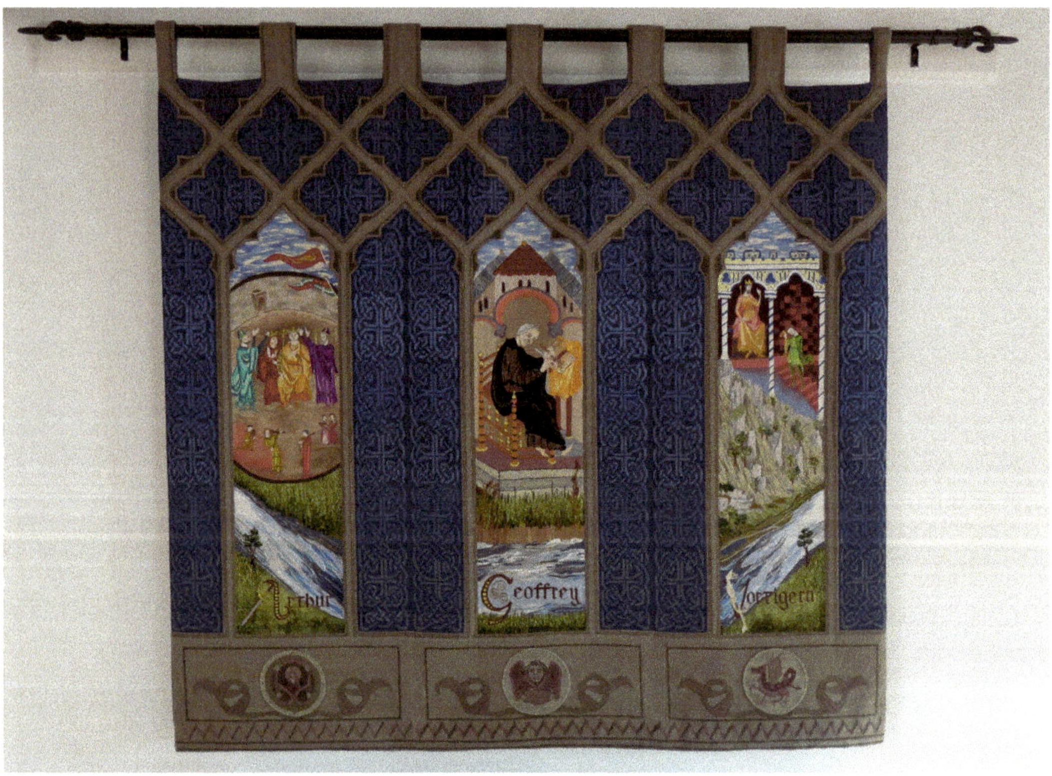

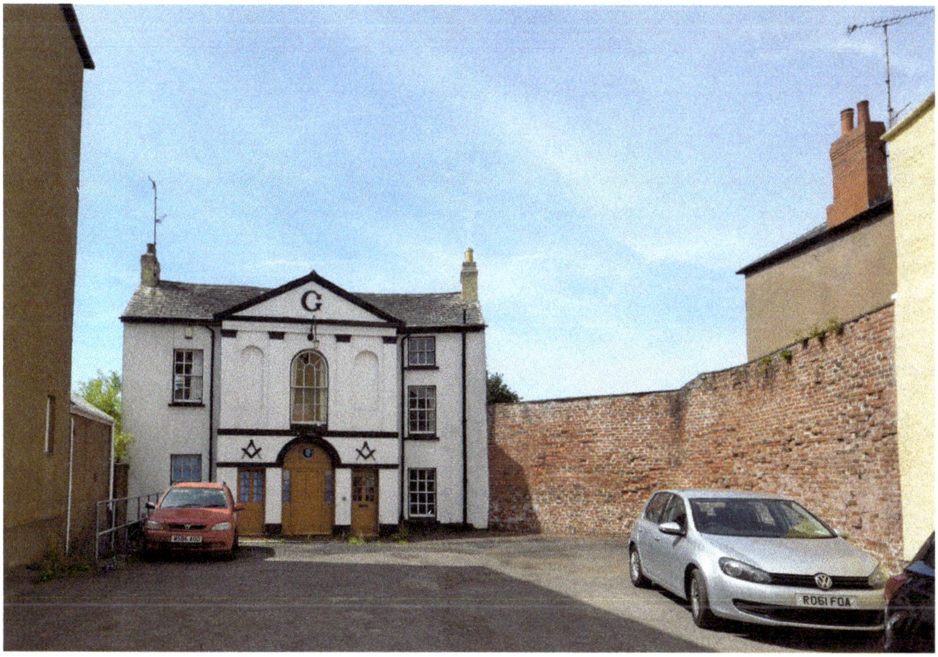

Masonic Temple, Monk's Gate and Market Hall

The Masonic Temple, as shown in the top photograph, is located on Monk's Street and is thought to be near the site of the town's medieval Monk's Gate. The lower picture is of the Old Market Hall in Priory Street. This is an early Victorian building constructed between 1837 and 1839 by the prolific Monmouth architect George Vaughan Maddox as the centrepiece of the town redevelopment. It was severely destroyed by fire in 1963 and partially rebuilt. Formally called the Nelson Museum, it is now the home of the Monmouth Museum. At the rear of the building are the original slaughterhouses that open onto the River Monnow.

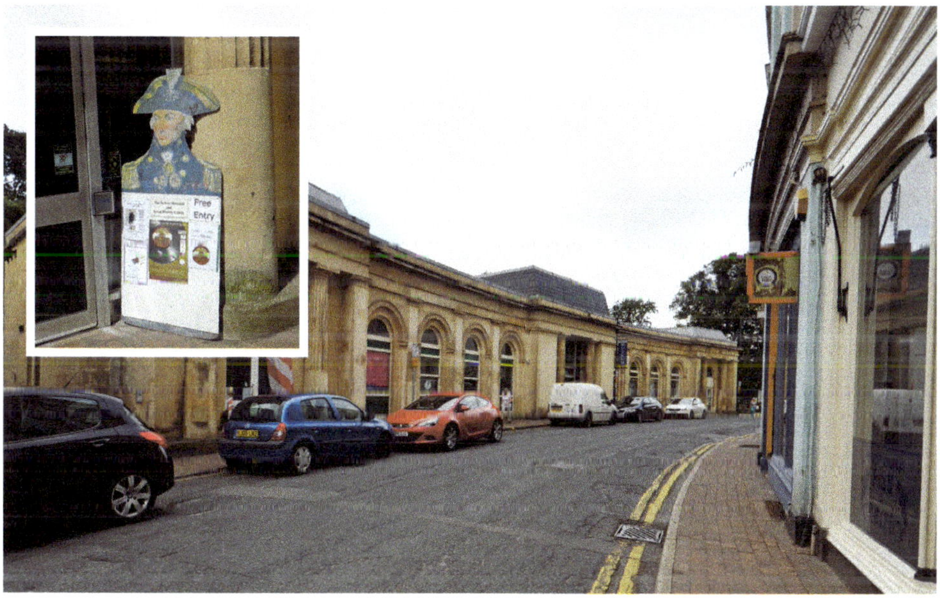

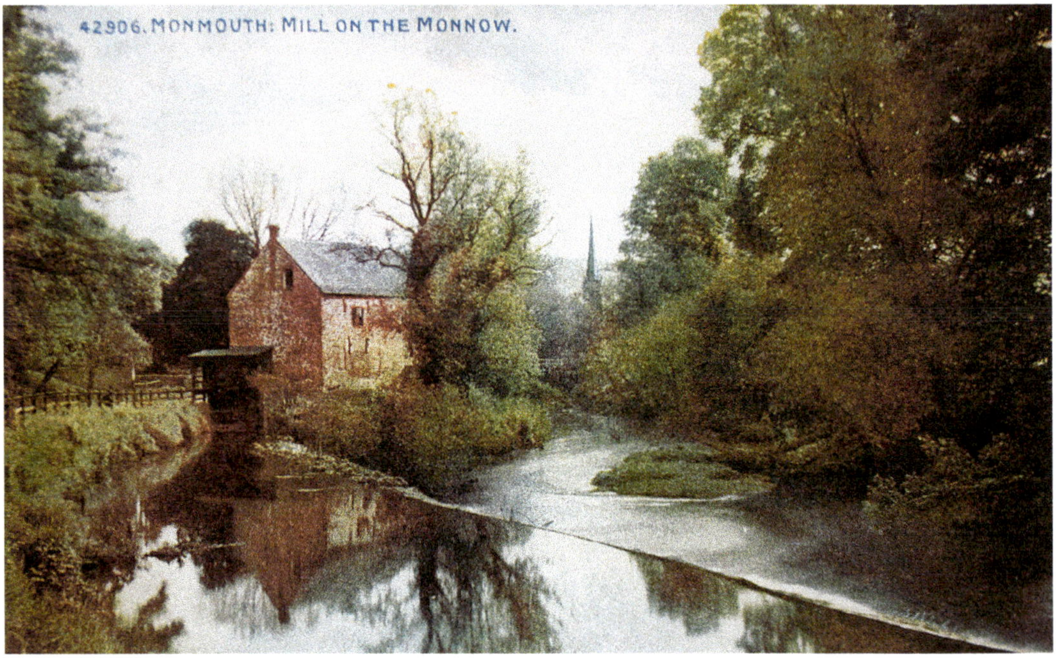

Monnow Mill

Just below the masonic temple on the bend of the Monnow River is the Monnow Mill, as captured in the top colour postcard, franked 14 May 1910. This clearly shows the weir and very short leat that, after 1895, fed two undershot water wheels 12 feet in diameter and 3 feet wide, which drove four pairs of millstones and rollers. The mill was a corn mill, producing flour, for much of its existence dating back to 1448. A Grade II-listed building and once known as Queens Mill, it is now a private residence. Today, it is impossible to take a photograph of the same view because of tree growth, but the remains of the weir and leat can still be seen from the riverbank at Forge Road.

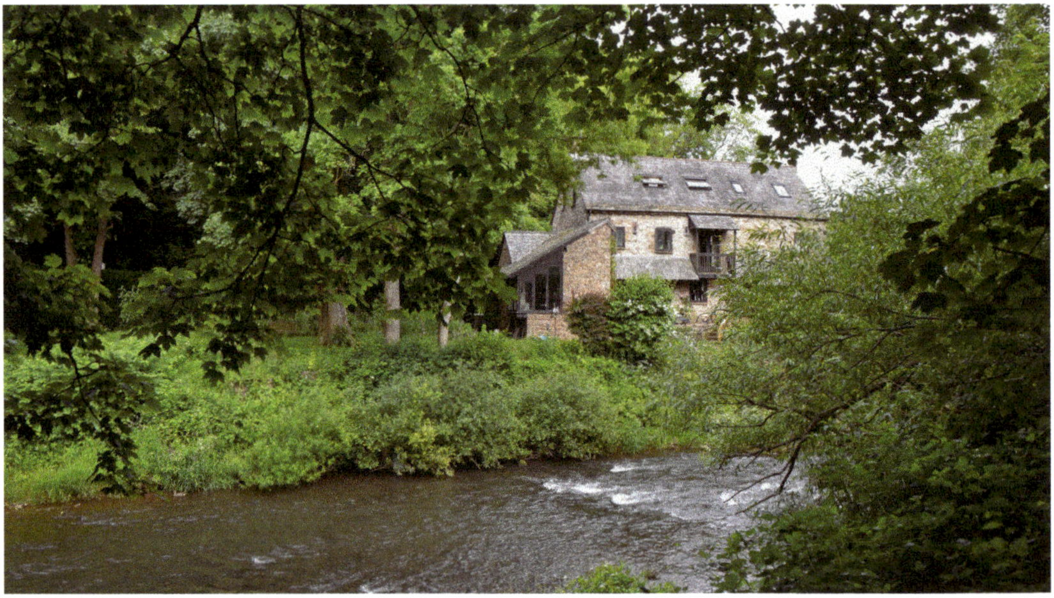

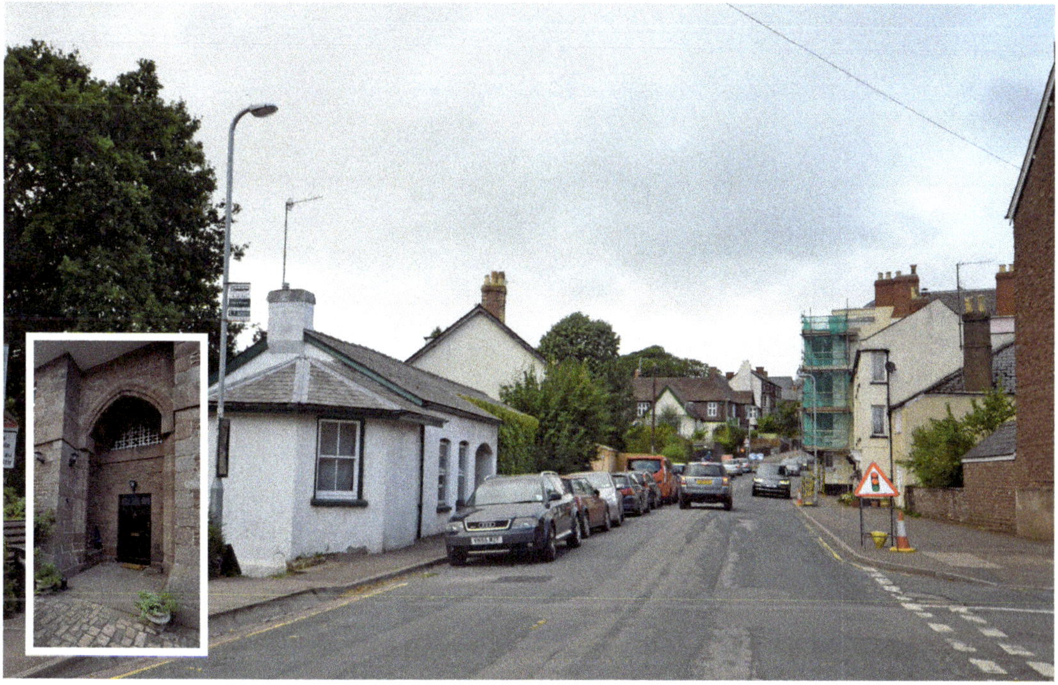

Monmouth Gaol

Looking up the Old Hereford Road past the Toll House on the left, the remains of the Monmouth Goal are to be found on the left-hand side and almost opposite the scaffold-clad building on the right. Only the impressive gatehouse of the gaol remains, as shown in the lower photograph, while the inset gives an impression of the size of the once massive gates that occupied the filled-in archway. Built in 1790, public hangings were held here until the 1850s, when the last execution attracted over 3,000 spectators. Closed in 1869, with the exception of the gatehouse (a Grade II-listed building), it was demolished in 1884.

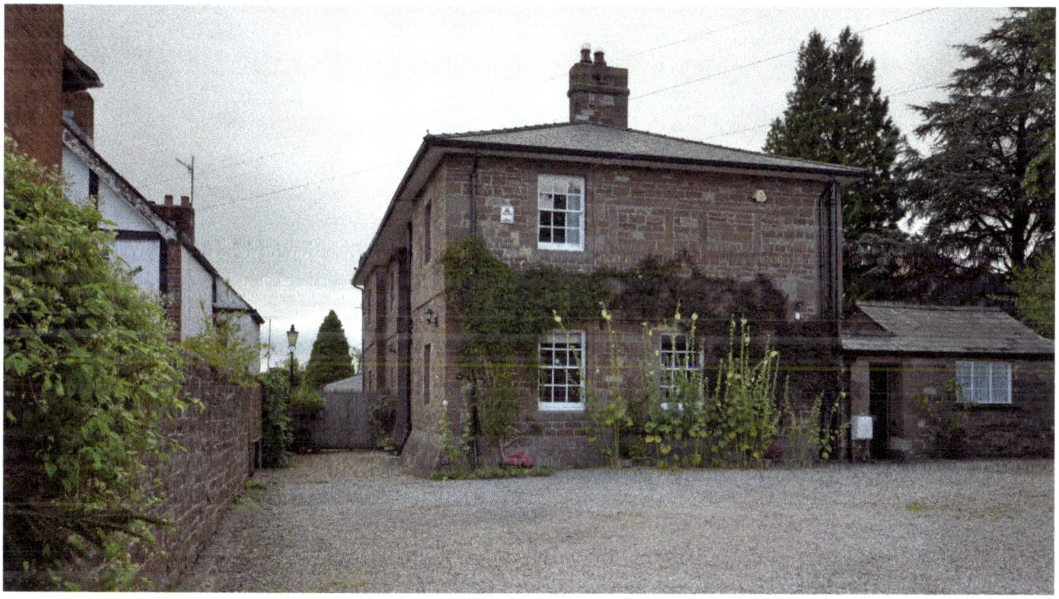

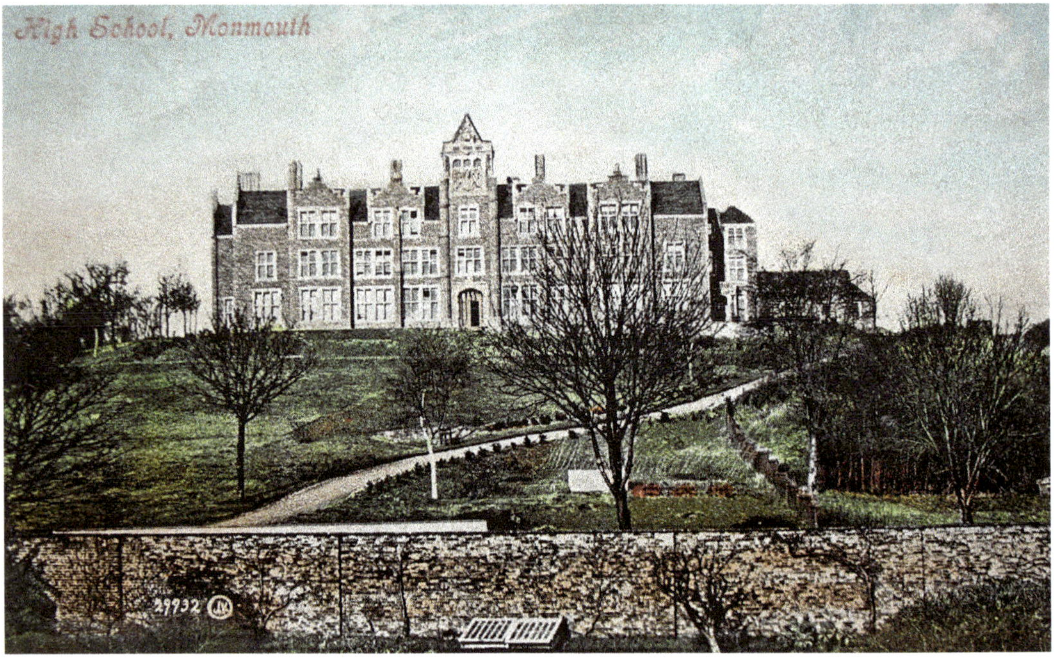

Haberdashers' Monmouth School for Girls

The Haberdashers' Monmouth School for Girls is an independent school that was first established in 1892 and is still supported by the Worshipful Company of Haberdashers. The company is one of the Great Twelve City Livery Companies of London; an ancient guild of the city dating back to 1371 and associated with the silk and velvet trades. The school, situated on the Old Hereford Road, takes girls from the age of seven to eighteen as both day and boarder pupils and has approximately 610 students. It is part of a family of schools known as the Haberdashers' Monmouth Schools.

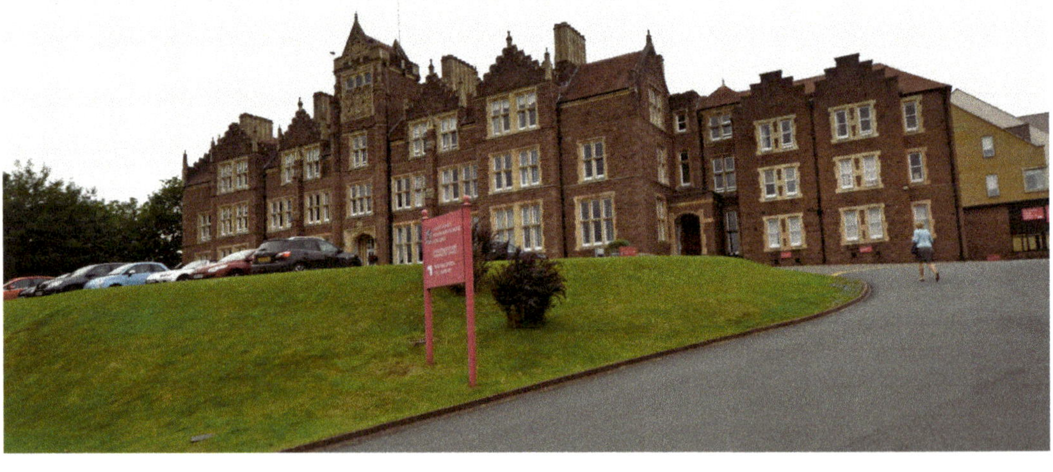

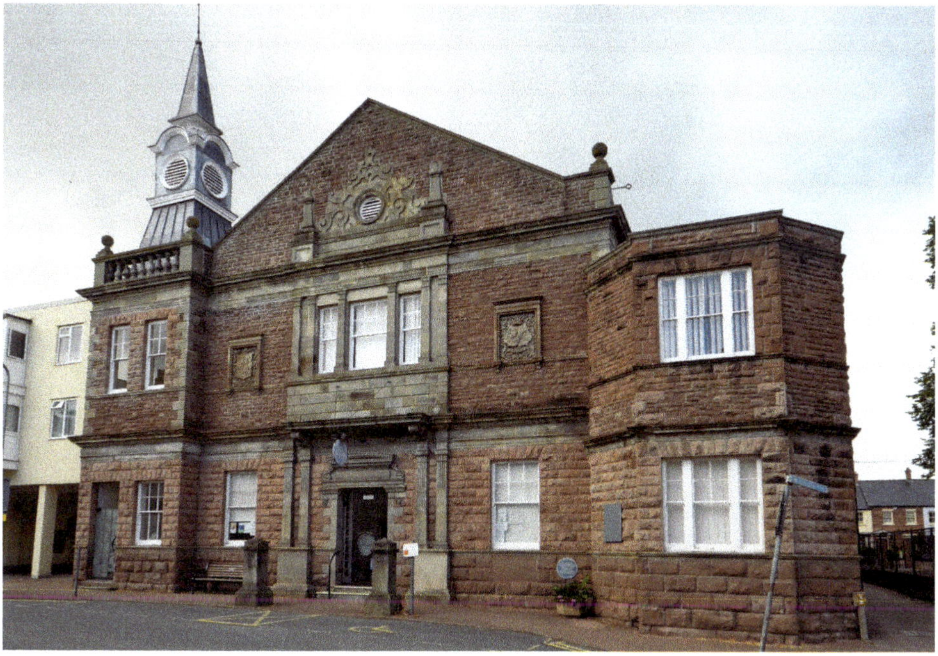

The Rolls Hall and St James Square

The top photograph is of the Rolls Hall in Whitecross Street. It was built in 1887–88 and presented to the town to celebrate Queen Victoria's Jubilee. It now serves as the public library and is near to St James Square where the town's War Memorial is located beneath the vast canopy of the historic Catalpa or Indian Bean Tree. The memorial was erected in 1921 whereas the tree had been planted around 1900. Both the memorial and tree are Grade II listed, as are a number of other buildings around the square, viz.: Numbers 12, 19, 25 and 33, the Dispensary, Ebberley House, the Old Nag's Head public house, the Dixton Gate/East Gate and the Old Toll House.

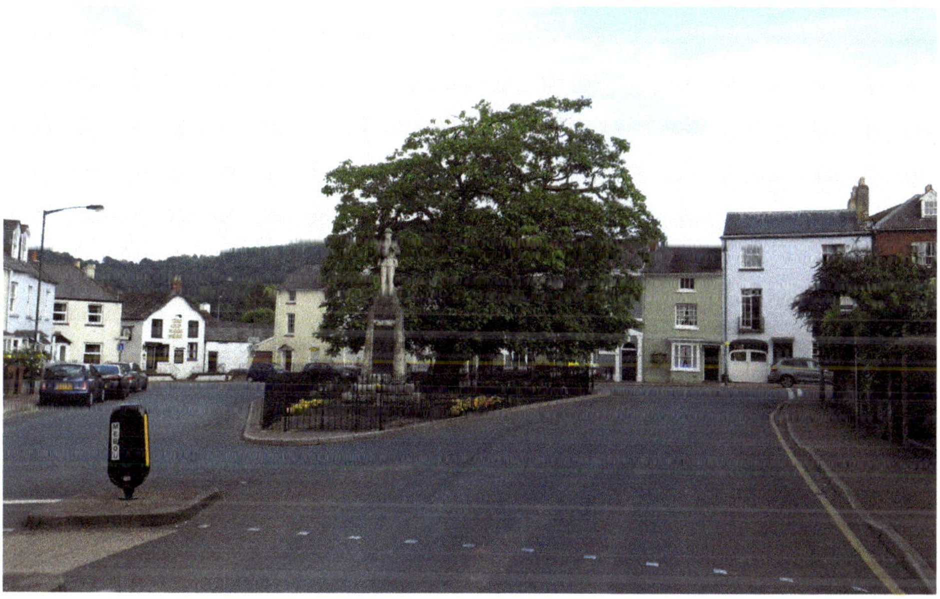

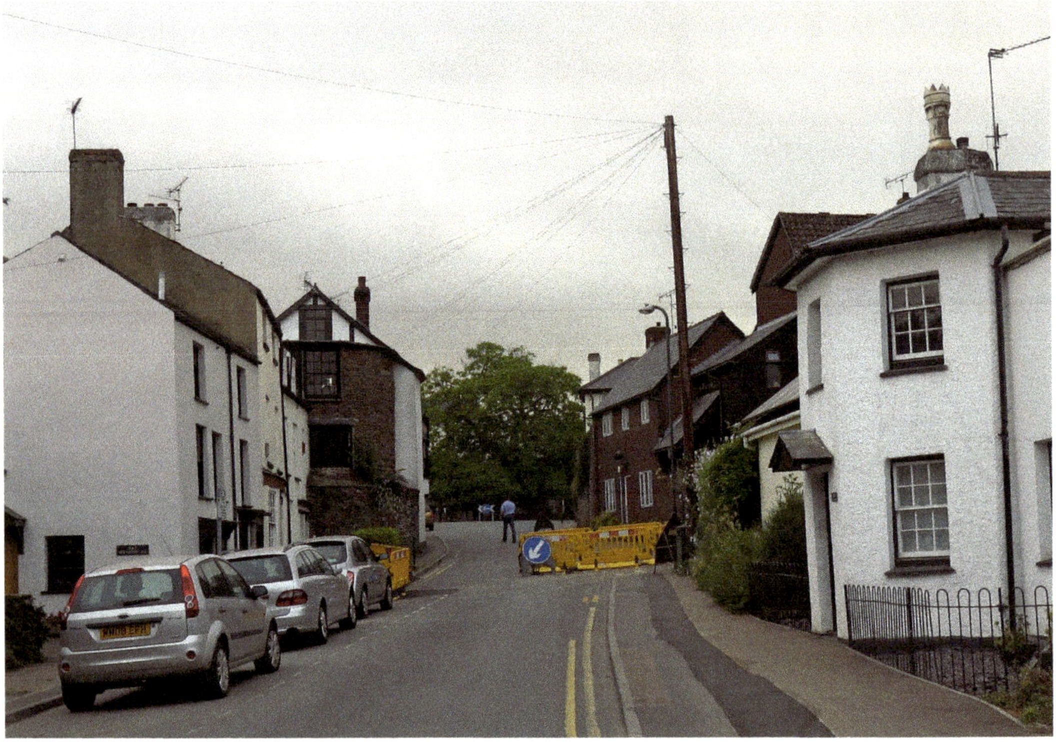

The Dixton Gate or East Gate

Apart from the Monnow Gate, the only other visible upstanding remains of the town's defensive wall system is the Dixton Gate or East Gate, which leads off from St James Square past an old Toll House towards Dixton. The remains of the town walls and gate, a stone drum gate-tower constructed between 1297 and around 1315, are built into the back of a nineteenth-century hostelry with medieval origins, the Old Nag's Head, which is a Grade II-listed public house.

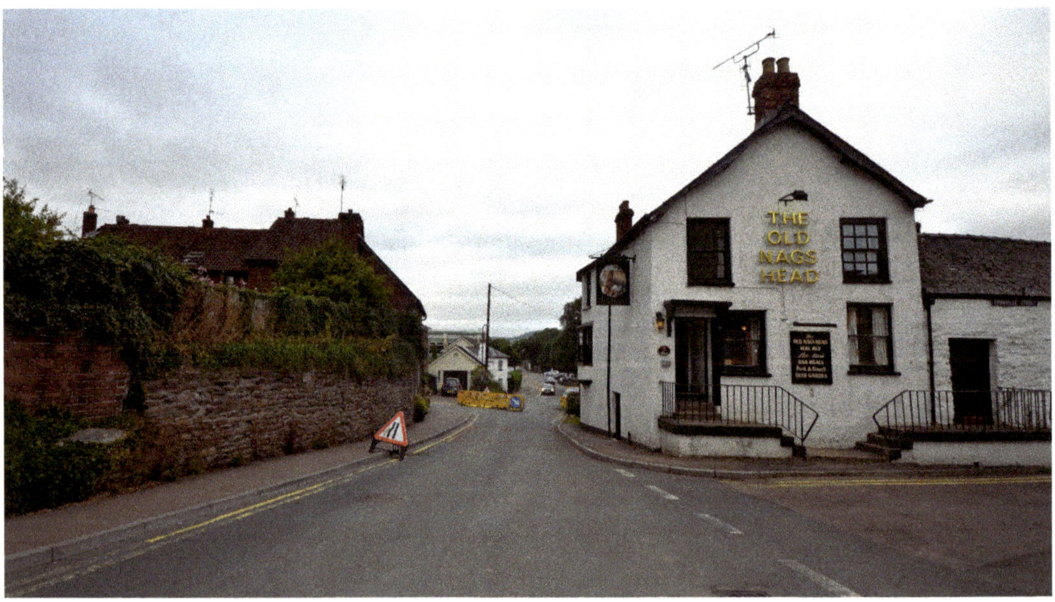

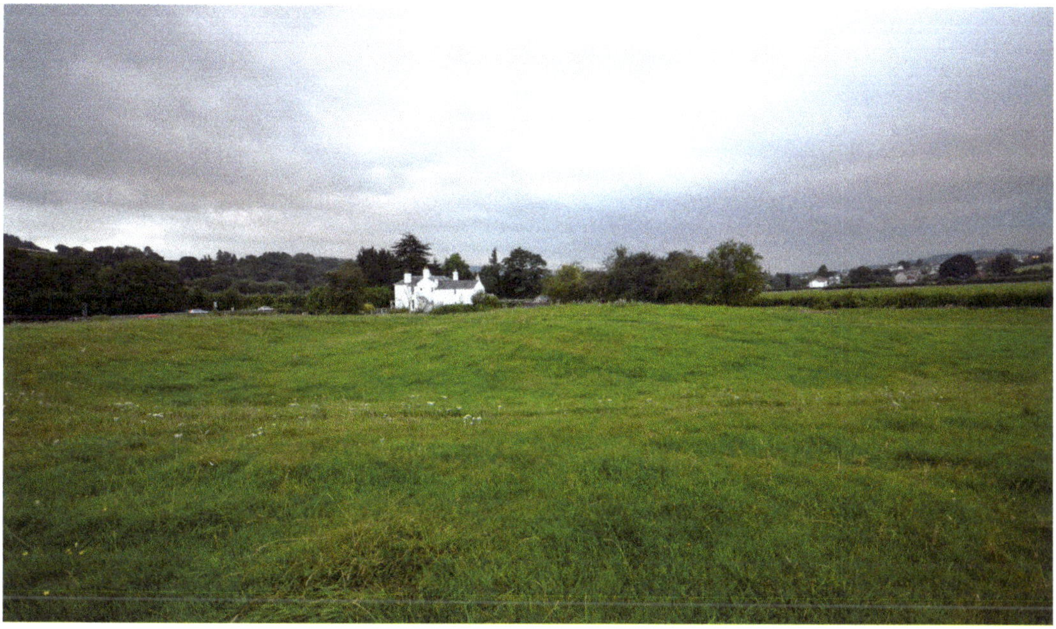

Dixton Motte and Church

Reputed to have been constructed by the Norman, William Fitz Osborn, Dixton Motte or Mound is a low oval earthwork, measuring some 18 metres north–south by 40 metres east–west and 2 metres high with steep sides and a convex summit. The motte is encased by an originally water-filled ditch 1.5 metres (5 feet) deep with a width ranging from 3 metres to 12 metres and a counter-scarped bank. Dated to around AD 1066–1540, the finds of pottery on the site may suggest a motte, perhaps later adapted into a moated site. The ancient St Peter's Church at Dixton is located on the banks of the River Wye across the A40 bypass from the Dixton Motte.

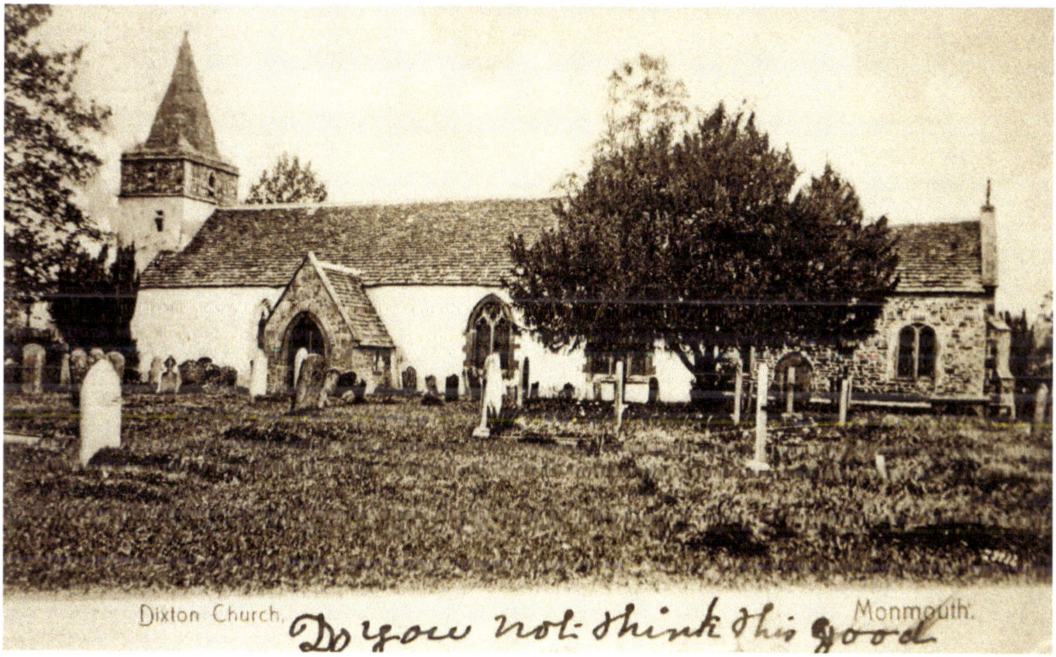

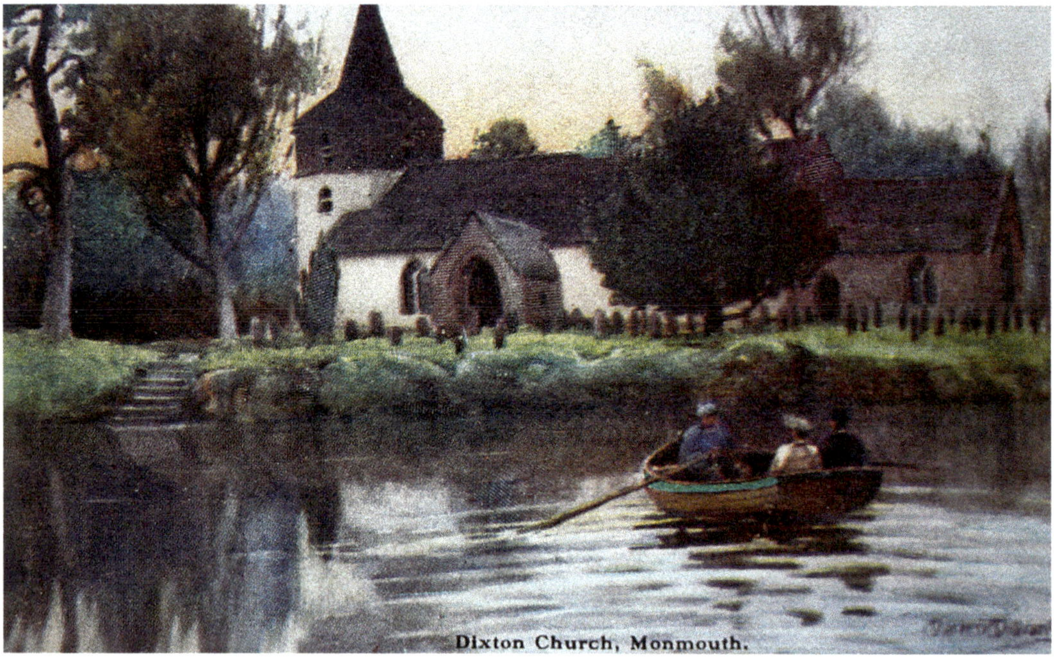

St Peter's Church, Dixton

There is something incredibly tranquil about the setting of St Peter's Church on the banks of the River Wye. People have been worshipping in this church for about 1,500 years; Celts were followed successively by Saxons and then Normans and yet, through the ages, Christian worship has not faltered. The *Book of Llandaff* refers to a place of religion on this site around AD 735 when it was already an old church dedicated to the Welsh saint Tydiwg/Tadeocus. The Welsh name of the parish is Llandydiwg, from which Dixton ultimately derives. The surrounding village has long disappeared and so has the ferry, leaving just a gate and steps to the river as a reminder, as shown in the inset image.

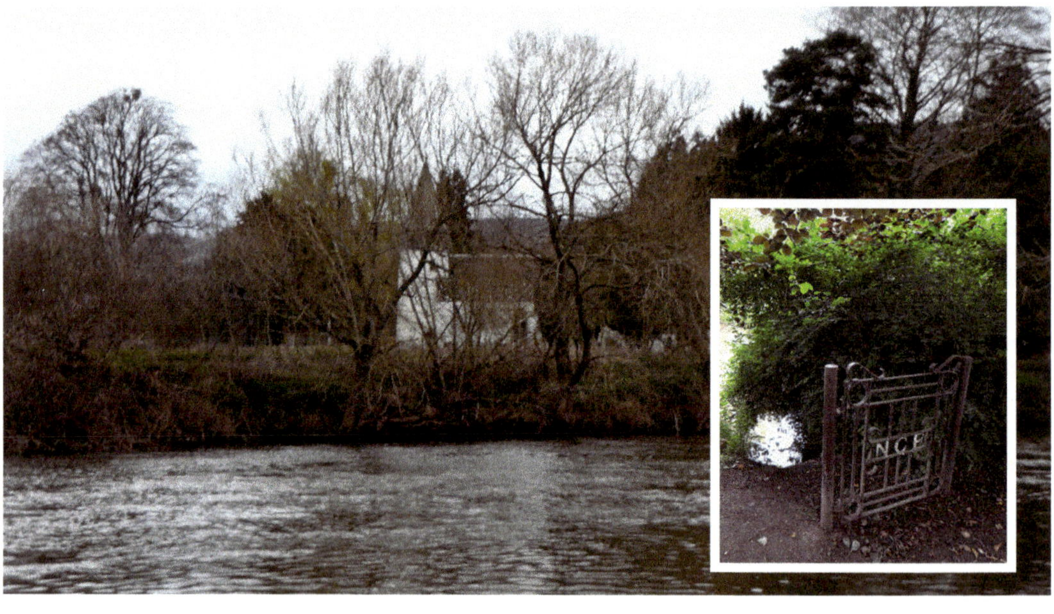

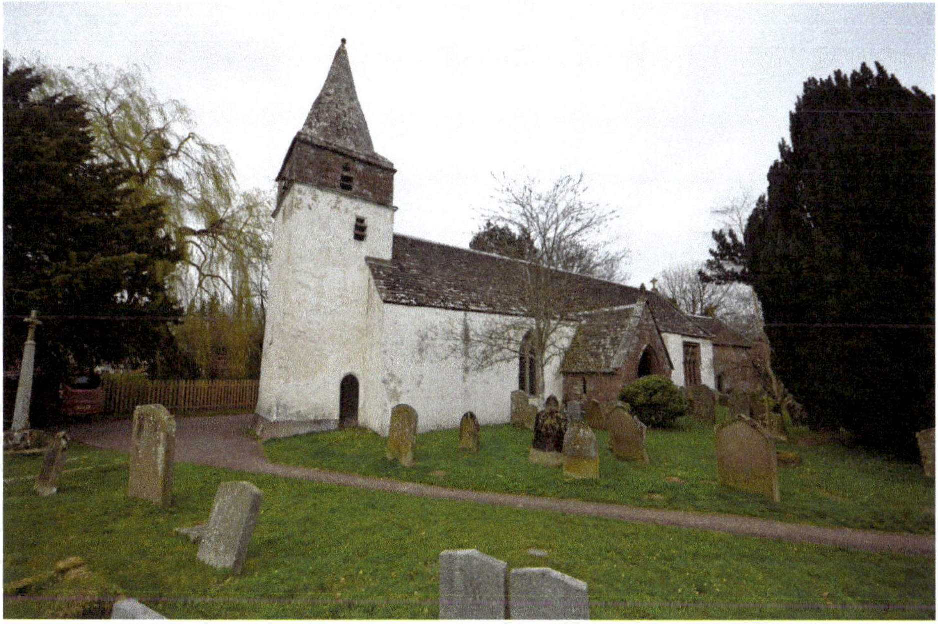

St Peter's Church, Dixton

St Peter's Church is a Grade II-listed building, as is the Preaching Cross in the churchyard. The church is low-lying and winter floods often enter the building from the River Wye, as indicated by the brass plates fixed to the west pillar of the Chancel Arch (*see* inset). These plates record the height to which flood water has reached in the past with the highest being recorded on 22 March 1947. St Peter's Church is unique – even though it is physically in Wales, the congregation voted in 1920 to remain in the Diocese of Hereford when the Church in Wales was disestablished.

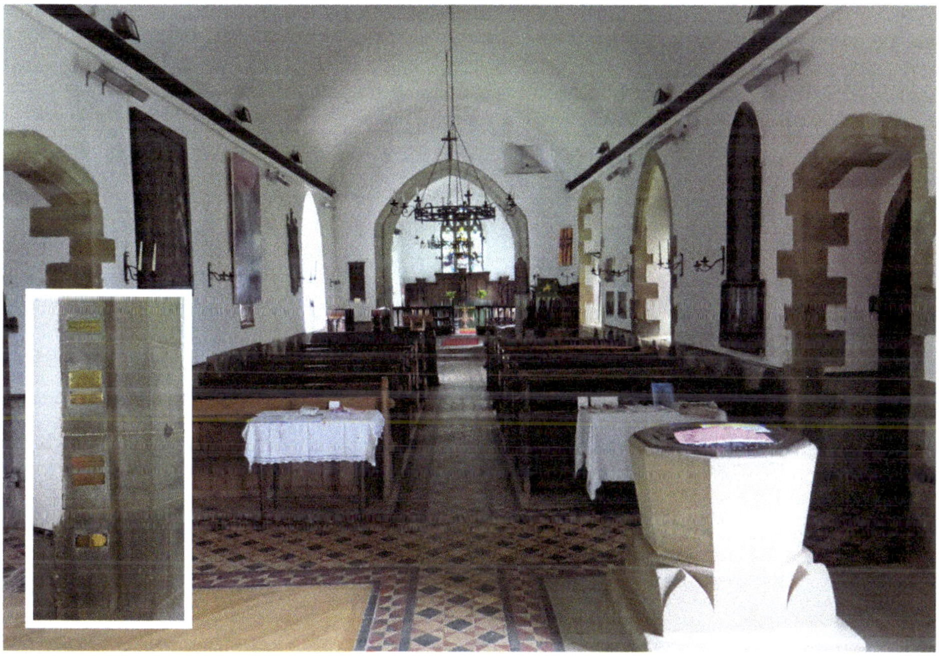

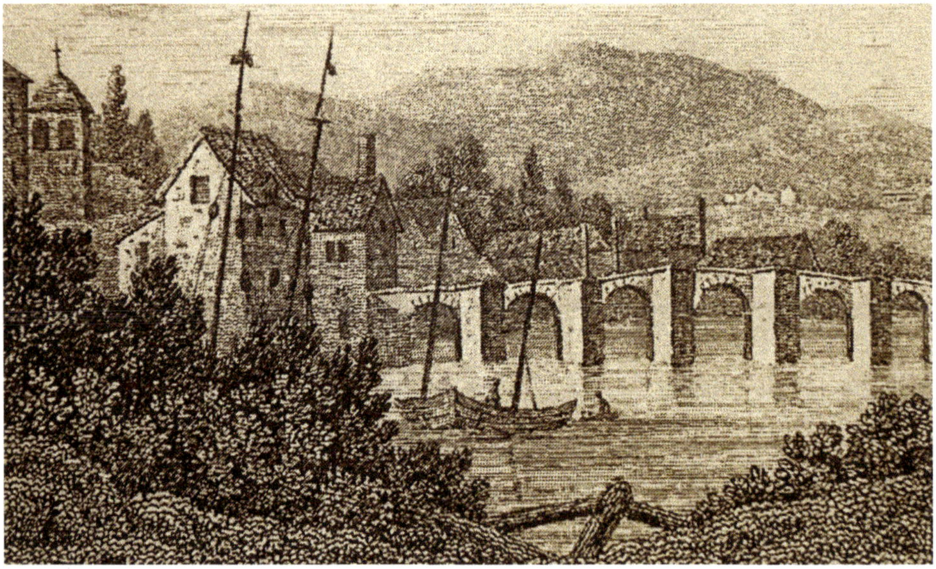

The Wye Bridge and Monmouth School

There has probably been a crossing and perhaps even a bridge over the River Wye (Welsh: *Afon Gwy*) at this spot since Roman times. The eventual medieval wooden bridge was replaced by the stone bridge, as shown in the top engraving from William Coxe's tome of 1801, while the lower tinted postcard is dated just over 100 years later in 1910. It depicts the Wye Bridge before 1890, with the famous and impressive Monmouth School surrounded by many buildings now demolished, including the Waterman's Arms Public House. Monmouth School, an independent day and boarding school for boys, was founded by William Jones in 1614 and is run today as a trust by the Worshipful Company of Haberdashers.

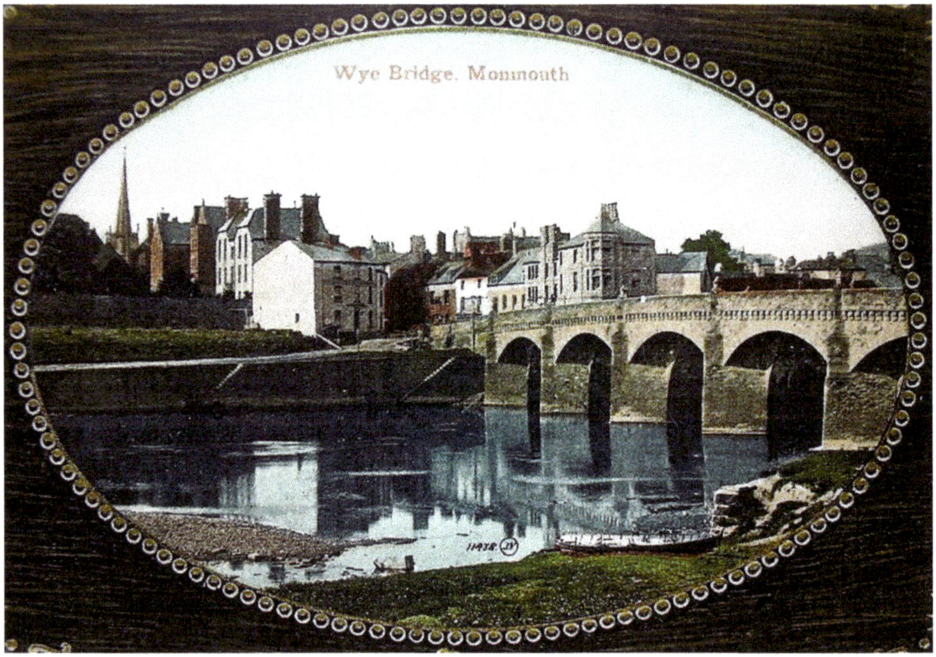

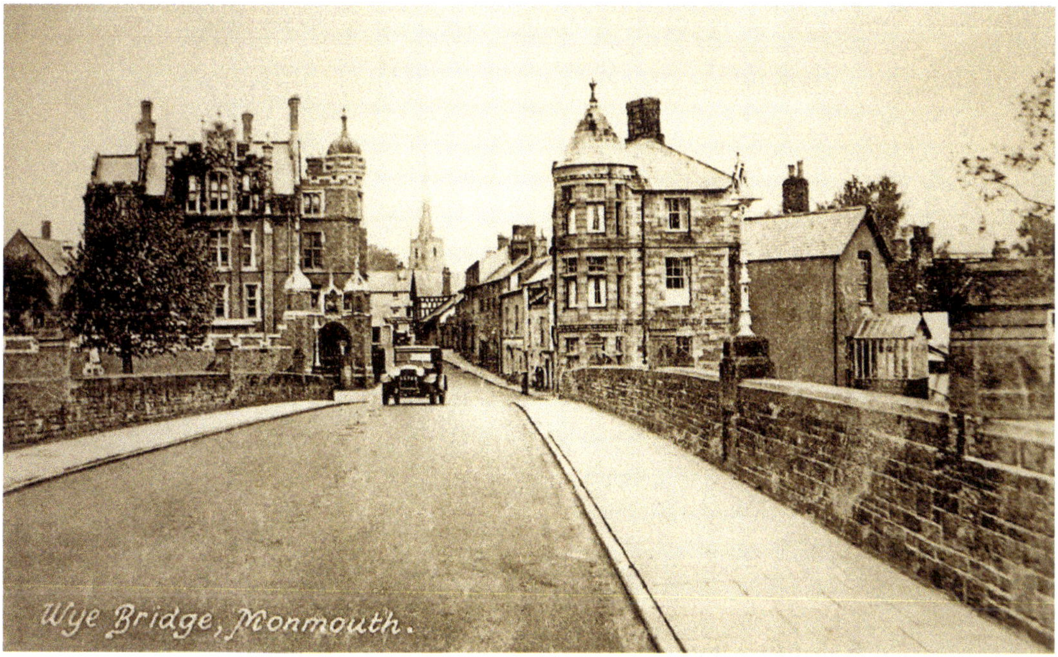

The Wye Bridge and Monmouth School

The top postcard view from the 1930s gives an impressive view of Monmouth School with just one car crossing the bridge in those far-off days of leisurely motoring. Today's view paints a different picture with the Wye Bridge choc-a-bloc with all different types of vehicle from cars to tractors, commercial vans to heavy articulated lorries. The present 71-metre-long five-span bridge was completely rebuilt between 1616 and 1617 and widened on both sides in 1879, as recorded by a plaque on the bridge parapet. A marvellous feat of engineering construction which, despite its age, has to cater for all types of vehicle, including continental juggernauts, traversing to and from the Forest of Dean and Wye Valley.

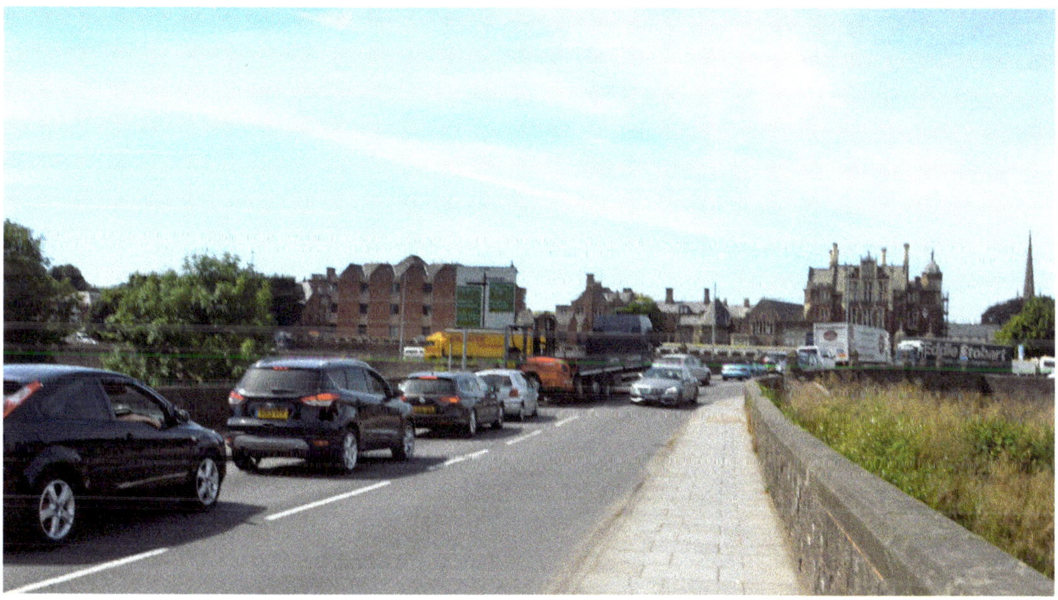

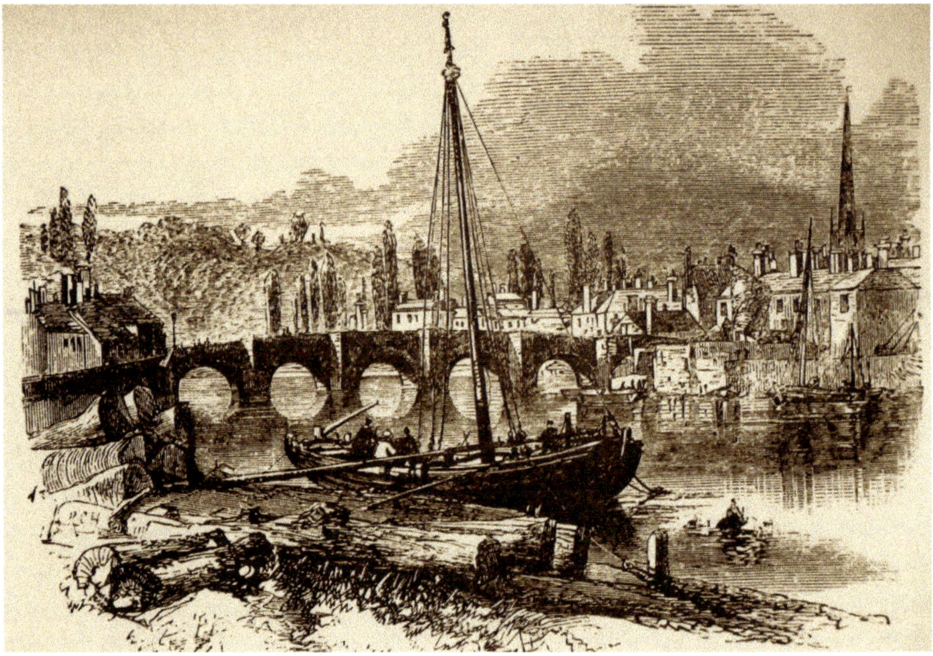

The Wye Bridge and Monmouth's Boating Heritage

The two views on this page demonstrate the strong boating heritage of Monmouth that has recently been highlighted by the discovery of 'The Lost Lake' by the Monmouth Archaeological Society (*see* pages 4–7). The top sketch is from the 'Book of the Wye' (1861) and shows the boatyards on the bank of the river from whence, in past times, seagoing vessels could reach the harbours at the Wye Bridge. The lower postcard view is of the more traditional fishing craft, the 'coracle'. A lightweight wattle and skin vessel of ancient British origins called a 'thoracle, 'trucle' and sometimes a 'coble' in Monmouth and Hereford.

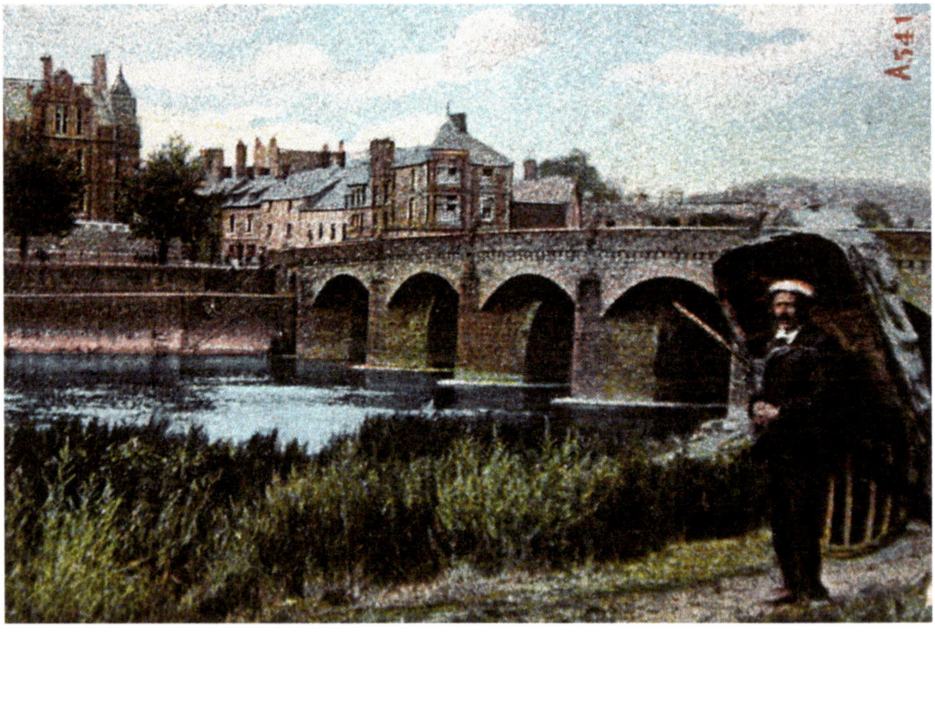

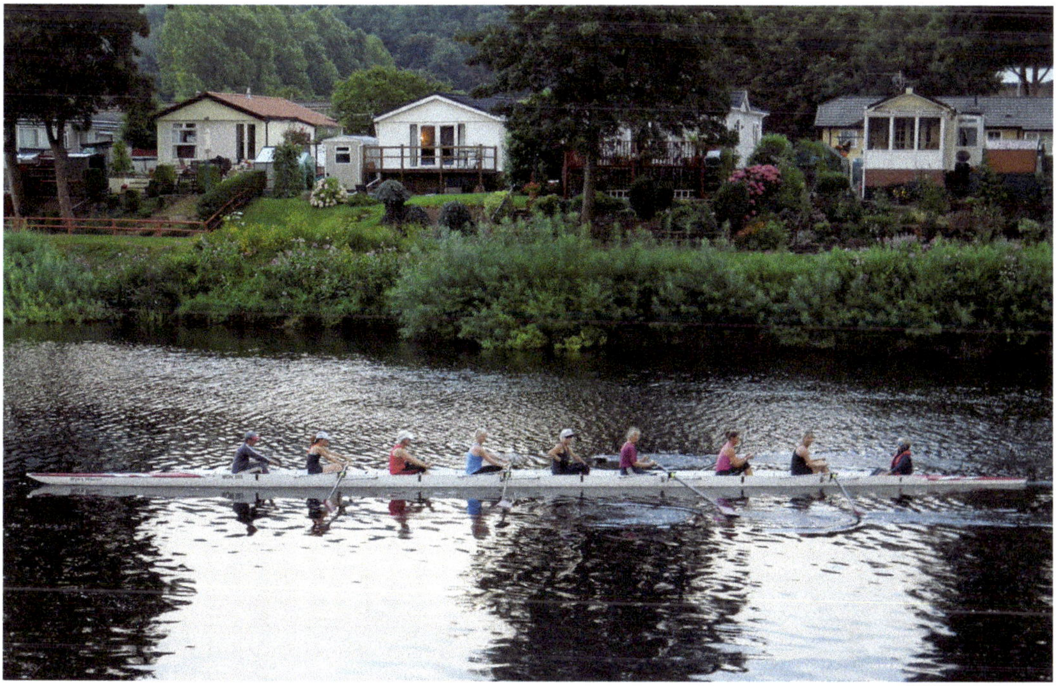

Monmouth's Boating Heritage – 'Wye's Women'

With Monmouth's boating heritage stretching back some 8,000 years, local residents can't fail to have boating in their blood and an insatiable urge to take to the water, as demonstrated by the nine female rowers captured on this page and the next. The Monmouth Rowing Club currently have a women's squad of thirty members. Of these, the crew of the 'Wye's Women' eight-sweep boat showed an admiring author not only how to row in style but also how to retrieve the boat from the river and get it back onto dry land.

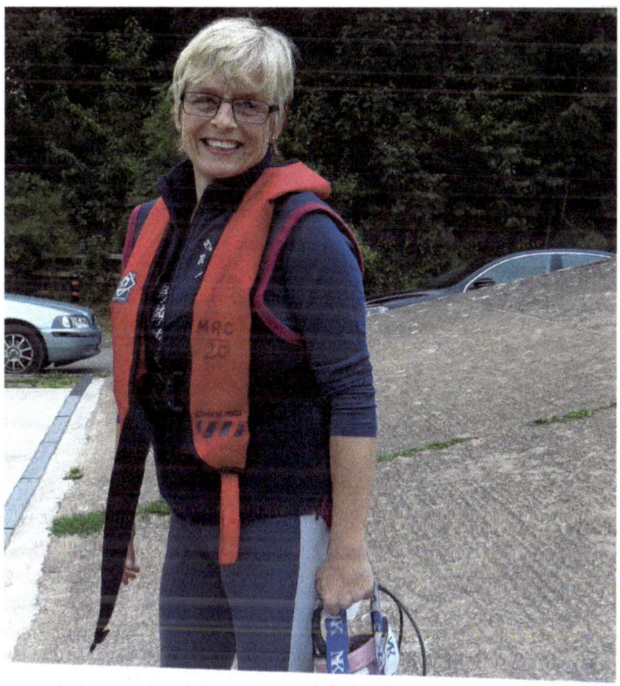

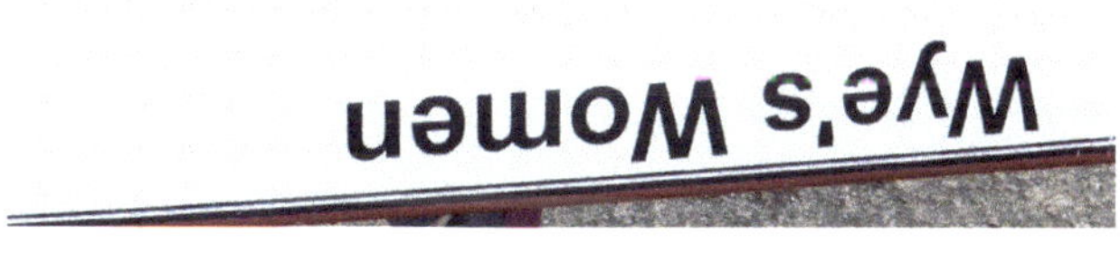

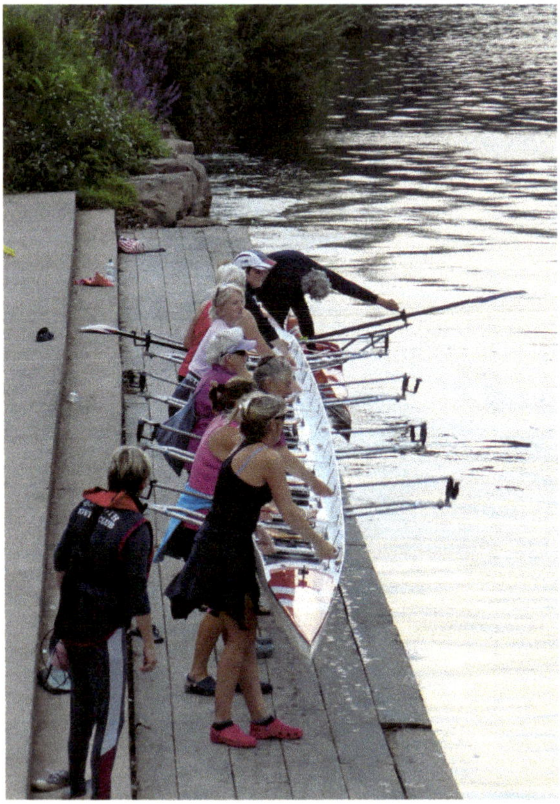

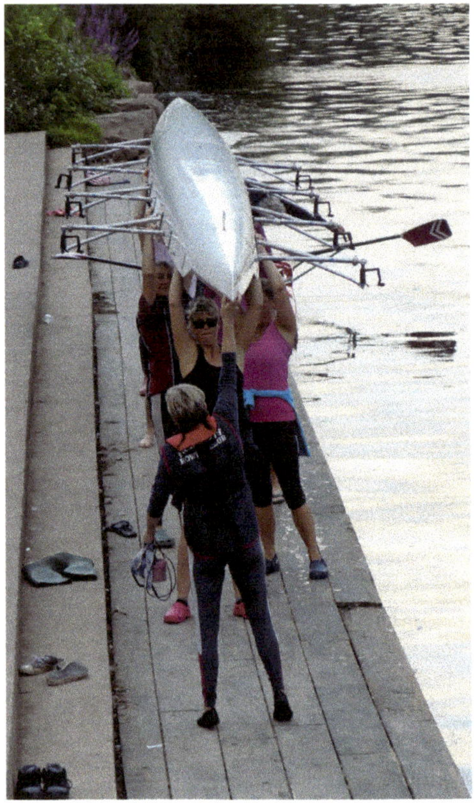

Monmouth's Boating Heritage – 'Wye's Women'

Not an easy boat to handle on the water or on land for that matter, the eight-sweep boat, the largest of the rowing boat classes, carries a crew of eight rowers plus a cox. It has an average length of 19.9 metres (62 feet) and a minimum weight of 96 kg (221 lbs), but the 'Wye's Women' took this in their stride and showed how it is done in style. They even had time for a group photograph once it was all over.

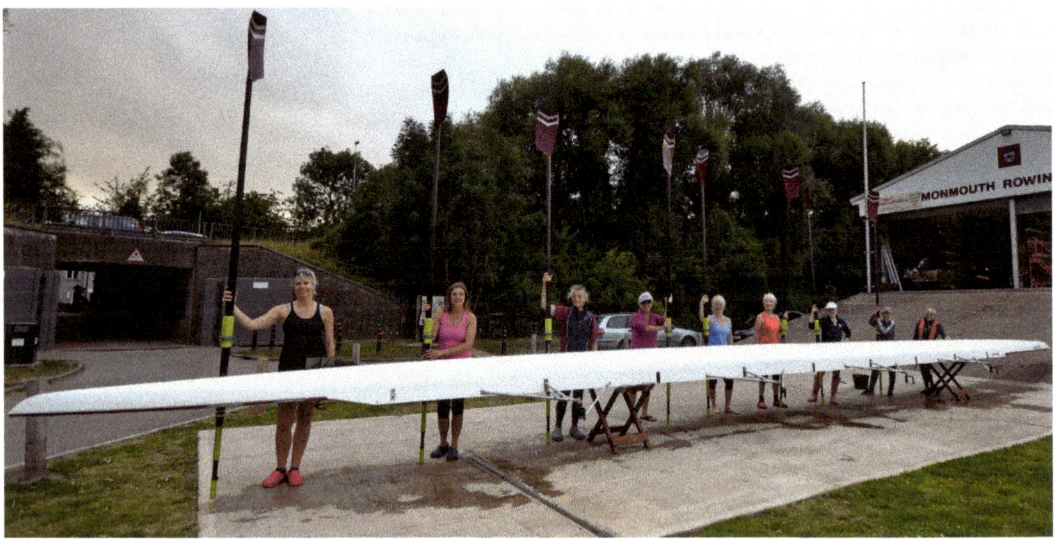

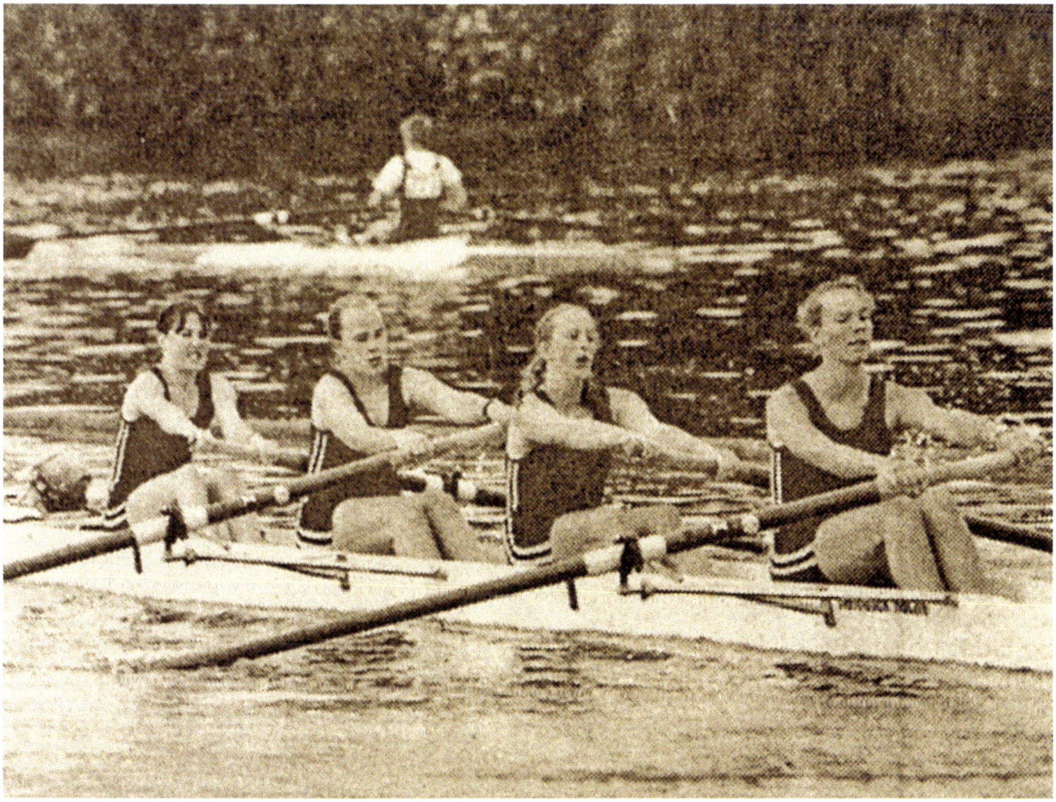

The Regatta

Rowing is not new to the female members of the Monmouth Rowing Club, as shown in the top 1996 photograph provided by the *Monmouthshire Beacon*. The four rowers were competing in the Quadruple Scull competition in the Regatta, an event that takes place every year on the river at Monmouth. Time rolls on and more ladies are taking to the water, as can be seen in the lower picture where two rowers in a double scull are trying to overcome the 'parking' of the boat so that they can disembark.

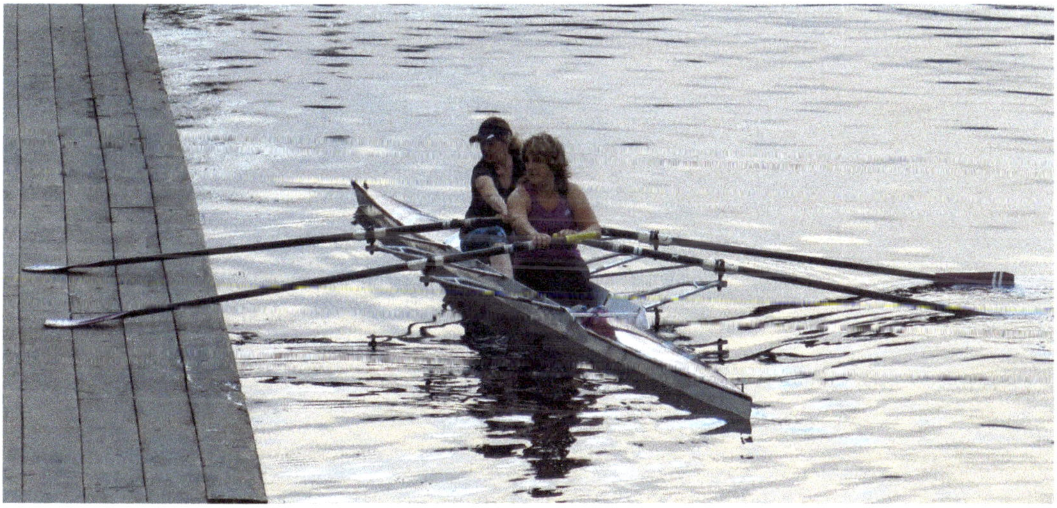

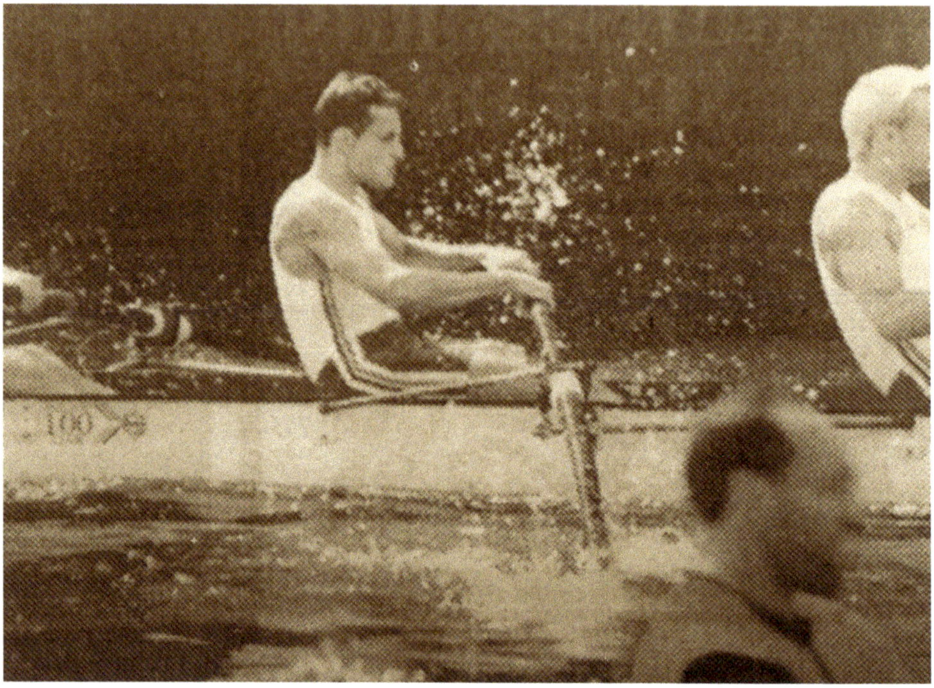

The Regatta

Another scene from the past, as provided by the *Monmouthshire Beacon*, this time of the men competing in the 1998 Regatta in the top photograph. Practice makes perfect as recognised by the male members of the Monmouth Rowing Club as they exercise their eight-sweep boat skills on the River Wye in August 2016. The Monmouth Rowing Club was founded in 1928 and is the furthest south of the three rowing clubs on the River Wye; the other two being Hereford and Ross-on-Wye.

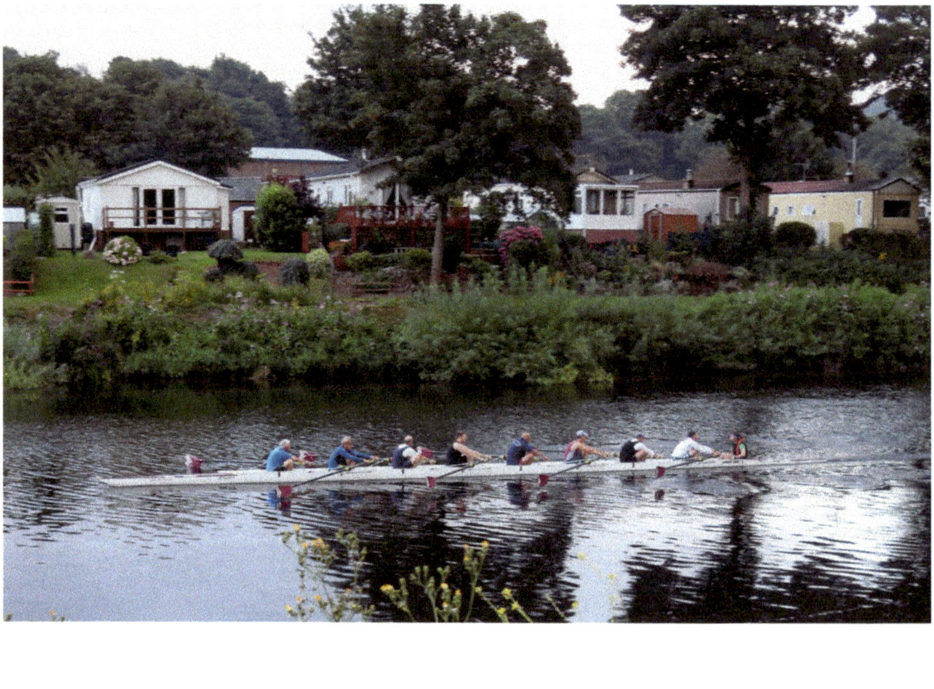

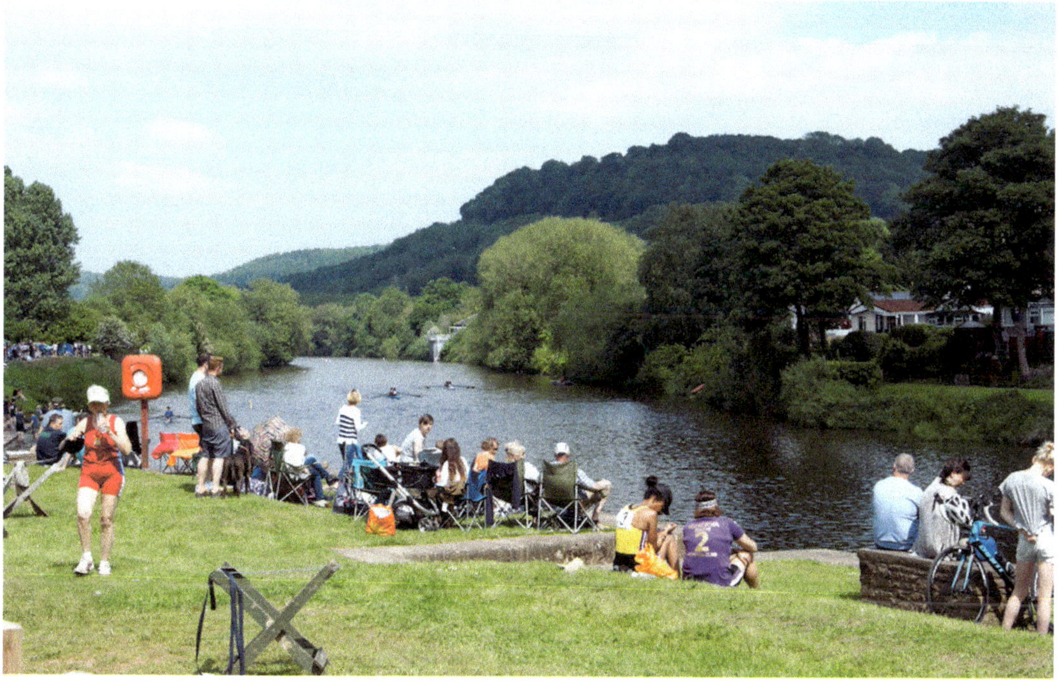

The Regatta

Traditionally, the Monmouth Summer Regatta has been held on the Sunday of the Spring Bank Holiday in late May with crews racing side by side over a straight 1,000 metre course for seniors and a 1,000 metre course for veterans and juniors. As shown by the *Monmouthshire Beacon* photographs taken at the 2016 Regatta, it is not just a day for rowers, but for spectators as well.

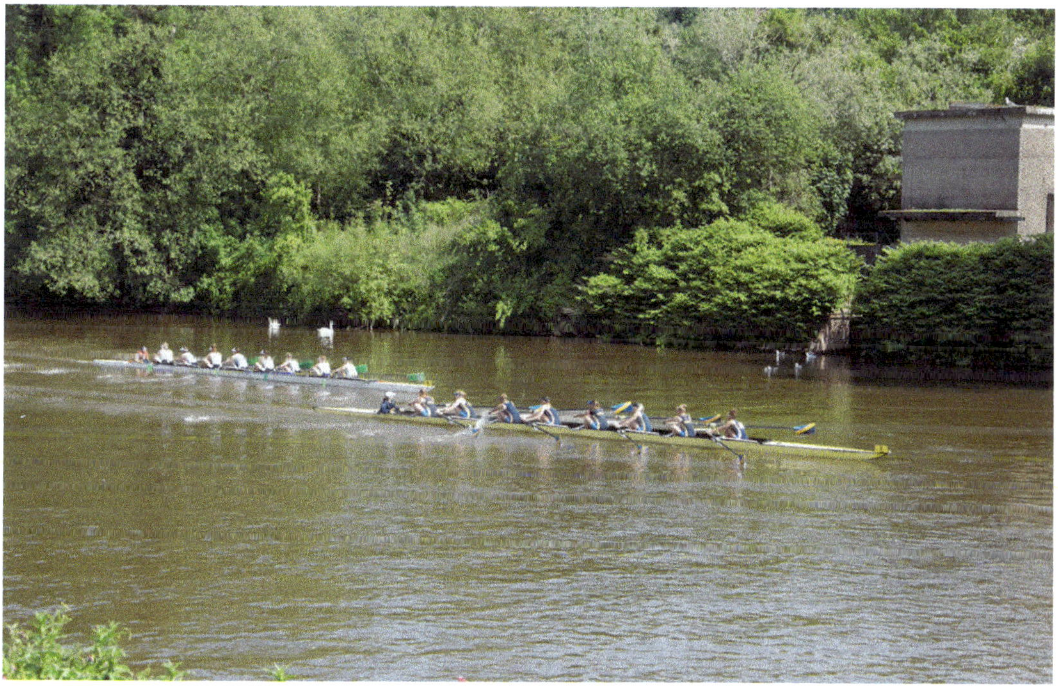

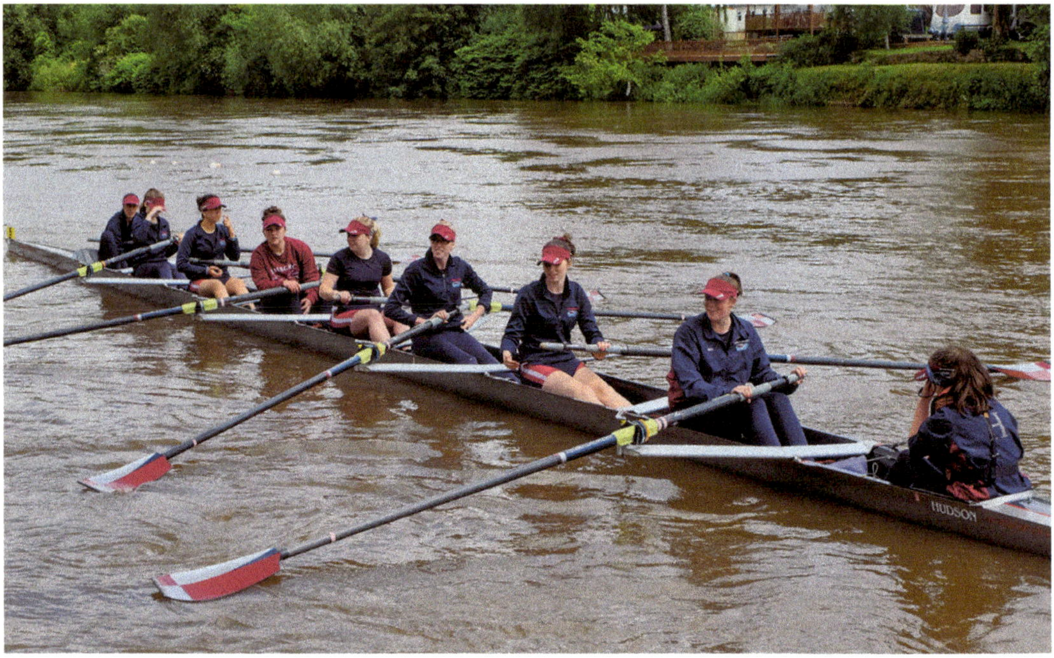

The Regatta

Two more photographs from the archives of the *Monmouthshire Beacon* with the top one being of the ladies' eight in 2014 and the lower picture being of an eight competition approaching the end of the race at the Wye Bridge in 2016. No rowing races are held below the Wye Bridge and in the summer the races extend 2.25 km upstream between Monmouth and Hadnock.

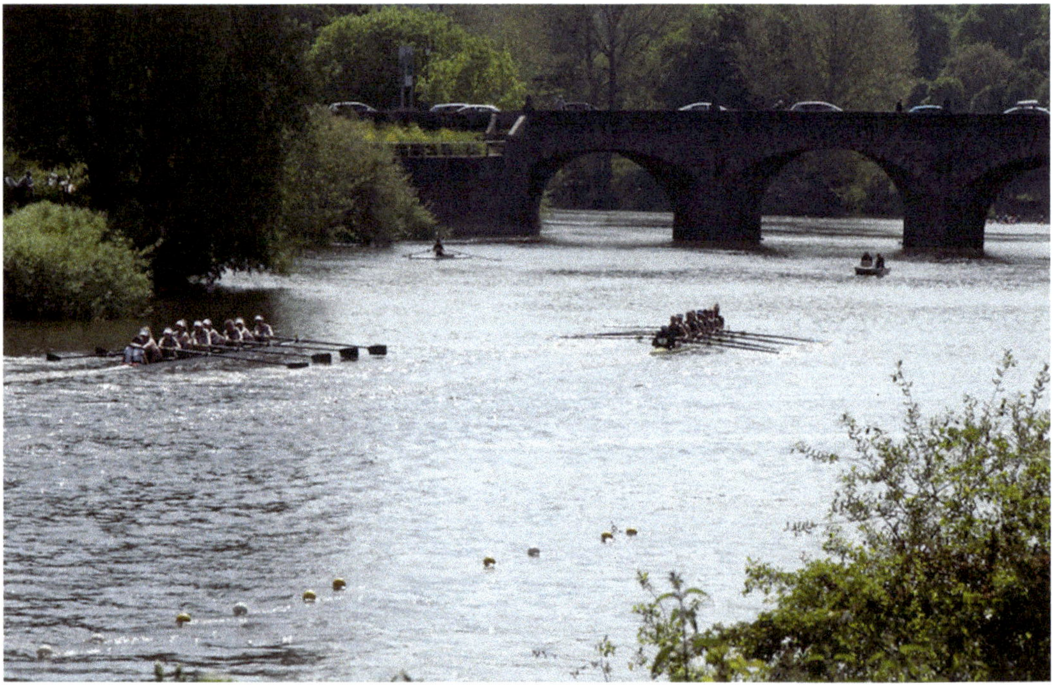

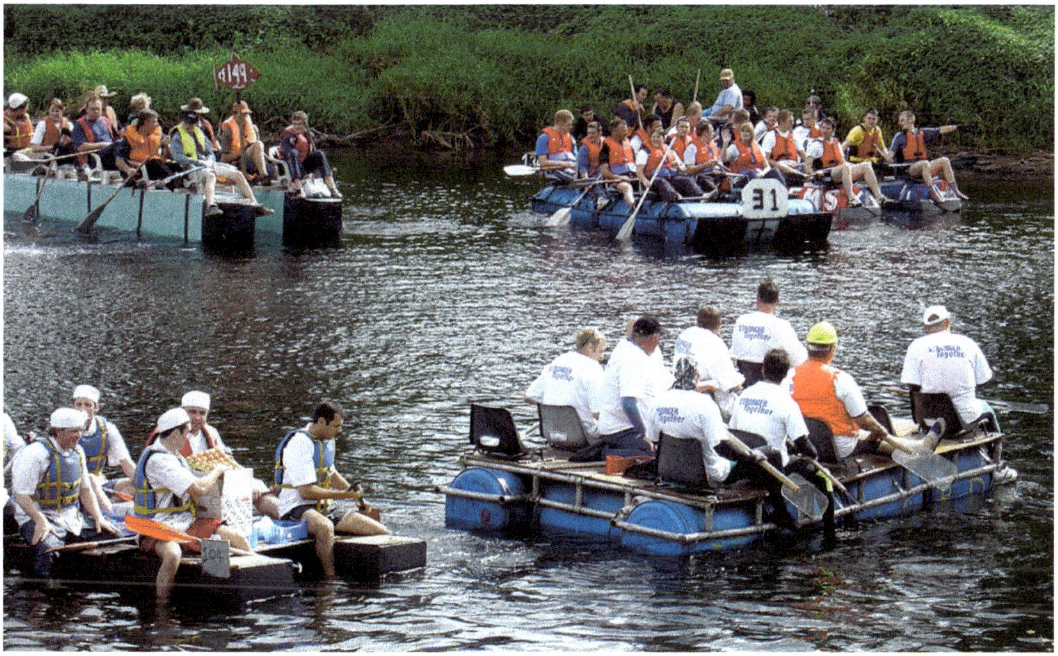

The Raft Races

The annual Rotary Club of Monmouth Raft Race celebrates its fifty-first year in September 2016 with a limit of 100 rafts. The event starts in Monmouth and ends a riotous 6.5 miles downstream at Tump Farm, Whitebrook, with all the proceeds going towards raising funds for St David's Hospice Care. Each year, the rafts get more and more sophisticated, as can be seen by comparing the two *Monmouthshire Beacon* photographs on this page; the top photo was taken at the 2007 event and the bottom one in 2015.

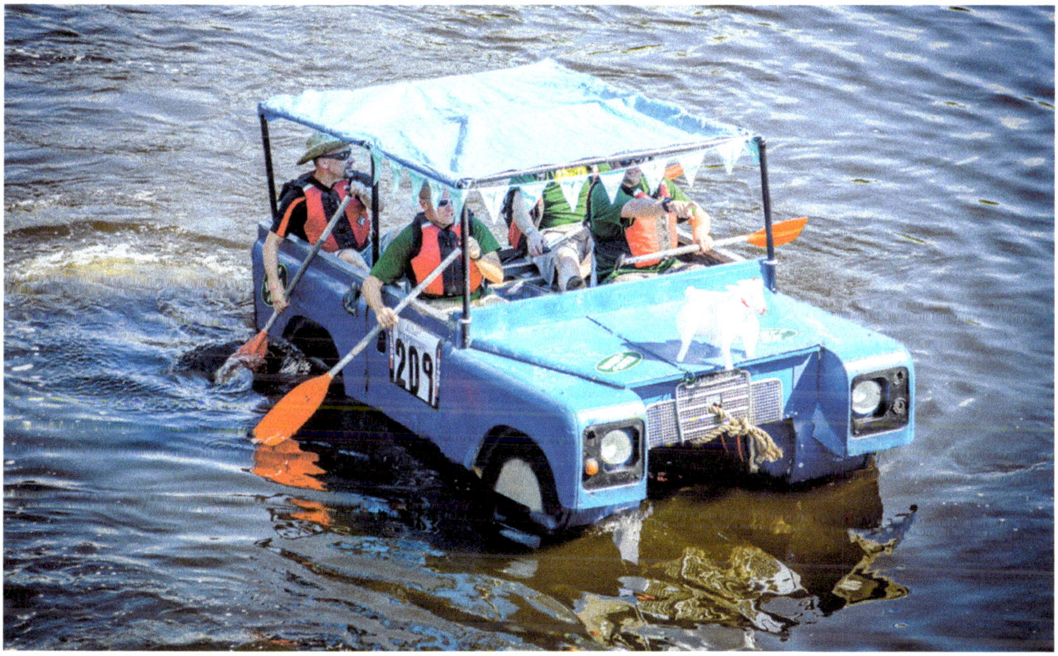

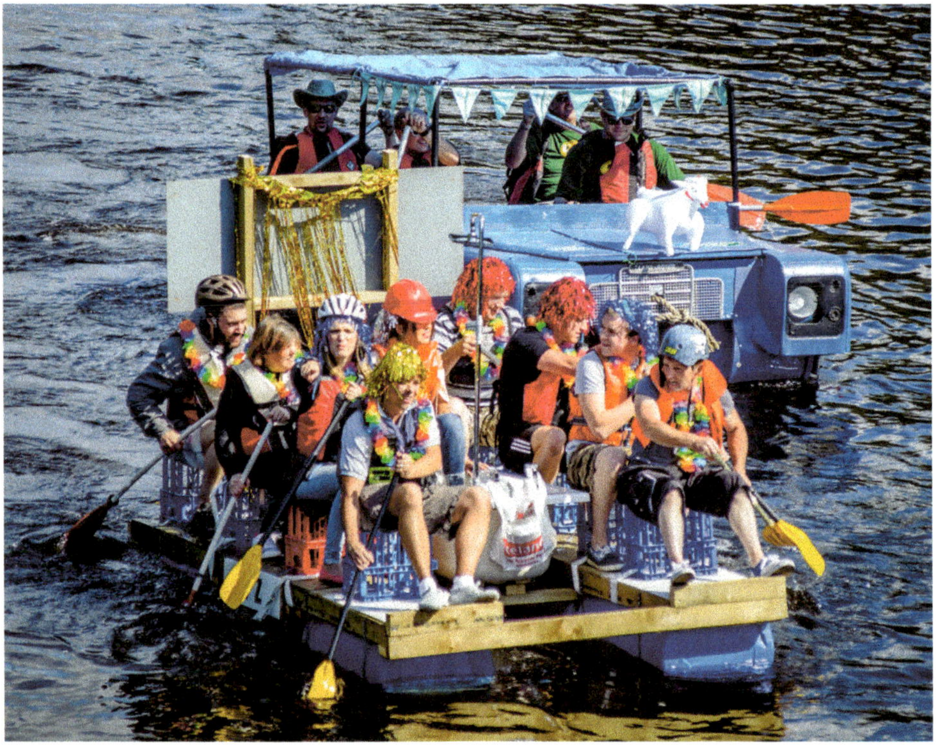

The Raft Races

Two more pictures taken by the *Monmouthshire Beacon* photographer of the 2015 Raft Race, in which the camera has captured the great fun and excitement enjoyed by all who take part in the annual event.

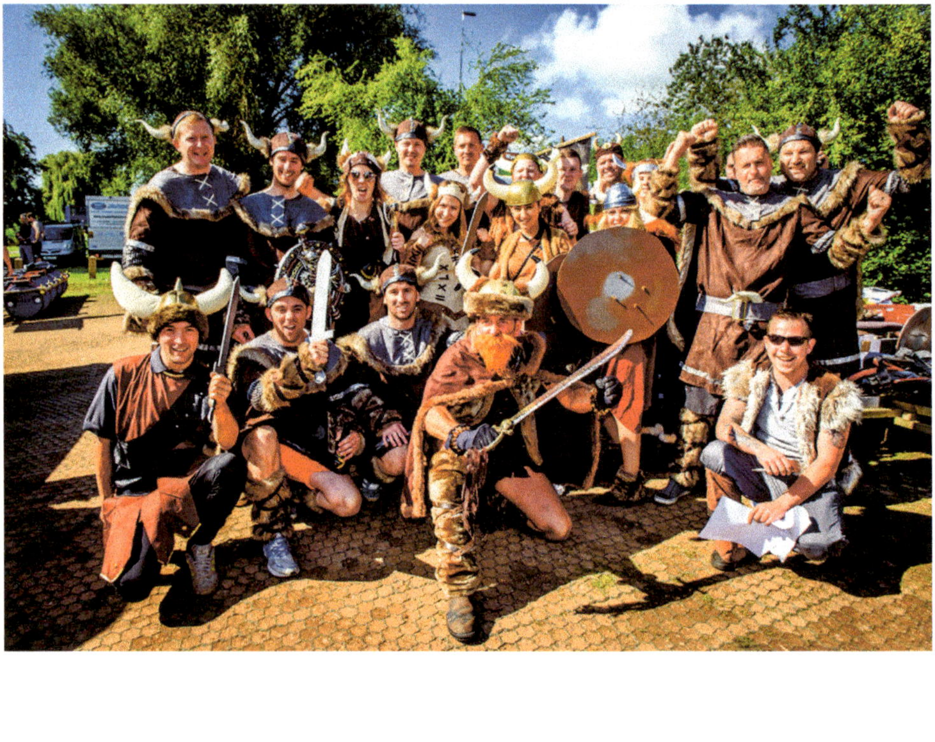

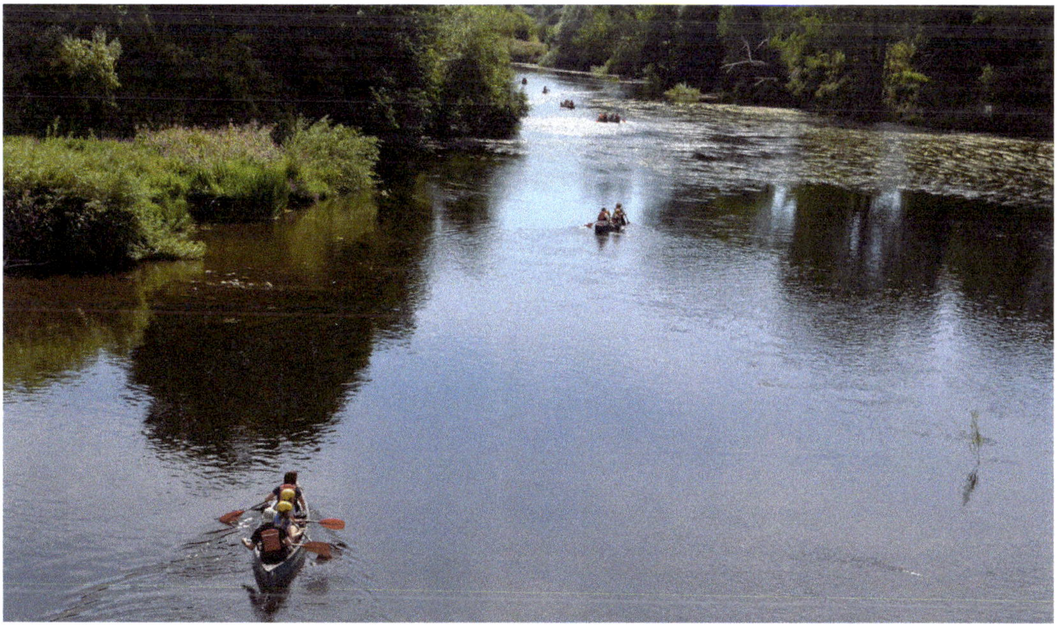

Boating on the River Wye

Boating on the River Wye is not just limited to the Regatta, rowing clubs and raft builders; it is an open waterway for pleasure craft as well. Rowing boats can be hired at the Wye Bridge, as show in the top picture and rowed down the river as far as Redbrook, some 3 miles downstream from Monmouth. After leaving the Wye Bridge, and within a short distance downstream, the pleasure craft will sail under the derelict metal bridge of the old Ross and Monmouth Railway before passing through the gap left in Wye Valley Railway viaduct. The lower photograph shows the metal bridge of the Wye Valley Railway when it was operational, while its derelict remains are highlighted in the inset picture.

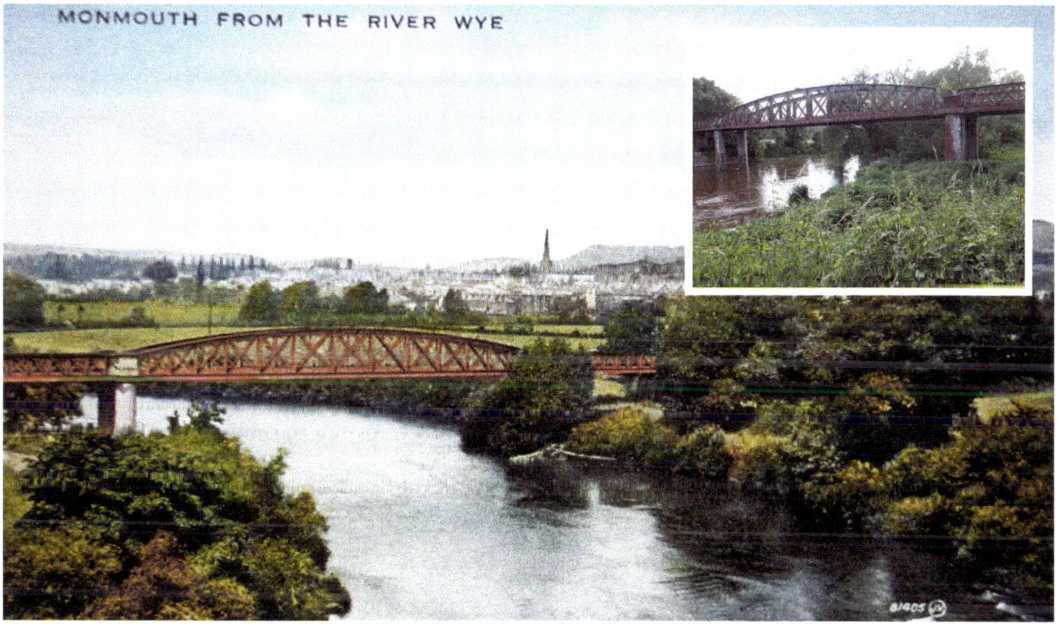

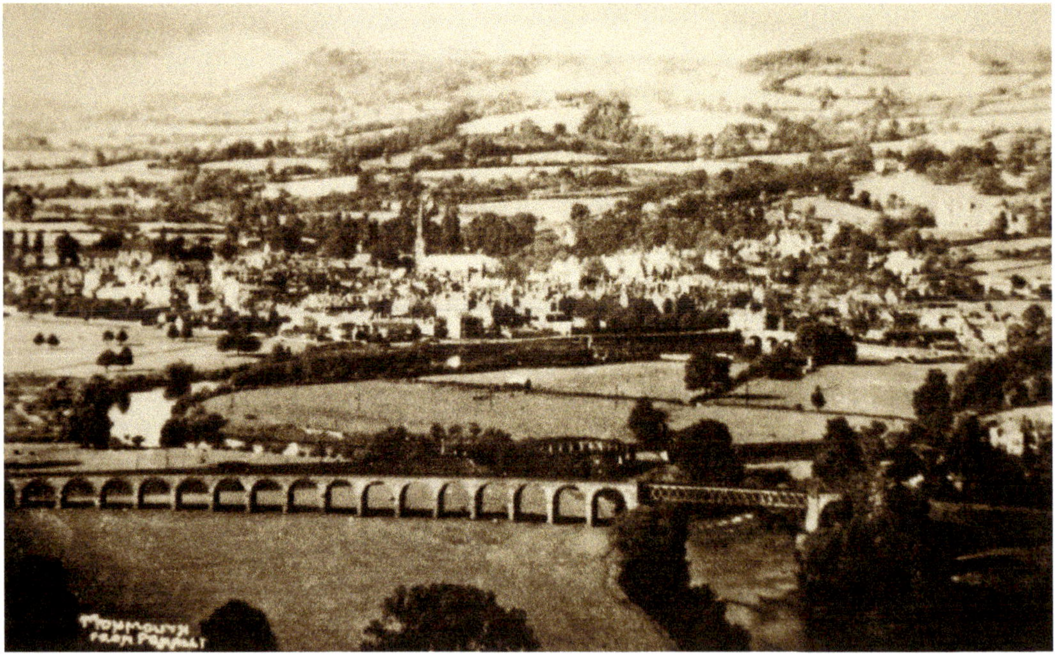

Bridges on the River Wye

Both panoramic photographs on this page are of the Wye Valley railway viaduct which was closed in 1964 and the metal bridge section across the River Wye recovered.

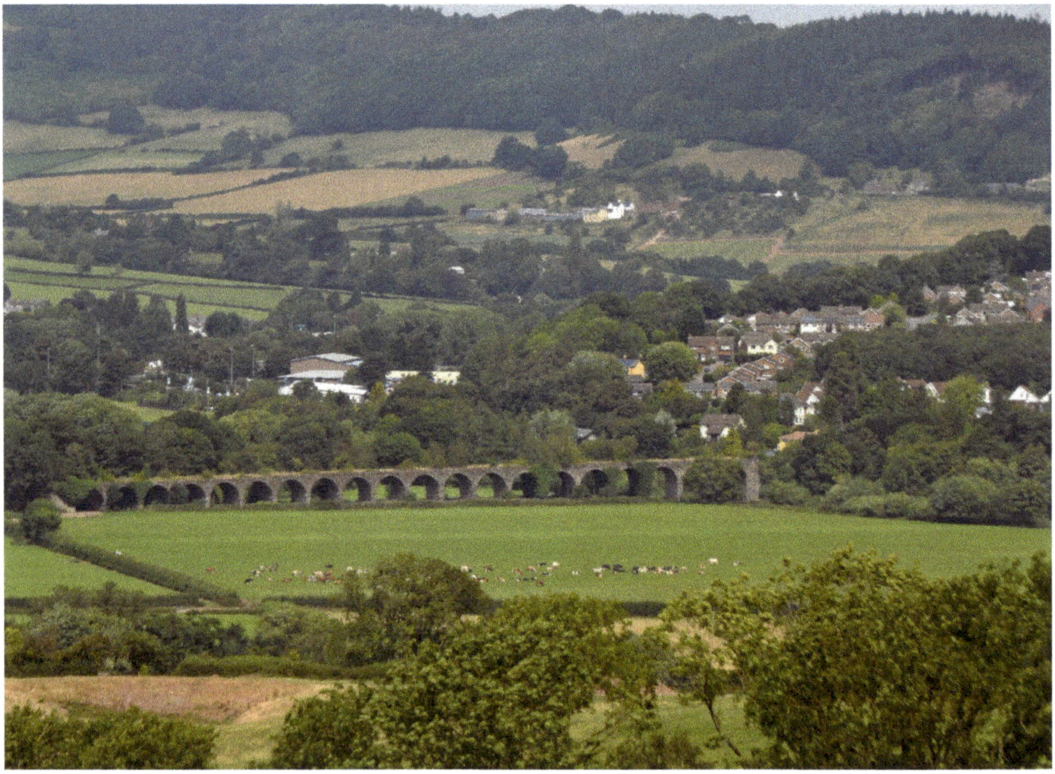

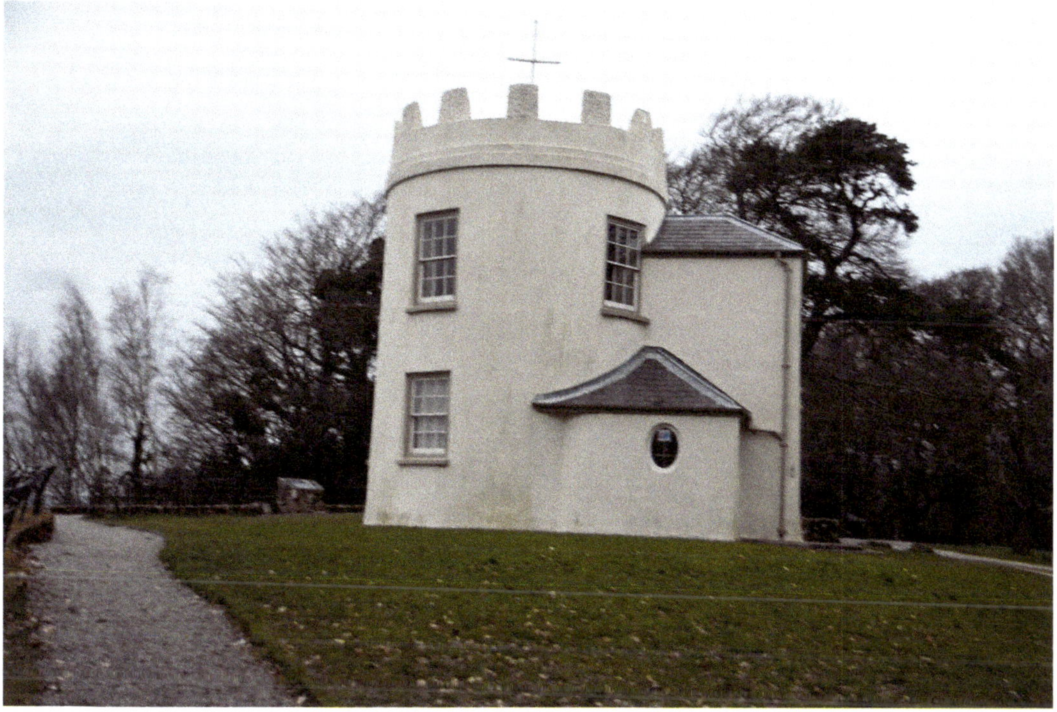

The Kymin or Kymin Hill and Naval Temple

The Kymin is a hill overlooking the town of Monmouth. It is about 800 feet above sea level and has some spectacular views over nine counties. The site is a designated Area of Outstanding Natural Beauty where there are two neoclassical monuments, the Roundhouse, which can be clearly seen from Monmouth, and the Naval Temple. The Roundhouse, construction of which was started by the Kymin Club in 1794 and finished in 1800, is a white round tower two stories high with a crenellated roof and is a Grade II-listed building. The Naval Temple was also built by the Kymin Club in 1800 to celebrate the second anniversary of the British victory at the Battle of the Nile in 1798. The site is managed by the National Trust.

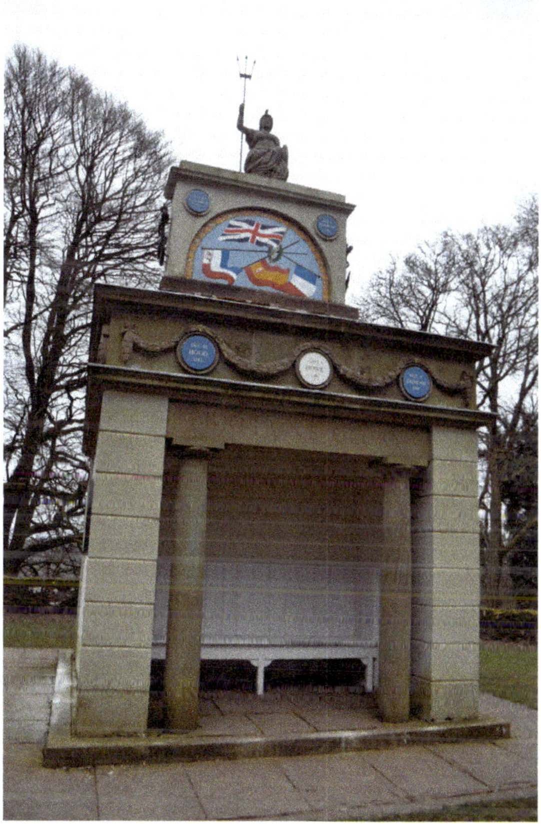

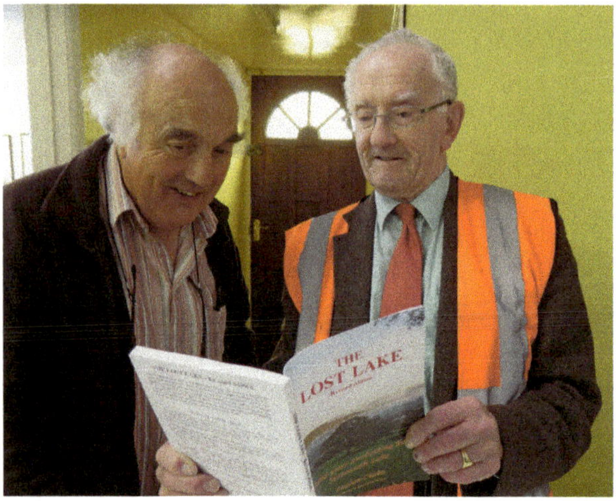

Fellow Authors
The author, with fellow author Stephen Clarke, MBE, chairman and founder member of the Monmouth Archaeological Society, discussing his latest revised edition of *The Lost Lake* and the continuing wonderful archaeological discoveries being made in the Monmouth area.

Acknowledgements

In compiling and preparing this book, I am grateful for the all the assistance and support that I have received from the following organisations and individuals, for which I offer my sincerest thanks and gratitude.

Stephen Clarke, MBE, FSA, MIFA, chairman and founding member of the Monmouth Archaeological Society, for his unstinting help and freedom of access given to use illustrations and photographs from his two books and the archives of the Monmouth Archaeological Society; I would also like to give my sincere thanks to Stephen for taking the time to proof read this book; Patricia Lynesmith, curator and Dr Eric Old, administrator, Castle and Regimental Museum, Monmouth for again unrestricted access to the museum's archives; Victoria Halifax, editor, *Monmouthshire Beacon,* for many marvellous photographs of the Regatta and Raft Races; Peter Bere, artist and illustrator, Monmouth Archaeological Society; Rhodri Clarke, Clarke Printing; John Davies, photographer, Monmouth; Aileen Atkinson, manager, Shire Hall, Monmouth; Bill Leddington, Church of St Thomas the Martyr, Overmonnow, Monmouth; Lloyds Bank, Monmouth branch; Mrs Shirley Meyrich-Evans, caretaker, Monmouth Castle; Graham Anderson, longbowman, and Terry Cristofoli, co-ordinator, the Priory, for permission to photograph in the Priory and to use an image from the booklet 'Stitches and Stories'.

My final accolade goes to the women of the Monmouth Rowing Club who very sportingly agreed to pose for me by their boat 'Wye's Women' after a very hard evening's workout on the river.

Please accept my apologies if I have inadvertently missed out anyone from the above list.

Reference has been made to the works of William Coxe; *An Historical Tour in Monmouthshire Illustrated with Views* by Sir R. C. Hoare Bart; *A New Map of the County and Other Engravings* (1801); *The Book of South Wales, the Wye and the Coast* (1861) by Mr and Mrs S. C. Hall; *The Chartist Riots at Newport* (1889) by W. N. Johns; *Down the Dig: Monmouth – An Adventure in Archaeology* (2008) and *The Lost Lake,* Revised Edition (2016) by Stephen Clarke, MBE.